GOLD,

A Garland Series

MONEY,

INFLATION & DEFLATION

René P. Higonnet & Mira Wilkins
ADVISORY EDITORS

MONETARY POLICIES AND FULL EMPLOYMENT

William Fellner

Garland Publishing, Inc.
New York & London • 1983

Reprinted by permission of
the University of California Press.
Copyright, 1946, by the Regents of the University
of California

Library of Congress Cataloging in Publication Data

Fellner, William John, 1905–
Monetary policies and full employment.

(Gold, money, inflation & deflation)
Reprint. Originally published: Berkeley :
University of California Press, 1946.
(Publications of the Bureau of Business and
Economic Research, University of California)
Includes bibliographical references and index.
1. Monetary policy.   2. Full employment policies.
I. Title.   II. Series.
HG230.3.F4   1983   339.5'3   82-48180
ISBN 0-8240-5232-3

Design by Jonathan Billing

The volumes in this series are printed on
acid-free, 250-year-life paper.

Printed in the United States of America

Monetary Policies and Full Employment

Publications of the
Bureau of Business and Economic Research
University of California

Monetary Policies and Full Employment

By

WILLIAM FELLNER

UNIVERSITY OF CALIFORNIA PRESS
BERKELEY AND LOS ANGELES
1946

UNIVERSITY OF CALIFORNIA PRESS
BERKELEY AND LOS ANGELES
CALIFORNIA

◇

CAMBRIDGE UNIVERSITY PRESS
LONDON, ENGLAND

PRINTED IN THE UNITED STATES OF AMERICA
BY THE UNIVERSITY OF CALIFORNIA PRESS

BUREAU OF BUSINESS AND ECONOMIC RESEARCH

◇

TO MY BROTHER PAUL

Introduction

As the title indicates, this volume is mainly concerned with the bearing of monetary policies on the problem of full employment. The earlier chapters of the volume lead up to a discussion of this problem.

It may be useful to express some of the propositions contained in the book in brief form before they are presented more fully and with the appropriate qualifications. The propositions listed here are not ordered consistently so as to represent the main themes of the successive chapters. However, most of what is contained in the volume is directly or indirectly related to the few simple statements which follow.

1) The equilibrium approach is justified because it is fruitful to *contrast* reality with hypothetical equilibrium positions, which usually have normative implications. Equilibrium positions, however, are not "observable" in factual material. Secular trend lines do not show the equilibrium path along which the economy would be moving in the absence of cyclical disturbances. A reduction in cyclical fluctuations would greatly affect the secular trend.

2) The analytical framework of the Keynesian theory, divorced from its equilibrium implications, serves as a convenient point of departure for a discussion of the savings-investment mechanism. As for the Keynes-Hansen hypotheses concerning the factors producing stagnant trends in "mature" economies, and particularly in the United States during the 1930's, these cannot be proved or disproved by statistical methods. However, the plausibility of some of these hypotheses does not seem to be great, if they are viewed in the light of the available material. Plausibility, of course, is a vague term and consequently there is room for legitimate differences of opinion in this respect.

3) Significant changes in the composition of output tend to develop into general growth of the economy as a whole. The shift

toward certain products stimulates investment more than is required to offset the undermaintenance in the fields adversely affected by the shifts. Consequently, tendencies toward changes in the composition of output may be important contributing factors of general expansion, which may extend even to the industries that would otherwise be adversely affected by the shifts. This is one of the meanings that can be attributed to the dictum that the proper functioning of a capitalistic system requires dynamic basic tendencies.

4) There exists a presumption that autonomous changes in money wage rates are associated with changes in real wage rates in the same direction. The reason is that not all new investment produces additional goods for future consumption. Part of the new investment produces additional goods for future new investment which, in turn, also partly produces additional goods for further new investment and so on. Therefore, it seems likely that the aggregate demand for goods (including the demand for investment goods) tends to rise, or decline, in a smaller proportion than money wage rates and the money wage bill.

5) It does not follow from what was said in the preceding paragraph that a decline of money (and real) wage rates always increases output and employment and that a rise in money (and real) wage rates always reduces these magnitudes. Lower unit costs and increased average and marginal profit rates need not always stimulate output, provided they are associated with an increase of the uncertainty attached to profit expectations; and higher unit costs and lower average and marginal profit rates need not always reduce output, provided they are associated with a lesser degree of uncertainty. A decline of real wage rates does tend to increase uncertainty because it reduces the average propensity to consume and because the market for consumers' goods is more stable than the market for producers' goods. There presumably exists a wage level that is optimal for output, in any given set of circumstances. (There may, of course, exist several optima.) This notion is quite different from Professor Lange's optimum propensity to consume, which is optimal merely for investment but not for output as a whole.

6) Price and wage rigidities presumably are important contributing factors of unemployment. Yet it cannot be taken for granted

that adjustments in the price and wage structure would always restore full employment. Nor can it be taken for granted that the lowering of interest rates and the liberalizing of credit conditions would always restore a high level of business activity.

7) In periods of underutilization the government may adopt various combinations of credit policies, price-cost policies, and tax policies aimed at increasing the level of private business activity without resorting to large-scale public expenditure. Aside from adopting these policies, the government may create reasonably full utilization by means of public spending. Moreover, if the other policies do not succeed in restoring a high level of private business activity, deficit-financed public spending is the only method that will eliminate mass unemployment. On assumptions that may frequently be realistic, public expenditure must be financed, directly or indirectly, by the central bank itself in order to possess expansionary effects. This circumstance per se does not, however, imply special dangers.

8) The dangers of an unconditional full employment guarantee stem mainly from the fact that such a policy would require a rigorous system of direct controls. Without these controls monopolistic groups could constantly raise wages and prices and reduce the quality of their services against the background of the full employment guarantee. The high degree of liquidity, existing under the conditions here postulated, would reinforce the inflationary pressure. This pressure would necessitate the adoption of comprehensive direct controls extending to the wage and price level to the factors affecting the mobility of resources, and probably also to the quality of goods and services. Persistent mass unemployment would be even more objectionable than are the trends that would be generated by the government policies in question, all the more so because mass unemployment would result in abrupt institutional changes of an unpredictable character. But the trends produced by a rigid full employment guarantee would prove to be objectionable enough, if a high value is placed on the present type of social and political institutions; and in the face of a chronic deficiency of private investment some such rigid policy of guaranteed employment might prove to be unavoidable.

9) Yet this dilemma does not have to arise unless there exists, in

the secular long run, a persistent tendency toward substantial under-utilization. The available evidence does not suggest that such a secular trend must be anticipated. Merely *cyclical* depression tendencies may presumably be counteracted effectively without "guaranteeing" the level of employment *de jure* or *de facto* and therefore such tendencies do not necessarily compel us to choose between mass unemployment and rigorous direct controls. In periods of high private investment expansionary policies would of course be unjustified. In early stages of recessions it should be possible to adopt effective expansionary monetary and fiscal policies and to make their timing dependent on price and wage trends and on the behavior of economic power groups in general. The expansionary policies should be discontinued when private investment revives sufficiently. They also should be discontinued if dangerous price and wage tendencies manifest themselves, regardless of the level of activity at which these tendencies develop. Such a policy might be capable of preventing major depressions and mass unemployment and of shortening business recessions materially. It would not guarantee economic impunity for concerted action of labor unions and producers' monopoly groups and therefore it presumably would not have to resort to systematic direct controls on a scale comparable to that on which a policy of rigid full employment guarantee would have to do so. If it should be necessary to apply large-scale antideflationary measures all the time (not merely "cyclically") then the difference between the rigid and the more flexible types of policy would tend to disappear and a *de facto* "guarantee" of the level of employment would gradually become established. But it seems likely that a sufficiently vigorous and effective cycle policy would produce a favorable long-run trend in private investment, and that, consequently, such a cycle policy could *stay* "merely" a cycle policy.

10) It seems, therefore, that permanent full employment, if it could be accomplished at all, would require far-reaching institutional changes of an abrupt (historically discontinuous) character. Preventing business recessions from developing into cumulative depressions with mass unemployment does not necessarily require abrupt institutional changes. Failure to accomplish this somewhat more modest objective in the United States would spell tragic con-

sequences both here and abroad. The accomplishment of this objective requires integrating monetary-fiscal policies with wage-price policies. The necessary processes of adjustment during periods of recession give rise to a cumulative shrinkage of aggregate demand by which the adjustments are substantially delayed and by which economic activity becomes paralyzed. The shrinkage in aggregate demand should be effectively counteracted before it is too late. However, if comprehensive controls of the "wartime" variety are to be avoided, it is imperative to adjust the timing of the expansionary policies to wage and price tendencies, and thereby, to the behavior of economic power groups. The behavior of these groups would presumably be much less harmful in these circumstances than in the event of an unconditional full employment guarantee. The policy of rigid guarantee could not afford to exert its influence in this way. It would have to adjust the other variables of the economy by legal compulsion to the rigid course of its own fiscal operations.

11) The more flexible line of approach here considered would not prevent occasional business recessions and limited periods of moderate unemployment, but it might well prevent major depressions and lasting unemployment without forcing discontinuous changes in the institutional setting. Political and economic trends are conceivable that would destroy the policy in question. The policy would prove unsuccessful if the behavior of economic power groups should become such that no amount of indirect pressure would be sufficient to influence them. If dangerous price and wage developments will consistently get under way at unsatisfactory levels of employment, unless the government discontinues its expansionary policies (and if they will get under way in spite of the fact that the government is known to discontinue its policies under such conditions), then we will have to have either substantial unemployment or far-reaching controls. The policy would fail also if, for other reasons we should be faced continuously with a large-scale insufficiency of private investment, in spite of the fact that the government develops a practice of stepping in at early stages of contraction. Such social and economic trends *would* bring about abrupt changes in our institutions because these institutions could survive neither protracted periods of mass unemployment nor the inflationary spiral

to be expected from a full employment guarantee in the absence of comprehensive controls. But predictions of these social and economic trends rest on mere guesswork and are quite unconvincing. The long-run economic trend and the cycle are interdependent. The past long-run trends, whenever they were unsatisfactory, were very largely influenced by the gross inadequacy of the monetary and fiscal policies applied in the early stages of some preceding business contraction and also by inconsistent attitudes of governments toward cost-price problems. This, it seems to me, is the most important single conclusion that can be deduced from modern monetary theory. It also is a distinctly hopeful conclusion. After all, would it not have been rather astonishing if the Great Depression and its aftermath could have been averted by policies based on the commercial loan theory of central banking plus the notion that it is always undesirable to run a large deficit and, at a later stage, on the idea that modest reflationary expenditures should be absorbed by price and wage increases?

While this study was being prepared, and after the completion of the first draft, I had the substantial benefit of Professor Howard S. Ellis' advice. The manuscript was read by Professors Norman S. Buchanan and John B. Condliffe, who made many valuable suggestions. I am greatly indebted to them and also to Mrs. Sanford A. Mosk, who eliminated many weaknesses by editorial and other changes. I was fortunate indeed to have the very able and competent assistance of Mr. Frank E. Norton, Jr., from the beginning to the completion of the study.

The editors of the *Journal of Political Economy* and of the *Quarterly Journal of Economics* gave their permission for the reprinting of diagrams which I have used in articles published in these periodicals. The Division of Research and Statistics of the Federal Reserve Board permitted the reproduction of one of its charts. The courtesy of all three is sincerely appreciated.

The study was essentially completed when Sir William Beveridge's *Full Employment in a Free Society* was published. However, in the last revision of the manuscript a few references were made to the argument contained in that work.

W. F.

Berkeley, 1945

Contents

Tables

[xvii]

Figures

Part One

CONCEPTS

CHAPTER I

Underemployment and Equilibrium

THE CONCEPT OF FULL EMPLOYMENT

THE TASK of defining full employment is an ungrateful one. When economists speak of reasonably full employment—or more briefly of full employment—they usually mean a condition in which job-seeking persons are not unemployed on any significant scale. Such a statement contains but a vague definition of the concept of full employment, but it frequently is true that more importance attaches to a deliberately vague statement of this character than to a pedantic technical definition which hides, rather than makes explicit, the ambiguities inherent in a problem. In this case, as in many others, the attempt at conceptual precision proves to be cumbersome and does not lead to a completely satisfactory result.

Full employment, of course, means the absence of *involuntary* unemployment: only the honestly job seeking have to be employed in "full" employment. The crux of the conceptual difficulty is that the stock of unemployed persons usually includes individuals who might obtain employment if supply conditions were different on the labor market, that is, if they sought a job on different terms. Whether an individual should be regarded as voluntarily or involuntarily unemployed has obviously something to do with the question whether he would remain unemployed even if he were willing to accept a lower reward for his services, that is, even if he changed his attitude as a potential supplier of labor services. The *voluntarily* unemployed may frequently be interpreted as demanding for their services a price at which these services are not bought. A wealthy rentier is voluntarily unemployed even if he were willing to work for high multiples of the current salary rates. In spite of this, it is not fruitful to maintain that all persons are voluntarily unemployed who fail to reduce the supply price of their

[3]

services sufficiently to gain employment. Such a definition, on which all unemployment might seem to be voluntary, possesses at least two fatal weaknesses. It presupposes that all persons could be employed if they accepted wages that are low enough; this is not necessarily true in dynamic conditions, characterized by the presence of uncertainty. Second, this definition would make the individual "responsible" for legal and institutional arrangements which preclude the prompt and unlimited downward flexibility of wage rates. Individuals may fail to reduce the supply price of their services in view of wage agreements based on collective bargaining, or in view of minimum wage laws, and so on. To argue that in such cases the unemployment is voluntary, would be highly artificial. The *voluntas* of the individual is not the cause of the downward inflexibility.

Lord Keynes suggested that this dilemma should be solved by postulating that persons are involuntarily unemployed if they would be willing to, and capable of, obtaining employment at a lower real wage rate provided the money wage rate was *not* reduced at the same time. This may be interpreted as one way of avoiding the conceptual difficulty arising from the legal and institutional arrangements preventing the individual unemployed from offering his services more cheaply. The arrangements in question typically relate to money wage rates; therefore, if the individual were unwilling to work for a lower real wage rate even though his money wage rate were not reduced, then his *voluntas* would have to be involved in his refusal to offer his services more cheaply. If this is true and if he *could* gain employment at a reduced real wage rate, he is voluntarily unemployed. Alternatively, the following definition is submitted to the reader: An unemployed individual is involuntarily unemployed if he is willing to accept employment at prevailing money wage rates, regardless of the height of the prevailing money wage rate.[1] The height of the prevailing money wage rates, of course, depends on legal and institutional arrangements and the individual is not indifferent to them. He obviously prefers to obtain employment at higher rather than lower wages; the point, however, is that, if he is to be regarded as involuntarily unemployed, his unwilling-

---

[1] This corresponds rather closely to Professor Pigou's definition of unemployment; cf. A. C. Pigou, *The Theory of Unemployment* (London, Macmillan, 1933), p. 4.

ness to work for a lower money wage must not stand in the way of his employment, provided wages in general are lowered. Persons who would be willing to work more hours than they actually do, are involuntarily unemployed to the extent of these hours, provided their willingness to work more is not dependent on the height of the current wage rate.

The Keynesian definition may not always be coëxtensive with the one suggested here. It is conceivable that a person should be willing to work for lower real wage rates provided his money wage rate is not reduced, but that at the same time he should not be willing to work for a lower money wage rate even if the greater part of the labor force is willing to do so (and even if therefore the "prevailing money wage level" does decline.) On the Keynesian definition, such a person would be involuntarily unemployed, whereas on the alternative definition here considered, his unemployment would be voluntary. On the other hand, it is conceivable that persons should be involuntarily unemployed on the definition here suggested, yet voluntarily unemployed on the Keynesian definition. It is submitted, however, that the boxes containing those who would be classified differently on the two criteria respectively, come close to being empty boxes; and the definition here considered seems to be simpler.

As was stated above, the conceptual precision gained by a logical excursion such as the foregoing one is partly fictitious. The seemingly precise criteria do not make it possible to classify all unemployed according to the voluntary or involuntary character of their unemployment. Much of what usually is considered frictional unemployment is a hybrid consisting of "voluntary" and "involuntary" elements. This type of unemployment frequently is involuntary if it is taken for granted that the individual unemployed is limited to a specific segment of the labor market (geographically, or as to the nature of the work that is sought); yet he may voluntarily so limit himself. Whether such persons should be considered involuntarily unemployed depends on whether we are willing to regard them as job seeking even though they limit themselves to specific segments of the labor market. Whatever technical definition we may favor, it is well to bear in mind that full employment essentially means a condition in which the number of honestly job-seeking persons who do not find employment—or who find less employment than they would like to—is negligible.

Sir William Beveridge's definition of full employment ("more vacancies than unemployed") obviously is intended to express the requirement that all unemployment should be frictional in the sense of being caused by the fact that the unemployed, as potential suppliers of labor, are limited to certain segments of the labor market. Furthermore, his "second" and "third" conditions of full employment (relating to the appropriate location of industries and to the mobility of labor) essentially express the postulate that frictional unemployment should be small.[2] The logical excursion here undertaken was concerned with such conceptual elements as lie behind definitions of the Beveridge type.

Periods of large-scale unemployment usually are periods in which material resources also are "underutilized." Although this statement will scarcely be contested, it should be recognized that, for the economy as a whole, it is impossible to lend logical precision to the concept of the underutilization of material resources. Underutilization exists, in a sense, if an individual firm operates to the left of the minimum point of its average cost curve. In another sense there exists underutilization if a firm operates to the left of the intersection of its average revenue curves with its marginal cost curve. Yet these deviations from perfect competition bear at best indirectly on underutilization in that sense of the term in which material resources are "underutilized" in depressions but are not underutilized in prosperity. The zero point of underutilization in the latter sense is arbitrary. It cannot be established by logical argument. Yet it is possible to lend somewhat more precision to concepts such as that of a substantial increase (or decrease) in the degree of underutilization of material resources. A substantial increase (or decrease) expresses itself in a sudden rise (or decline) of the ratio of real capital to real output which is accounted for neither by a change in relative factor prices nor in the setting up of new production functions. It is impossible to find out from statistical time series alone what accounts for a change in the capital-output ratio. But a

---

[2] William H. Beveridge, *Full Employment in a Free Society* (New York, W. W. Norton, 1945). Sir William Beveridge's first condition relates to the sufficiency of aggregate demand.

method will be described in chapter iii by which it is possible to construct index numbers expressing, at least crudely, the changes in the ratio of capital to output. For depressions and recessions these index numbers indicate increases which could scarcely be attributed to changes in relative factor prices or to innovations alone.[3]

EQUILIBRIUM ANALYSIS IN A DYNAMIC WORLD: THE DEVIATIONS FROM EQUILIBRIUM

Full utilization is assumed in some of the traditional equilibrium theories. The time-honored theories of economic equilibrium do not, however, relate to a "representative" level of economic activity. They are not, and they do not purport to be, realistic in this sense. For example, the neo-classical theories of perfect competition—with their implications of full utilization and of ideal allocation of the available resources—obviously do not describe an existing state of affairs. They may be considered valuable tools of analysis because it is possible to explain certain properties of the real world (e.g., the malallocation of resources) by the deviations of our economies from the equilibrium conditions postulated. An infinite number of systems could be described from which our actual economies deviate, and the properties of the actual economic systems could be "explained" by the deviations. However, such an analytical procedure is fruitful only if it can be justified by some independent criterion. The justification of the neo-classical general equilibrium theories rests largely on the fact that normative significance is attached to the equilibrium conditions in question. The deviations from some of the equilibrium conditions described in the theory are fairly generally considered harmful, although, for example, the stationary character of the systems in question is not considered a desirable objective. The limitations of the approach derive mainly from the circumstance that in most respects the actual deviations from the norm of perfect competition are not (or are very incompletely) under control. For this reason, and because of the stationary character of the neo-classical general equilibrium, it is necessary to have more than this one equilibrium concept at our disposal.

[3] The material substantiating this statement is found partly in chap. iii and partly in my earlier article, "The Technological Argument of the Stagnation Thesis," *Quarterly Journal of Economics* (August, 1941).

It should be added that the particular equilibrium approach is frequently handled merely as a method of looking at a segment of a dynamic economy for a moment of time. In this event it is not part of an equilibrium approach proper but it is an indispensable tool of analysis, especially if used in the framework of the more realistic theory of monopolistic competition. However, the long-run solutions of monopolistic competition theory *are* equilibrium theories in the true sense and they describe the condition of specific industries not on realistic assumptions but on the assumption of perfect foresight. They are useful, by contrast, in the analysis of the consequences of imperfect foresight. But it cannot be maintained that in the real world there exists a tendency toward these long-run equilibria. Such a tendency would exist if certain functions remained stable which do not in reality remain so. Consistently abortive tendencies are not properties of economic reality. They are properties of an analytical framework that by implication focuses attention on the forces that render the tendencies abortive and illustrates the consequences of these forces.

The significance of the concept of *monetary equilibrium* may also be attributed to the possibility of explaining economic reality by deviations from the equilibrium conditions. In the Wicksellian tradition, periods of expansion may be characterized by the condition that investment exceeds savings, and periods of contraction by the condition that savings exceed investment. Savings may be defined in the manner suggested by Professor Robertson, in which case the excess of investment over savings means rising aggregate money income, and the excess of savings over investment means declining aggregate money income; or, savings may be defined in the manner suggested by the Swedish economists, in which case the excess of investment over savings (*ex ante*) means that realized aggregate income exceeds expected income, and the excess of savings over investment (*ex ante*) means that realized income falls short of the expected.[4] If, in the course of cyclical development, investment exceeds savings in certain phases, whereas savings exceeds investment in others, it seems convenient to contrast these developments

---

[4] Cf. for example Gunnar Myrdal, *Monetary Equilibrium* (London, William Hodge, 1939).

with conditions that would be prevailing in a hypothetical economy in which savings would equal investment. The hypothetical
economy in question is said to be in monetary equilibrium regardless of the amount of unemployment existing in the conditions
postulated. The "equilibrium" under consideration is of the "dynamic" variety, unless net savings and net investment do not merely
equal one another but are also equal to zero. In other words, the
magnitudes of the system shift gradually in directions determined
by the long-run tendencies prevailing in the economy.

The concept of monetary equilibrium has proved useful in business cycle theory, although the Wicksellian emphasis on interest
rates in the description of the hypothetical equilibrium condition
and in the discussion of disequilibria has been largely replaced by
an emphasis on various other determinants of savings and investment. But again it should be realized that the fruitfulness of the
equilibrium concept rests on the relative ease with which certain
characteristics of our economies may be approached by the way of
contrasting real systems with the hypothetical equilibrium economy.

Figure 1 illustrates the "Swedish" rather than the "Robertsonian"
version of the analysis because the Robertsonian equilibrium condition (constancy of money income), although more precisely ascer-
tainable, is of a more limited applicability than is the Swedish
equilibrium condition (realized values = planned values).[5] If aggregate money income is expected to change, Robertsonian S = I should
hardly be considered a condition of equilibrium; and in a growing
economy $(I > 0)$ aggregate money income *is* expected to rise, unless
prices are expected to decline.

The figure shows the money value of present consumption (C),
of present net investment (I), and of present consumption plus net
investment, that is, of present *earned income* (Y), plotted against

[5] The figure has various features in common with expository devices that have been
used by other authors in the presentation of their own theories. (Cf. Paul A. Samuelson,
"A Synthesis of the Principle of Acceleration and the Multiplier," *Journal of Political
Economy* (December, 1939), 786–797; Michal Kalecki, "A Theory of the Business Cycle,"
Essays in the Theory of Economic Fluctuations (London, George Allen Unwin, 1939),
pp. 116–149; Mabel F. Timlin, *Keynesian Economics* (Toronto, University of Toronto
Press, 1942), pp. 101–116, 117–129, 152–161; Nicholas Kaldor, "A Model of the Trade
Cycle," *Economic Journal* (March, 1940), 78–92. Cf. also my note on "Period Analysis
and Timeless Equilibrium," *Quarterly Journal of Economics* (February, 1944).

the money income expected for the present period. The "period" must be defined in such a manner that consumption plans, which are conceived of as being always realized and as being governed by income expectations, should not be changed during any one period.

Where a line drawn at a 45° angle through the origin intersects with the Y curve, expected income equals the earned income of the period. This point of intersection (P) expresses monetary equilib-

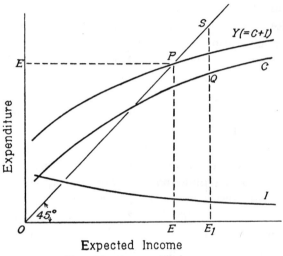

Fig. 1. Monetary equilibrium.

rium.[6] To the left of this intersection investment exceeds expected savings, whereas to the right of the intersection investment falls short of expected savings. Magnitudes such as SQ stand for expected

[6] At this point all investment is planned; there takes place no undesigned accumulation or reduction of inventories. Consequently, if merely planned investment had been included in the I function, rather than all investment, the intersection of the 45° line with C + I would still mark monetary equilibrium. In fact monetary equilibrium is defined as a condition in which expected and realized income are equal (as in point P) *and* in which there is no undesigned change in inventories. But due to the actual methods of inventory valuation, the second condition is always satisfied if the first condition is. Consequently, figure 1 expresses merely the first condition and it thereby implies the second. The second condition as well as the first would be expressed in figure 1 explicitly if merely planned investment were included in the I function and if the intersection of the 45° line with the C + I function (so defined) would be said to mark monetary equilibrium. This, however, would render the figure less suitable for other purposes (such as that of showing the difference between expected and realized income in disequilibrium, etc.)

savings.[7] The magnitudes in question appear as vertical distances between the 45° line and the C curve, and it is this distance which equals investment (Y–C) at the intersection of the 45° line with the Y curve.

Both the C and the I curve, especially the latter, must be assumed to shift from period to period since the expenditure undertaken at a given level of income expectations depends on a variety of unstable circumstances. Consequently, it is necessary to introduce an arbitrary distinction between factors expressed in the basic functions of the graph on the one hand, and factors expressed by shifts of these functions on the other. Considering that the C function is more stable than the I function the simplifying assumption will temporarily be made that the C function remains entirely stable and that consequently all determinants of aggregate consumption are expressed in the shape of the function as it is drawn in the graph. As to the I function, the assumption is made that the slope of the curve is determined exclusively by the relationship that exists between the increase in consumption accompanying a rise in income (dC/dY), on the one hand, and investment on the other. The increase in consumption accompanying a rise in income, such as occurs when investment takes place, is by no means the only determinant of the amount of net investment that can be undertaken profitably; yet the I curve, as drawn in the graph, implies that the other determinants of net investment are given; that is, that they are not functionally related to the magnitudes measured along the axes. Whenever the other determinants of investment change, the I curve must be said to shift. On these definitions, the I curve slopes downward if, as income rises, the increase in consumption accompanying a further unit rise in income becomes smaller. Assuming that the marginal propensity to consume is known to decline, the I curve is negatively sloped. If the C function were assumed to be linear, the I function would be horizontal.[8]

---

[7] $0E_1 = SE_1$ stands for expected income, and if, from this magnitude, consumption (QE_1) is deducted, then expected savings is obtained.

[8] It will be argued later that it might be preferable to conceive of the C function as being approximately linear, but for the moment the more usual notion concerning the shape of this function is accepted because the difference does not bear on the problem here considered.

A brief comment is necessary before turning from the shapes of the basic functions to their shifts. Expected income is not in reality a definite magnitude. This is an important fact, but it is impossible to allow for it in a simple diagram. There is a temptation to measure along the abscissa the "most probable" income expectations but, like all other simple solutions, this would be unsatisfactory. Plans are not determined by most probable expectations alone, and they are not necessarily changed when the outcome is different from what was considered "most probable," as long as the actual outcome is within a range that was regarded a priori as "fairly" probable. If a simplified model is used, with "expected income" measured along the abscissa, it should be borne in mind that what is really wanted expressed is somewhat different and less precise than what is expressed by the model. What is wanted expressed is that certain types of instability would not arise (or would not acquire importance) if the money income realized by the bulk of the income recipients were in the more or less close neighborhood of what was regarded a priori as most probable. The intersection of the Y curve with the 45° line represents such a hypothetical condition, termed monetary equilibrium. As the graph is drawn, the equilibrium is stable, if the basic functions are stable, because the Y curve intersects with the 45° line from above, so that to the left of the intersection expansionary forces are generated, whereas to the right a contractionary movement is started.

However, the basic functions obviously are not stable and there is no reason to assume that the shifts of the I curve—and consequently those of the Y curve—would be gradual or that they would be predictable. In consequence of the sudden, discontinuous shifts of the I curve, the intersection of the Y curve with the 45° line may, in reality, never occur at the level of the simultaneous expected income. But even if the shifts of the Y curve should accidentally be continuous enough to move the intersection through the region of the simultaneous expected income, the equilibrium conditions are still not satisfied. Equilibrium requires that slight movements away from that position should generate forces that bring the system back to equilibrium; "unstable equilibrium"[9] in a system that is

---

[9] That is, equilibrium that is not restored if the system is exposed to a slight disturbance.

being continually "disturbed" is a concept of no significance. The stability condition is satisfied with respect to movements along the curves as they are drawn in the figure. The condition is not, however, satisfied for shifts of the Y curve. Even if in the course of the discontinuous shifts of the Y curve the intersection with the 45° line should "for a moment" occur at the expected income of the period,[10] the curve will have shifted in the next period and no forces will have been generated that would prevent further shifts of the curve in the same direction. The actual behavior of the system suggests that the shifts of the I curve do not take place in accordance with dependable "functional relationships" and that they cannot be correctly anticipated.

The analysis illustrates the complete arbitrariness of statements according to which the system tends toward equilibrium positions, but, by a distinct set of disturbances, is prevented from reaching them. If the curves are drawn so as to imply stable equilibrium, except for possible shifts of the curves, then it is true that the assumed equilibrium would be approached and ultimately reached were it not for the shifts. Yet this tendency toward equilibrium is a property of the model rather than of the economy; it exists only so long as the factors expressed in the shapes of the basic functions are arbitrarily distinguished from the forces expressed by shifts. It may be fruitful to set up models in such a manner as to imply the existence of an equilibrium which the system would be approaching, were it not for a distinct set of disturbing forces. But the value of this method must be established by some independent consideration. With respect to monetary equilibrium, the significance of the concept rests on the fact that a variety of dynamic processes has been conveniently represented as being produced by the constant discrepancy between investment and savings. Moreover, it is also true that some of the factors producing the discrepancy under consideration can be controlled, and that the elimination of these factors is generally considered a desirable objective. The level at which it would be desirable to establish monetary equilibrium is, of course, that of full utilization.

---

[10] That is to say, at a point the abscissa of which is the expected income of that same period.

A weakness of the analytical conditions of monetary equilibrium as usually presented is that they do not extend to the requirements of a dynamic equilibrium over intervals of time longer than a "unit period." A hypothetical system that is *continuously in monetary equilibrium* may be said to satisfy the requirements of *dynamic equilibrium* during its growth (or decline); and certain types of instability may be analyzed fruitfully by contrasting the actual dynamic development of economies with the hypothetical developments that would occur in dynamic equilibrium. Yet, the conditions of monetary equilibrium cannot be satisfied over longer intervals unless the basic functions of figure 1, translated into "real" terms, behave in a certain way as time passes. The "real" physical magnitudes of the system cannot of course remain stable in dynamic equilibrium; they must change in accordance with such capital formation as satisfies the condition $S = I$, and also in accordance with population changes, and so on. The monetary magnitudes may or may not remain stable, depending on price behavior. In order to increase the usefulness of the analysis it should be extended so as to cover the conditions of the consistency of monetary equilibrium over time. This problem will be considered in the next chapter.

The conclusions so far reached may be briefly stated.

1. The time-honored equilibrium theories such as, for example, the neo-classical general equilibrium theories, on the one hand, and the theory of monetary equilibrium, on the other, do not purport to explain factually representative levels of activity. They are not realistic in this sense. They also cannot be defended on the grounds that they describe a situation toward which there constantly exists an abortive tendency. To defend equilibrium theorizing by such a statement is meaningless, because the statement characterizes a method of approach rather than establishes its usefulness. The method is that of describing some hypothetical condition and of viewing the processes preventing its realization as "disturbances." The significance of the condition so chosen must then be established independently. The case for equilibrium theories which do not purport to relate to factually representative levels of activity must rest on the claim that the actual *deviations* from the equilibrium conditions explain important processes conveniently.

2. For a discussion of policies, it is convenient to describe equilibrium systems in such a fashion that most of the actual deviations from equilibrium should fairly generally be regarded as undesirable; and it is also convenient to establish the theoretical framework so as to have the "deviations from equilibrium" at least partly under control.

DOES A DYNAMIC SYSTEM PASS THROUGH EQUILIBRIUM?

So far we have been concerned with varieties of the equilibrium approach that do not aim at representing a "typical" level of business activity. However, since the depression of 1929–1933, the opinion has frequently been expressed that certain theories of underemployment equilibrium—such as the Keynesian theory—are *realistic* tools of economic analysis. This opinion is based on the fact that the theories in question recognize the possibility of chronic unemployment, and that in the decade of the 1930's, there actually existed a chronic tendency toward underemployment in some of the leading industrialized economies. It is generally realized, of course, that the economies under consideration were not actually in a condition of equilibrium. Actual economic development is always dynamic, and it was very markedly dynamic in the period in which theorizing in terms of underemployment equilibrium became popular. Yet, once the fluctuations occur within a range of substantial underutilization, it becomes tempting to divide theory in two parts, one of which is concerned with a hypothetical equilibrium level around which the system fluctuates, and the other with the "business cycle" occurring around this equilibrium level. At any rate, this notion seems to be implicit in the claim that theories of underemployment equilibrium are more "realistic," or more "useful," than the classical or neo-classical equilibrium systems.

It is by no means obvious, however, that some intermediate level between the high and low points of economic fluctuations can legitimately be singled out as an equilibrium level. This procedure has certain very definite implications that cannot be accepted generally, although the procedure may be convenient for a limited number of specific purposes. Uncritical acceptance of the hypothesis that underlies the procedure in question would indicate uncritical belief in arithmetic averages as "significant" magnitudes. Arithmetic averages do not generally reflect any significant property of a universe; they mean what they are defined to mean and nothing more. The same is true of average levels between high and low points of fluctuating economic time series. They must not be considered equilibrium levels unless some independent reasoning estab-

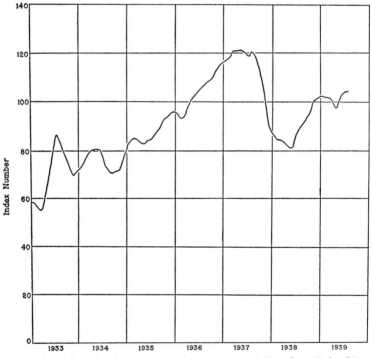

Fig. 2. Industrial production, 1933–1939 (1935–1939 = 100). Data from *Federal Reserve Charts on Bank Credit, Money Rates, and Business,* Board of Governors of the Federal Reserve System.

lishes them as such. It would, of course, be equally meaningless to choose one of the extreme levels or any intermediate level as typical of the entire range without making clear of what property that level is assumed to be typical and without demonstrating that it truly is representative of that property.

To illustrate this proposition there is reproduced here the chart of the Federal Reserve Board with respect to industrial production,[11] for the period between the depression and the outbreak of the war in Europe. The period was one of chronic underemployment even if the peak level of 1937 is included; and the fact-interpreting usefulness of underemployment equilibrium theories has frequently been asserted with reference to this circumstance, or to similar developments in other economies during the same period.

The reader may notice in figure 2 that the rise from the trough of the depression to the peak level of 1937 exceeds 100 per cent, and that the abrupt decline from the summer of 1937 to the summer of 1938 amounts to about 33 per cent. It is true of British as of American developments that the rise in activity from the trough of the depression to the upper turning point of 1937 was very significant. In Great Britain, where the contraction was less abrupt during the depression of 1929–1932,[12] the post-depression recovery carried the economy (in contrast to American developments) substantially beyond the 1929 level.[13] Looking at the period as a whole, however, unemployment was also a serious problem in the British economy.[14]

---

[11] Industrial production includes manufacturing and mining. The figure is drawn on the basis of monthly data.

[12] The preceding expansion also was much less vigorous.

[13] The available Board of Trade Index of Production indicates a 61.3 per cent rise (of what corresponds broadly to American "Industrial Production") from the lowest quarter in 1932 to the highest quarter in 1937 and a 14.2 per cent decline from the latter to the lowest quarter in 1938. The index for the year 1937 was 24.6 per cent higher than that for the year 1929. (Cf. *Board of Trade Journal*.) In the United States the index was less than 3 per cent higher for the year 1937 than for 1929.

[14] In the United States the peak level of total unemployment in 1933 seems to have been between 14 million and 16 million persons, and the lowest level in 1937 between 6 million and 8 million persons. (Cf. Russell A. Nixon and Paul A. Samuelson, "Estimates of Unemployment in the United States," *Review of Economic Statistics*, August, 1940.) In Great Britain the peak level of registered unemployment in 1932 was 2.8 million persons and the lowest level in 1937 was 1.5 million persons. (Cf. *Ministry of Labor Gazette, Supplement*, February, 1939.) Colin Clark estimates *total* unemployment for 1932 at 3.7 million persons; since the difference between Clark's figures for total unemployment and the ministry's figures for registered unemployment corresponds to about one-third of the latter throughout the period lying between 1932 and the first quarter of 1936, total unemployment for 1937 may be put at about 2 million persons. (Cf. Colin Clark, *National Income and Outlay*, London, Macmillan, 1937, p. 208.) Considering that during the period in question the British labor force was approximately 40 to 45 per cent of the American (about 22 million persons, as compared with the 50 to 54 million in the United States), unemployment must be said to have been relatively less significant in Britain than in the United States. However, the British figures undoubtedly indicate a substantial volume of unemployment. In relation to the labor force, the peak level of unemployment seems to have corresponded to about 30 per cent in the United States and to about 14 per cent in Great Britain, whereas the 1937 low

It may be convenient to summarize and to interpret certain properties of an economy, the behavior of which is partly reflected by the foregoing figure (or by similar figures for other countries) so as to substitute hypothetically *some* definite level of activity for the changing levels actually experienced. We shall not resort to this procedure, but we do not wish to deny that it has its advantages in certain specific contexts. It is necessary, however, to be aware of the fact that developments such as those sketched above do not truly display an equilibrium tendency. In particular, it should not be implied that a system behaving in this manner tends to show a relatively high degree of stability at some intermediate level, say at the average level between the two extremes. The notion that the properties of a fluctuating economy should be studied by postulating a hypothetical equilibrium level around which the oscillations take place, suggests that the system, in the course of its oscillations, passes through a distinct level of potential stability. There is nothing, however, in the facts that would bear out such an assumption. There is no reason to assume that "in the absence of cyclical disturbances" our economies would have moved along paths that are distinguishable in economic time series.

The question of whether our economies should be said to fluctuate around distinct levels of potential stability may also be viewed in terms of statistical techniques. The charts reflecting actual economic development do not show the marked regularity of simple periodic functions. Certain kinds of regularity might indeed lend plausibility to the assumption that our economies are oscillating around a distinct level of potential stability. The material does not, however, offer itself readily for this technical procedure.[15]

Generally speaking, the concept of a factually observable "normal" is misleading, regardless of the method by which the fluctuations around the normal values are "found" statistically and are

seems to have corresponded to about 13 per cent in the United States and to about 9 per cent in Great Britain. (On the labor forces of the two countries respectively, cf. Colin Clark, *op. cit.*, p. 208, table 94, column 3, and *idem, The Conditions of Economic Progress,* London, Macmillan, 1940, p. 79, column 5.)

[15] For example, as concerns the results obtained with the periodogram analysis, cf. W. L. Crum, "Cycles of Rates on Commercial Paper," *Review of Economic Statistics* (January, 1923), 17–29.

analyzed theoretically.[16] It is preferable to speak of fluctuations around a trend line (admittedly arbitrary) than to postulate fluctuations around "normal." To distinguish between "the" trend and fluctuations around it is convenient, because the forces producing the long-run drift of time series are *partly* distinct from those producing their oscillations and vice versa. But if this method is adopted, it is necessary to take into account the interaction of the two types of forces, before conclusions are reached. If the trend were different, the fluctuations would also be different; and in the absence of the forces producing the fluctuations, the long-run drift of the time series would undoubtedly be quite different from anything actually observable. This is another way of saying that "normal" or "equilibrium" cannot be observed in statistical material. Trend lines or the loci of any statistically observable points do not describe paths along which the system would be moving in the absence of "cyclical disturbances."[17] By influencing the "cycle" we also influence the trend. Economic systems do not pass through equilibrium positions, nor do they "tend" to reach these positions—unless, by affirming this tendency, the intention is to express the sterile tautology that any condition would be realized if the forces preventing its realization were absent.

This may also be expressed by saying that the underemployment equilibrium through which our systems are supposed to pass in the course of their fluctuations is indeterminate. Technically it could also be said that the underemployment equilibrium in question is "unstable." Yet it is preferable not to speak of "determinate" but of unstable equilibria that are being constantly disturbed. Such a conception would be meaningless, since unstable equilibrium plus

---

[16] Professor Schumpeter points out rightly that the concept of "normal business" is not unknown to businessmen. (Joseph A. Schumpeter, *Business Cycles*, New York and London, McGraw-Hill Book Co., 1939; cf. the introduction.) But business is considered normal or abnormal depending on how closely it accords with the tendencies that are taken for granted in any specific short-run period, and the notions about what should be taken for granted change fast and "without notice." Employing the terminology of pages 10–11 above, we may express this by saying that even if in some period the intersection of the Y curve with the 45° line should accidentally occur at the expected income of the same period, the Y curve will soon have shifted away and no forces will have been generated that would bring the curve back.

[17] Cf. Wesley C. Mitchell, *Business Cycles: The Problem and its Setting* (New York, National Bureau of Economic Research, 1927), p. 376.

disturbances add up to disequilibrium. The indeterminancy of underemployment equilibrium is expressed in the fact that some of the basic functions, which must be assumed as given if the equilibrium solution is to be calculable, are not merely volatile but that an infinite number of positions assumed by these shifting functions is equally "legitimate." In other words, it is impossible to attribute normalcy, in the given conditions, to any distinct position assumed by the basic functions during their fluctuations. Normalcy may be attributed to some position which appears to be desirable, and thereby, a value judgment may be expressed. But presumably the aim is dynamic equilibrium,[18] with reasonably full utilization, and this is not a condition "through which the system passes."

---

[18] That is, at a condition in which monetary equilibrium is satisfied consistently over time.

CHAPTER II

The Indeterminateness of Underemployment Equilibrium

THE PROBLEM OF INVESTMENT FOR FURTHER INVESTMENT

THE CONCEPT of underemployment equilibrium is older than the Keynesian analysis. In pre-Keynesian days the conditions of this equilibrium were expressed in terms of the behavior of the relative cost structure, on certain simplifying assumptions concerning aggregate money flows. This type of statement is found, for example, in Professor Hicks' *Theory of Wages,* where the question is raised as to what occurs, in a stationary closed community, if the general level of real wages is raised and maintained at a height inconsistent with full employment. Hicks' answer is: "The final position thus reached is one of equilibrium if the existence of the unemployed is left out of account."[1]

On the other hand, the Keynesian type of analysis is concerned with money flows and it has definite implications on cost behavior. The conditions of Keynesian equilibrium may be provisionally stated in terms of figure 1 (p. 10). In the Keynesian analysis the position of the I function is determined by the marginal efficiency schedule and the rate of interest; and the rate of interest is in turn determined by the demand for money and the supply of money (but it *could* be regarded as being determined by the demand for loans and the supply of loans). The basic assumption is that the intersection of the Y curve with the 45° line occurs "in the real world" at a level of money income equivalent to a physical output which can be produced with much less than the available labor force. This implies that the Y curve tends to a distinct position around which it

---

[1] J. R. Hicks, *The Theory of Wages* (London, Macmillan, 1932), pp. 198–199. Cf. also A. C. Pigou, *The Theory of Unemployment* (London, Macmillan, 1933), p. 252.

oscillates under the impact of certain disturbances; and that the behavior of the cost structure is such that the equilibrium position of the Y curve is not rendered unstable by "adjustments," even though the number of unemployed is large in the equilibrium position.

The fact that the I function oscillates is recognized, and even emphasized, in the Keynesian reasoning; but if the equilibrium solution is to be meaningful it has to be assumed that some distinct level occupied in the course of these oscillations represents the true level of the function, and that the function is being moved around this position by specific disturbances. This notion of the "true level" is essential for the determinancy of the equilibrium solution. It will be argued that there is nothing in the real world, or in the Keynesian analytical framework itself, that would substantiate this notion of the "true level."

The intersection point to which the Keynesian analysis relates (point **P** in fig. 1, p. 10) fails to exhibit an equilibrium tendency, so far as shifts of the functions are concerned. This becomes obvious as soon as the question is raised: Why does the intersection occur where it does at any moment of time? Assuming that the position of the C curve is relatively stable, the answer is: Because producers believe that a certain amount of investment can be undertaken profitably, given all actual and assumed conditions of the system at that time. If they believed that more investment could be undertaken, the investment flow would be higher, provided that resources were available for more investment. Whether the improved expectations of the producers would be justified depends on what their expectations would be in subsequent periods. Optimism that is consistent over time necessarily justifies itself for the economy as a whole, unless interference on the part of the monetary authority or some other outside disturbance prevents it from justifying itself; and pessimism that is consistent over time necessarily justifies itself for the economy as a whole, unless the deflationary consequences of pessimism are effectively counteracted by monetary policy or by an outside impact. As long as undesirable price developments, stemming from scarcity, do not occur, the monetary authority should not be assumed to counteract consistent optimism.

It should, of course, be realized that a psychological theory in which a statement such as the foregoing one belongs does not carry very far. Any worthwhile theory must go beyond statements like this and it must do so by raising the question of what normally influences producers in forming their expectations and also of what expectations are likely to remain fairly consistent over time. Furthermore, certain expectations almost necessarily lead to developments that will be counteracted by deliberate action of the monetary authority or by other outside disturbances. All this should lead to an analysis of real factors underlying the psychological surface of dynamic theory. At the same time it must always be remembered that expectations are the immediate determinants of entrepreneurial activity and that consequently no doctrine holds true that leaves out of account the interaction of real developments with entrepreneurial expectations. In order to argue that a level of expectations producing an underemployment intersection in figure 1 is a true level, it would have to be shown that shifts away from that level give rise to certain developments preventing these shifts from becoming permanent. This, however, cannot be argued convincingly unless certain basic postulates of the underconsumption theories are implied.

The underconsumptionist justification of the doctrine of the "true" level of underemployment would have to be about as follows: Given the C function of figure 1, entrepreneurs have objective reasons for undertaking no more and no less than a definite amount of investment at each income level. If they undertake more investment they will soon discover that they were too optimistic and consequently they will reduce their investment activity; if they undertake less investment than would correspond to the true level, they will discover that they were too pessimistic, and consequently they will increase the scale of investment. They do so because any given marginal propensity to consume "calls for" (by which is meant objectively calls for) a certain amount of investment. Hence, given the C curve, the true level of the Y curve is objectively determined. The relationship between the C curve and the Y curve is considered to be an objective one because it is assumed that producers invest in order to satisfy consumer demand. Given, therefore, the C function of figure 1, that is, the so-called consumption function, the true level of investment for each point along the abscissa is that amount which will give rise to an increase in output no greater than is warranted by the marginal propensity to consume.

This notion would be correct only if investment were governed exclusively by the increase in consumption that can be achieved when output (income) rises. However, it can be shown that the capitalist economy would be involved in a continuous process of contraction if the investment-consumption relationship actually were as simple as this. Once it is assumed that the marginal propensity to consume, in real terms, typically is smaller than unity, it must be taken for granted that part of the investment undertaken during any period does not serve to increase the consumption of the subsequent period in which output rises but, on the contrary, serves to bring forth further investment in the subsequent period. This may be expressed briefly by saying that only part of the investment of any period is "for (subsequent) consumption," the other part is "for (subsequent) further investment." The *additional* output attributable to investment serves these two purposes respectively. The net investment of a period must be assumed to increase the real output produced subsequently beyond the level at which the subsequent output otherwise would be. This increase corresponds to the marginal productivity of capital.[2] If the marginal propensity to consume is smaller than unity, part of this subsequent increase in output will have to consist of a further increase in new investment *and the same proposition will hold true of any sequence of periods.* This is another way of saying that *any* amount of net investment may be "justified" per unit of expected consumer demand, provided a high rate of investment per unit of consumer demand will be considered justified also in the future. *Aggregate* consumer demand of course rises if more investment is undertaken per unit of additional consumer demand (i.e., if more investment for further investment is undertaken) because in this event aggregate income rises. Within the limits set by the availability of resources, any amount of output

---

[2] The concept of investment for further investment could also be defined in gross terms (i.e., as part of gross investment). For the purpose here the net concept is more convenient. In declining economies the net magnitudes would become negative and the increases would become decreases.

can be maintained indefinitely, regardless of the shape and the slope of the consumption function, provided the willingness to invest for further investment is sufficient.

It also is possible to indicate what fraction of the aggregate net investment of each period must turn out to be investment for further (or subsequent) *planned* investment, in order to avoid an *unplanned* accumulation (or decumulation) of stocks.[3] *The fraction is one minus the marginal propensity to consume*, in real terms. This is true because the additional output attributable to the net investment can be only partly sold to consumers; and the fraction that can be sold to consumers is measured by the marginal propensity to consume. The remaining output attributable to the net investment must be for subsequent (further) planned investment, if unplanned changes in stocks are to be avoided. Investment for further investment always turns out to be the amount of net investment times one minus the marginal propensity to consume, but if the economic process is to show stability over time, the subsequent investment flows must be deliberately generated and must not express themselves in undesigned changes of inventories.

The lag between the "investment" and the "subsequent further investment" is merely that extending from the acquisition of a new physical asset to the appearance of such additional output as must be allocated either to consumption or to investment. This is a lag of infinitesimal length; when commodities are being produced, the "goods in process" produced in the first infinitesimally short period coöperate in the production of the goods in process produced during the second period of infinitesimal duration.[4] It does not follow, however, that a new decision to invest the product of the preceding investment must be made in each period of infinitesimal length. One and the same "decision" may cover the subsequent reinvestment of the product of investments for a considerable period in advance. The investor decides in advance that the goods in process

[3] Investment for further planned investment may be, of course, in part, a matter not of actually selling to another investor, but of satisfying one's own reservation demand for physical assets in the next period. This, however, is true of all demand-supply propositions.

[4] Cf. Earl R. Rolph, "The Discounted Marginal Productivity Theory," *Journal of Political Economy* (August, 1939), 542–556. Cf. *ibid.*, pp. 548 ff.

produced in the first infinitesimally short period will be used to produce further goods in process, and so on: he decides to produce "finished" products. The individual makes new decisions at discrete points of time.

From the standpoint of the *ex ante–ex post* distinction, investment for further planned investment is a hybrid because it is characterized by a relationship between investment plans and the *result* of preceding investment. The investment plans call for using the product of preceding investment in the framework of further investment. Nevertheless, for a community as a whole, it is possible to speak of a high or of a low willingness to invest for further investment. The willingness to invest for further investment is high if, consistently over time, a substantial amount of investment is undertaken that results in products used for further investment. Consistency over time must be required in order to exclude investment that leads to unplanned additions to inventories. In the event of unplanned accumulation, aggregate investment declines after a brief interval, so that there exists no "consistency over time"; and, of course, there also exists no "willingness to invest for further investment."

The "real" conditions of dynamic equilibrium, which will now be formulated, are, as will be argued, interdependent with the monetary conditions discussed in chapter i (that is, with the modernized version of the Wicksellian $S = I$). In figure 3, the expected real income of a planning period is measured along the abscissa; the aggregate consumption (C), the aggregate planned investment (I_p), and the sum of these two ($C + I_p$) are measured along the ordinate in real terms and for the identical period.[5] Assuming that the marginal propensity to consume declines with rising real income, the C function tends to flatten out; and assuming, as in figure 1, that the inducement to invest for further investment is given (i.e., is not functionally related to the magnitudes measured along the axes),

---

[5] "Real" means that the magnitudes in question are expressed in the prices of some base period. As was pointed out in footnote 6, p. 10, it would have been possible to use the monetary I_p function instead of the monetary I function in figure 1; and it would be possible to use the real I function instead of the real I_p function in figure 3. But some of the points involved in the discussion of chapter i could be brought out better by using the I function, and the main point involved in the present context can be illustrated more conveniently by using the I_p function.

the I_p function slopes downward. Investment for further investment should be represented by a horizontal line, and the other constituent of aggregate planned investment, namely planned investment for subsequent consumption, depends on the marginal propensity to consume, which here is assumed to decline. If a linear consumption function (i.e., a constant marginal propensity to consume) were assumed, the I_p function would have to be drawn horizontally. It will be argued later that it may be realistic to conceive of the C curve as a linear function, although it is more usual to assume that the marginal propensity to con-

sume declines with rising income. This difference possesses no significance in the present context.

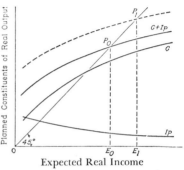

Fig. 3. "Real" determinants of dynamic equilibrium.

Dynamic equilibrium requires that expected real income should equal $C+I_p$; this condition is satisfied where the 45° line of the figure intersects with $C+I_p$. The same condition cannot, however, be satisfied in the subsequent period, unless the I_p curve shifts upward from the "present period" to the next. This is clearly reflected by figure 3, since the real income of the next period will be higher than that of the present period by a magnitude that depends on (although is not uniquely determined by) the investment of the present period. Assuming at first a relatively stable C function, it is obvious that the higher real income can correspond to a new intersection point with the 45° line only if the I_p curve shifts upward. The necessary degree of shift may be read from the figure if it is known at what rate the system moves to the right along the abscissa in consequence of the net capital formation that takes place. The $C + I_p$ function must shift upward so that the abscissa of its intersection with the 45° line should move to the right at the same rate. Assume, for example, that the investment of the present period is the height of the I_p curve for E_0 (this must equal the planned saving for the real income level OE_0); and assume that, from the present to the next period, this investment raises the rate of real income from OE_0 to OE_1; then the curves of the chart must shift to the "dotted" levels corresponding to an intersection with the 45° line at OE_1. In fact, an upward shift of the I_p function becomes necessary not merely if the C function is stable; it becomes necessary whenever the historical consumption function (which *may* result from upward shifts of analytical consumption functions) possesses a slope of less than unity. This condition is realistic. Dynamic equilibrium requires upward-shifting I_p functions.

It also becomes obvious from these considerations that investment for further planned investment must increase from one period to the other (unless either the marginal propensity to consume or the average propensity to consume, or both, *increase* markedly with rising income). Constancy of both the average and the marginal propensity to consume would require an increase of aggregate investment for further investment in the same proportion as that in which real income rises, because both aggregate consumption and investment for consumption would be increasing at this same rate. Decline of both the average and the marginal propensity to consume would require an increase of investment for further investment at a rate exceeding that of the rate of increase of real income, because both aggregate consumption and investment for consumption would account for smaller shares of an increased output.

If the "real" conditions of dynamic equilibrium—those expressing themselves in the upward shift of the intersection from P_0 to P_1 in figure 3—are not satisfied, then the monetary conditions (*ex ante* S = I) can also not remain satisfied for more than a period of negligible duration. If the I_p function of figure 3 does not shift upward from period to period in accordance with the requirements of dynamic equilibrium,[9] an unplanned accumulation of inventories takes place and this must be expected to result in monetary and real contraction. On the other hand, if the "real" conditions are satisfied, then the actual development corresponds to expectations, and hence a discrepancy between the money value of *ex ante* savings and investment cannot arise. The conditions expressed by figure 1 and those expressed by figure 3 are therefore interdependent con-

---

[9] Dynamic equilibrium was defined in chap. i as a hypothetical state of affairs in which the condition of monetary equilibrium is satisfied consistently over time; and monetary equilibrium was defined as satisfying the condition S = I, *ex ante*.

ditions of what may be called *dynamic equilibrium,* but it is impossible to express the two sets of conditions in one and the same diagram, unless a constant price level is postulated. With a correctly foreseen continuous decline of the price level, dynamic equilibrium might, for example, require stability over time of the basic functions of figure 1, but the functions of figure 3 would still have to shift in accordance with the requirements here discussed, to allow for the rise of real income in consequence of the net capital formation. It may be repeated that the underlying definition of dynamic equilibrium requires that actual economic development must not deviate from plans and that this concept, although obviously unrealistic, is believed to be fruitful in the analysis of phenomena of instability, such as are attributable to deviations from planned developments (i.e., to unforeseen events).

The existence of periods of expansion refutes the assumption according to which all investment is determined by the rising consumption by which it is accompanied. What part of investment is "spontaneous" (in the sense of not having been induced by a *preceding* rise in consumer demand) is a question of no significance whatsoever from this point of view. Regardless of whether a flow of investment is or is not "spontaneous," it is true that part of the additional output must subsequently be absorbed by further planned investment, if no unplanned accumulation of inventories is to occur. If all investment was intended to be for consumption rather than for further investment, the economy would be contracting without interruption, provided that the marginal propensity to consume is smaller than one. In these circumstances, the investment activity of any period would prove to be too high in the next period. If, accidentally, there were no contraction in some period, the process of contraction would set in with a negligible lag.

Since it is realized that the investment activity of any period is partly for consumption and partly for further investment, it cannot be maintained that the shape of the C curve determines the true level of the I curve of figure 1 and thereby of the Y curve. The I curve is determined partly by the amount of investment that is undertaken in order to supply increased output for consumption and partly by the amount of investment that is undertaken to supply increased output for further investment. The inducement to invest for further investment must be distinguished from the inducement to invest for consumption; and the amount of investment serving the purpose of further investment has no objectively determined "true level" as long as resources are available for this type of activity and as long as these resources are of the kind that is demanded. If it is consistently assumed that more investment for further investment is justified, then actually more proves to be justified; whereas if it is consistently assumed that less of this activity is justified, then actually less proves to be justified.

So far as the mechanics of the capitalist process are concerned, there is no more inherent truth in the statement that investment is for the sake of consumption than in the statement that consumption is for the sake of investment (or production). If producers were consistently willing to use for investment all resources that are not being used for the production of consumers' goods, they would find this behavior to be profitable regardless of the position and of the slope of the consumption function. To say that investment for further investment would involve an absurdity because producers would always be producing partly for producers instead of for consumers, means calling an entirely normal, and even indispensable, feature of an expanding economy, absurd. In Professor Knight's words:

The increase in wealth is to a large extent an end in itself as well as a means to the increase of *income,* and this also again to a rapidly increasing degree as the standards of life are advanced. Men work to get rich in a large proportion of cases not merely in addition to, but in place of, consuming larger amounts of goods. It is a grave error to assume that in a modern industrial nation production takes place only in order to (increase) consumption. It is true to a great and ever-increasing degree that consumption is sacrificed to increase production. Whatever our philosophy of human motives, we must face the fact that men *do* "raise more corn to feed more hogs to buy more land to raise more corn to feed more hogs to buy more land," and in business generally, produce wealth to be used in producing more wealth with no view to any use beyond the increase of wealth itself.[7]

---

[7] F. H. Knight, *Risk, Uncertainty and Profit* (Boston and New York, Houghton, Mifflin, 1921), cf. p. 319; cf. also *idem, The Ethics of Competition and Other Essays* (New York-London, Harper, 1935), p. 26, n. 2.

If, however, for some reason it is determined to press reality into a model in which all investment is undertaken "ultimately" to satisfy consumer demand, this may be done, provided a sufficiently complicated terminology is used, and provided care is taken to avoid the pitfalls of that terminology. This procedure is not going to be applied here, but it may be pointed out that since total consumption is increasing with total real output, it is always possible to maintain that all investment activity is aimed at letting total consumption rise. Moreover, instead of saying that part of the present investment serves the purpose of subsequent further investment rather than that of additional consumption, it is possible to say that part of the investment of the present period will prove profitable because of consumption occurring at a distant future rather than in the immediately following periods. All this, however, constitutes a difficult attempt to save a preconceived model in the face of a nonconforming reality. Clearly, since the marginal propensity to consume is positive (which means that aggregate consumption is rising with aggregate income), dynamic lags may be defined into the system, the investment of the present may be associated with the consumption of distant periods, and consequently all economic activity may be represented as being undertaken to realize higher and higher points along the aggregate consumption function, at increasingly distant dates. Then, of course, the length of the "dynamic lag" becomes variable and this becomes the reason for the variable relationship between the C and the I function. Unfortunately for the terminology in question, it would have to be added that the investment of the present serves effectively the consumption of n periods from the present only if in the course of these n periods further investment will be undertaken that will have to serve the consumption of periods following the nth period from the present.[8] This kind of terminology does not recommend itself because it obscures an essential fact, on which economic analysis should be focused. It is a fact that contraction cannot be avoided if a certain fraction of the products of the net investment activity of each period fails to be used subsequently for further (additional) planned net investment. This is true of any sequence of periods. An

---

[8] There exists an obvious analogy with the pitfalls of the "Austrian" capital theory, and, in general, with views rooted in the wage-fund theory.

economy intended to be completely "geared to consumption" is by necessity a contracting economy, if the marginal propensity to consume is less than unity.

The foregoing analysis relates to the mechanics of the capitalist process. On the level of value judgments it could scarcely be contested that normally all investment derives its "justification" from being associated with rising consumption. But this is an altogether different question.

THE CONSUMPTION-INVESTMENT RELATIONSHIP

Factual observation does not suggest any simple relationship between the aggregate flow of investment, on the one hand, and either the marginal propensity to consume or the time rate of increase in aggregate consumption, on the other. The apparent lack of a significant relationship between these variables supports the view emphasizing the importance of investment for further investment, and makes it difficult to argue that the "true" position of the investment function is determined by the character of the income-consumption relationship or by the expected rise in aggregate consumption. Figures 4 to 10 are presented here to justify these statements.

Figure 4 shows yearly data for consumers' outlay in constant prices and for net private capital formation in constant prices for the period 1919–1938. The underlying data are taken from Professor Kuznets' study on income and its composition during this period.[9] The figure is drawn on an arithmetic scale because it is primarily the absolute rather than the relative rate of increase in consumption that might be assumed to bear a relationship to the flow of new investment. It should be added, however, that plotting of the data on a logarithmic scale would not suggest the existence of the relationships between the change in consumption, on the one hand, and the amount of investment, on the other, such as appear to be absent when the data are plotted arithmetically.

It is seen that on the whole consumers' outlay tends to rise at a decreasing rate during the expansion period of the 1920's. In other words, the absolute amount of investment justified by the time rate

---

[9] Simon Kuznets, *National Income and Its Composition, 1919–1938* (New York, National Bureau of Economic Research, 1941), I, 269.

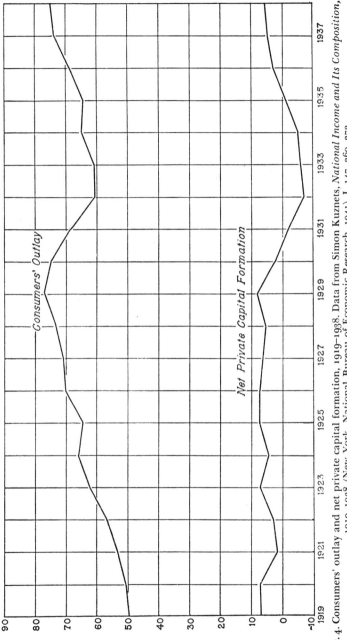

Fig. 4. Consumers' outlay and net private capital formation, 1919–1938. Data from Simon Kuznets, *National Income and Its Composition,* 1919–1938 (New York, National Bureau of Economic Research, 1941), I, 147, 269, 272.

of increase in consumption tended to decrease. Despite this, net private capital formation is well maintained during the 1920's; in fact it exhibits a slight upward tendency.[10] Prior to the collapse of 1929 the curve expressing consumer outlay does not show properties which would distinguish it from its previous course. For the entire recovery period of the 1930's the trend of the rate of increase in

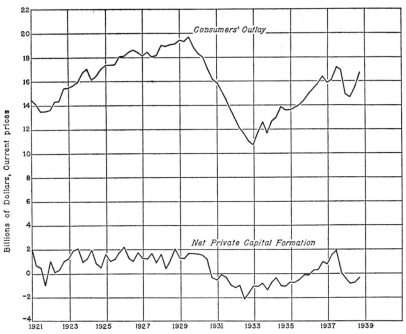

Fig. 5. Consumers' outlay and net private capital formation, quarterly, 1921–1938 (current prices). Data from Harold Barger, *Outlay and Income in the United States, 1921–1938* (New York, National Bureau of Economic Research, 1942), pp. 114–119.

consumers' outlay appears to be linear; however, the rate of increase is sharper immediately prior to the downturn of 1937, than in the early stage of the recovery. Net private capital formation rises at first at an increasing rate and thereafter continues to rise, although at a decreasing rate. The figure does not suggest any simple relationship between the aggregate amount of private investment and the time rate of increase in consumption.

---

[10] This does not contradict the Acceleration Principle because consumers' demand is not coextensive with "direct demand," nor is investment coextensive with derived demand.

Figure 5 contains quarterly data for consumers' outlay and net private capital formation for the period 1921–1939. These data are taken from Dr. Barger's study.[11] They differ from the data underlying figure 4 in several respects. In the first place, the Barger data are not corrected for price changes. In addition, there unfortunately exist certain definitional differences between the concepts used by Kuznets, on the one hand, and by Barger, on the other. In spite of this, it would be just as easy to illustrate the previous statements with reference to the figures based on Barger's estimates as it is to justify them with reference to the estimates of Kuznets.[12] There does not appear to be any simple relationship between the time rate of increase in consumption and the absolute amount of investment. At the same time, the figure based on Barger's estimates shows that after the depression of 1929–1933, net private investment reached its lower turning point one-half year (two quarters) earlier than consumers' outlay. The same is true of gross private investment, and of aggregate investment inclusive of public outlay, although this is not indicated in figure 5.[13] Not much meaning can, in these circumstances, be attached to the opinion frequently voiced that in the 1930's, as opposed to the 1920's, investment was "geared to consumption."[14] It is true, of course, that the average propensity to consume was lower in the 'thirties than in the preceding decade,[15]

---

[11] Harold Barger, *Outlay and Income in the United States, 1921–9138* (New York, National Bureau of Economic Research), pp. 114–119.

[12] Consumers' outlay tends, on the whole, to rise at a decreasing rate during the 'twenties, whereas investment exhibits an approximately horizontal trend in the same period. For the 'thirties, the conclusions would also be identical with those derived from the Kuznets' data.

[13] The investment "lead" on the upturn is a consequence of the fact that inventory accumulation reached its lower turning point in the third quarter of 1932, that is, one-half year prior to consumers' outlay. The aggregate of the other constituents of private capital formation turned up in the first quarter of 1933, that is, simultaneously with consumers' outlay. The upturn of inventory accumulation in the third quarter of 1932 is reflected in the fact that the corresponding figure for the third quarter of the year is a smaller negative figure than that relating to the second quarter. The series here used are corrected for seasonal variations.

[14] On the contrary, figure 5 indicates a consumption lead for upturns after the minor recessions of the 'twenties in 1924 and 1927. All downturns of the 'twenties, however, are more readily interpreted in terms of an investment lead. In 1921 (upturn), 1937 (downturn), and 1938 (upturn), consumers' outlay and investment turned in the same quarter.

[15] Cf. e.g. Harold M. Somers, "The Performance of the American Economy Since 1860," in *The Growth of the American Economy,* ed. Harold F. Williamson (New York, Prentice Hall), p. 777.

but this is merely another way of saying that the decade of the 'thirties was a relatively depressed period. Investment always corresponds to a reduced share of output, when the level of activity is low.

In the historical long run the amount of investment also does not seem to have been "geared" to the time rate of change in consumption. Figures 6 (arithmetic scale) and 7 (logarithmic scale) show consumption and capital formation for the period lying between the 1880's and the depression of 1929–1933. The data are taken from

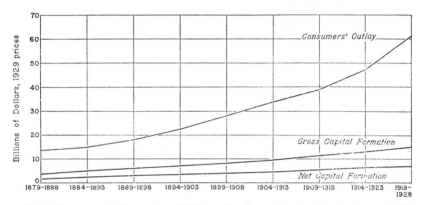

Fig. 6. Consumers' outlay and capital formation for overlapping decades (1929 prices). Arithmetic scale. Data from Simon Kuznets, *Uses of National Income in Peace and War*, Occasional Paper, 6 (New York, National Bureau of Economic Research, March, 1942), pp. 30, 31, 39.

Professor Kuznets' recent study *Uses of National Income in Peace and War;*[16] they express average values for overlapping decades (such as 1878–1888, 1884–1893, 1889–1899, etc.) and they are corrected for price changes. On the whole, consumption and net capital formation tended to rise at a similar rate, logarithmically. (At first net capital formation rose at a somewhat higher rate than consumers' outlay, logarithmically; for the later part of the period, the reverse is true.) Arithmetically, the rate of increase of consumers' outlay shows rising trend and so does the absolute amount of investment, for the period as a whole. This, of itself, might suggest a relationship between the two magnitudes. Closer analysis, however, contradicts

---

[16] *Uses of National Income in Peace and War*, Occasional Paper 6, National Bureau of Economic Research (March, 1942), cf. p. 31. Capital formation (gross and net) is "total" rather than "private" because the data do not permit of the separation of public from private investment.

such a hypothesis. For example, the absolute (arithmetic) rate of increase in consumers' outlay was approximately constant from the decade 1894–1903 through the decade 1909–1918; the absolute amount of net capital formation, however, increased continuously during this period with the result that it was approximately two-

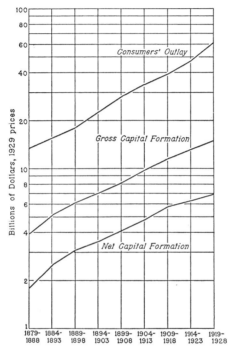

Fig. 7. Consumers' outlay and capital formation for overlapping decades (1929 prices). Semilogarithmic scale.

thirds higher in the decade 1909–1918 than in the decade 1894–1903. Moreover, after the decade 1909–1918 the absolute rate of increase in consumers' outlay increases sharply, whereas the amount of net capital formation increases less sharply than was true in previous decades in which the rate of increase in consumers' outlay was approximately constant.

It might be maintained that the consumption-investment relationship should be interpreted as a relationship existing between the marginal propensity to consume and the amount of investment,

rather than as a relationship existing between the time rate of increase in consumption and the absolute amount of investment. In
fact, such an interpretation would accord well with several versions
of the underconsumption theory. The factual material previously
used does not, however, substantiate this hypothesis any more than
the hypothesis linking investment to the time rate of change in
consumption. Figure 8 shows the lack of consistency in the relation-

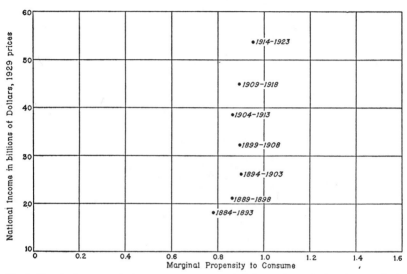

Fig. 8. Marginal propensity to consume—net capital formation relation (1929 prices).
Data from Kuznets, *Uses of National Income*, p. 31.

ship between the marginal propensity to consume and the amount
of net capital formation, for the "historical long-run." The data are
derived from Kuznets' study (*Uses of National Income . . .*), where
the figures for capital formation, in constant prices, can be found
directly. The data expressing the marginal propensity to consume
have been calculated for any one decade by averaging $\triangle C/\triangle Y$ from
the preceding decade to the decade in question with $\triangle C/\triangle Y$ from
the decade in question to the subsequent decade. This is the closest
approximation obtainable from the Kuznets' data to the $\triangle C/\triangle Y$
of the decades to which the capital formation data relate. We have
also experimented with lags, implicitly introduced by *not* averaging
in the manner indicated, but the scatters obtained in that fashion

are quite similar to the one in figure 8. The data indicate that aggregate investment is not "geared" in any observable manner to the marginal propensity to consume. Investment for further investment accounts for varying shares of total investment and of total output.

Figure 9 indicates the historical long-run relationship between the aggregate level of output and the marginal propensity to consume, in constant prices.[17] The absence of a significant relationship

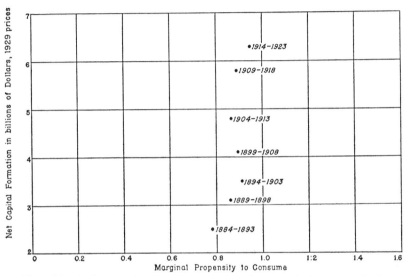

Fig. 9. Marginal propensity to consume—national income relation (1929 prices). Data from Kuznets, *Uses of National Income*, p. 31.

is suggested immediately by the middle range of the scatter (five readings). It may be objected that the first and the last reading, in time, lends the scatter the semblance of an upward slope. This is produced by the fact that in the first of the decades included, the marginal propensity to consume was low in comparison to its long-run average, whereas in the last decade it was high. Output was rising continuously throughout the period considered and consequently the first and the last readings, in time, show a low output level paired with a low marginal propensity on the one hand, and a high output level paired with a high marginal propensity, on the

[17] The marginal propensity to consume is obtained for the single decades by the same process of averaging as was described above.

other. Yet in the entire intermediate range, the marginal propensity to consume oscillates, whereas output rises continuously, so that no consistent relationship whatsoever emerges.

As for the period of the 1920's and 1930's, the yearly data, taken from Kuznets' *National Income and its Composition*, indicate a

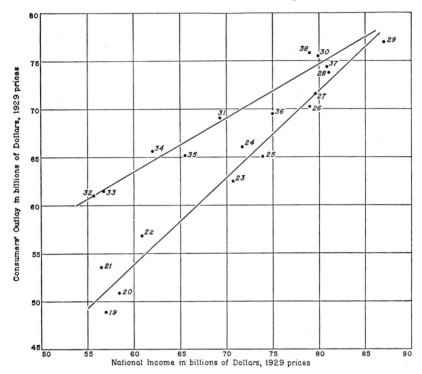

Fig. 10. Consumers' outlay—national income relation, 1919–1929 and 1930–1938 (1929 prices). Regression equations: 1919–1929, C = 0.0364 + 0.898 Y ± 1.635; 1920–1929, C = 4.76 + 0.835 Y ± 1.405; 1930–1936, C = 29.9 + 0.559 Y ± 1.228 where C and Y are expressed in billions of dollars. Data from Kuznets, *National Income and Its Composition*, I, 147.

decline in the marginal propensity to consume for the transition from 1928 to 1929 as compared with preceding pairs of years. This decline precedes the collapse of 1929.[18] Yet, the opposite situation exists in the period immediately preceding the decline of 1937, that is, for the transition from 1936 to 1937. Here the marginal propensity to consume rises from low level, in the early 'thirties, to a level

---

[18] The analogous statement does not hold for the minor recessions of the 'twenties.

similar to that of the 'twenties. Figure 10 shows these relationships. The consumption function, in constant prices, distinctly appears to be "linear" during the period between the First World War and the Great Depression, but the point for 1929 lies below the line of average relationship,[19] and the slope of the line connecting the point for 1928 with the point for 1929 is distinctly smaller than the slope connecting the immediately preceding years. The data for the 1930's appear to be placed around a straight line of smaller slope;[20] yet the points for 1936 and for 1937 could be said to belong just as well in the universe of the 'twenties as in their own universe. The two latter points (1936 and 1937) are placed very close to the line of average relationship applying to the period 1919–1929, and $\triangle C/\triangle Y$ for the transition from 1936 to 1937 is 0.862, which is almost precisely identical with the slope of the line of average relationship applying to the decade preceding the Great Depression (0.898). The yearly data suggest a decline in the marginal propensity to consume prior to the Great Depression, but a rise in the marginal propensity to consume prior to the downturn of 1937.

National income has also been plotted against consumers' outlay in current prices and aggregate (individual) income payments against consumer outlay in both constant and current prices, from the Kuznets' data. These scatters, not included here, differ from those in figure 10 in certain respects.[21] From the present point of view, the differences are of no great significance, however, because all these scatters suggest approximate linearity of the consumption function,[22] and they also suggest a decline in the marginal

---

[19] $C = 0.0364 + 0.898$ Y. The standard error of estimate is 1.635. If the year 1919 is omitted, the equation is $C = 4.76 + 0.835$ Y; the standard error of estimate is 1.405.

[20] $C = 29.9 + 0.559$ Y. The standard error of estimate is 1.228.

[21] In two of these other scatters (national income *versus* consumption in current prices, and income payments *versus* consumption in constant prices), the line of best fit for the 'thirties lies much closer to the line of best fit for the 'twenties than in figure 10; yet the two lines still appear to be distinct. In the third scatter (income payments *versus* consumption in current prices) a single linear function suggests itself for the entire universe of 1919–1938. For an interpretation of differences between the national income-consumption relationship and the income payments-consumption relationship, cf. Paul A. Samuelson, "Appendix to Chapter XI," in Alvin H. Hansen, *Fiscal Policy and Business Cycles* (New York, Norton, 1941).

[22] This, of course, does not mean that it is impossible to refine the linear income-consumption relationship by introducing further variables. Cf. Mordecai Ezekiel, "Saving, Consumption, and Investment," *American Economic Review* (March and June, 1942).

propensity to consume prior to the downturn of 1929, but a rise prior to the downturn of 1937.

If the relationship between the marginal propensity to consume and investment or output is investigated on the basis of Dr. Barger's quarterly estimates,[23] the inference that the marginal propensity to consume rose prior to the downturn of 1937 is confirmed. However, the validity of the statement that there occurred a decline prior to the collapse of 1929 is much less clearly confirmed, although it is not exactly refuted.[24] On the other hand, the Barger data do seem to contain some indication to the effect that the marginal propensity to consume showed an unfavorable tendency prior to the investment downturns of the minor recessions of the 1920's.

In conclusion it may be stated that the available factual material does not lend itself to the verification of simple underconsumptionist hypotheses concerning the relationship between consumption and investment. No simple relationship is found between the time rate of change in consumption on the one hand, and the absolute amount of investment, on the other. This does not contradict the Acceleration Principle because "direct demand" and "derived demand" are not coëxtensive with consumer demand and investment demand, respectively. But the lack of relationship in question contradicts one simple underconsumptionist hypothesis, and another is contradicted by the fact that the marginal propensity to consume does not seem to govern the flow of investment or its turning points. All this obviously does not answer the question whether certain underconsumptionist elements could be fitted into more complex hypotheses, statistically or analytically.

---

[23] These run in current prices.

[24] The "upper turning point" of capital formation falls in the fourth quarter of 1928, yet after some decline there again occurred a rise from the second to the third quarter of 1929, which carried capital formation to a slightly lower level than that of the fourth quarter of 1928. After the third quarter of 1929 capital formation declined continuously. The upper turning point of total income clearly falls in the third quarter of 1929 rather than in the fourth quarter of 1928 because, although income also shows a double peak with a decline and a subsequent rise between the two, the income peak of the third quarter of 1929 is higher than that of the fourth quarter of 1928. Now, the marginal propensity to consume shows an "unfavorable" tendency immediately preceding the fourth quarter of 1928. Yet, between the fourth quarter of 1928 and the third quarter of 1929 the tendency is not consistent. In one of the quarters lying between these two, consumption rose in spite of a decline in income and in the quarter of the income turning point and of the second investment peak (i.e., in the third quarter of 1929) $\Delta C / \Delta Y$ was approximately at the level of the early 'twenties.

THE ELEMENT OF TRUTH BEHIND THE UNDERCONSUMPTION THEORIES

The element of truth behind the underconsumptionist reasoning may perhaps be expressed by saying that the amount of investment is "psychologically determined" in a higher degree than the amount of consumption. Consumers' expenditures are less sensitive to consumers' income expectations than are producers' expenditures to producers' income expectations. If entrepreneurs become less optimistic, and, consequently, the income of consumers as well as that of producers declines, then expenditures on consumers' goods are typically better maintained than investment expenditures. It is true both of the demand for consumers' goods and of the demand for producers' goods that the general expectation of high demand on the part of entrepreneurs actually results in high demand, unless the authority exerts deflationary pressure; yet an unsatisfactory state of mind leading to reduced output translates itself less readily into a precipitous decline in consumer demand than into an abrupt shrinkage of the demand for producers' goods. The reason for this phenomenon is that consumer saving is more elastic to incomes and to income expectations than is consumer spending, whereas the willingness of producers to invest undoubtedly depends, in a large measure, on their recent incomes and on their income expectations. The comparatively small elasticity of consumption to income is a consequence of biological and institutional circumstances which introduce a large amount of rigidity into consumption habits. In this sense it may be said that the amount of investment is psychologically determined in a higher degree than the amount of consumption; or that the market for consumers' goods is more dependable, viewed from the angle of the producer, than is the market for investment goods.

Consistent optimism tends to justify itself *ex post*,[25] and so does consistent pessimism.[26] But there is some reason to assume that optimism might not long remain consistent if the share of the demand for consumers' goods in the total demand for goods becomes

---

[25] As long as the economy does not run into scarcities.
[26] As long as it is not effectively counteracted.

"unusually" low, and that an "unusually" high share of consumer demand may tend to reverse the pessimistic trend of which it is the product. The reason is that the producer can shift his demand curves for goods, within a significant range, much more easily than the consumer. Consequently the fear that he might do so is greater than the fear that consumer demand would shift violently. The fear that the investor might prove to be an unreliable customer may very well lead to the discontinuation of a period of optimism, once a "high" stage is reached in which investors buy a substantial share of total output. Awareness of the fact that consumers are more reliable customers may lead to an increased willingness to produce, once a "low" stage is reached in which a very substantial share of output is bought by consumers. Knowledge of the fact that biological properties and rigid habits underlie a considerable portion of consumer demand make the producers of consumers' goods less likely to change their output abruptly. The fact that a buyer who is a producer is in a position to change his demand suddenly is likely to render the willingness to produce for producers unstable and also to reduce the average level of this activity. Obviously, if the willingness to produce for producers declines, then the demand of producers for investment goods also declines. In this case the fact that producers mutually know of one another that their demand is potentially unstable, actually leads to a reduction of their demand. This, I think, is the element of truth lying behind the underconsumptionist doctrines, which, however, misrepresent the case by disregarding the phenomenon of investment for further investment. It is also the element of truth behind the paradox that an equitable distribution of income may be conducive to entrepreneurial interests. The average degree of uncertainty is smaller in an economy in which consumer demand accounts for a high percentage of aggregate demand than in an economy of which the opposite is true. This is a consequence mainly of the greater stability of the market for consumer goods.

However, full employment with a low average propensity to consume might also be associated with a high degree of uncertainty for a further reason. Given the initial capital stock and the rate of increase in man-hour output from period to period, there exists a definite rate of net capital formation that would be required to keep the ratio of the real capital stock to real output constant (assuming that the output of a full-employment economy expands at the maximum rate made possible by the rise in man-hour output.) However, if the average propensity to consume is low a higher rate of capital formation than that just described may be required to absorb the *ex ante* savings at full employment. In this event, continued full employment requires a continuous increase in capital intensity per unit of output. Such a reorganization of the factors of production would have to be brought about by spontaneous decisions of the producers (possibly under the impact of relative price changes, as in the well-known models of Böhm-Bawerk and Hayek). It still remains true that the investment decisions in question would justify themselves *ex post* if the willingness to invest for further investment were maintained at a sufficiently high level in the long run. But, unless changes in technological knowledge or spontaneous changes in consumers' preferences lead to using different methods of production, the degree of uncertainty is greater if unfamiliar factor combinations have to be tried out continuously than if identical methods can be "duplicated."

In short, full employment with a very low propensity to consume is quite conceivable. Yet the degree of uncertainty would be high in these circumstances, mainly because producers' markets are more unstable than consumers' markets. In addition, constantly changing methods of production might be required under such conditions, quite apart from such changes as are induced by technological progress or by spontaneous changes in consumers' preferences.[27]

This element of truth behind the underconsumption theories is,

---

[27] The reader may convince himself of the following algebraic relations. If the ratio of the capital stock to output is a constant K_1 and the average propensity to save is a constant K_2, then output must rise at the percentage rate K_2/K_1 in order to bring forth the amount of new capital formation *the ratio of which to output* equals the average propensity to save. If, owing to a slower rise in man-hour output, aggregate output rises at a smaller rate, "savings exceeds investment" unless the ratio of capital to output increases; if, owing to a more rapid rise in man-hour output, aggregate output rises at a more rapid rate, "investment exceeds savings" unless the ratio of capital to output declines. The formula assumes that K_1 is the ratio of the stock existing at the beginning of each accounting period to the output of that period. If K_1 is the ratio of the stock existing at the end of the period to the output of the period, then the required percentage rate of increase in output is $K_2/K_1 - K_2$. Population changes are disregarded.

of course, insufficient to establish an equilibrium level for aggregate output, given the consumption function. Merely the presumption is established that output may tend to decline when a level implying a very low average propensity to consume is reached, that is, when investment has become very high per unit of consumption expenditure; and that output may tend to increase when a very high average propensity to consume is reached, that is, when investment has become very low in relation to consumption. But the range between the "very high" and the "very low" seems to be a wide range indeed.

SUMMARY

Investment and output, as a whole, have no determinate equilibrium level "around which" they might be said to fluctuate. This is not to deny, of course, that the level of output always is "determinate" in the tautological sense that the interaction of a great many circumstances makes it to be what it is at any moment of time. The factors determining the output and the employment of any moment may be subsumed under a few headings, and the Keynesian headings seem highly convenient in many cases, especially if the approach is integrated with the quantity theories by realization of the fact that the consumption function and the marginal efficiency of capital may be affected by the size of the existing money stock. Given the production functions and given the wage unit, the schedule of the marginal efficiency of capital in conjunction with the rate of interest and with the consumption function may be said to determine the size of output in wage units and thereby the magnitude of employment.[28] Yet unless monetary equilibrium is postulated, it is necessary to transform the Keynesian consumption function[29] into a function relating the consumption of a period to the income *expectations* of the same period or to the actual income of some preceding period; and an attempt must be made to explain the income expectations or the disposable income with reference to other variables. If so

---

[28] In the Keynesian system, the rate of interest, in turn, is said to be determined by the demand for money and the supply of money. The system would remain "the same" in all essential respects, and certain problems could be approached more conveniently, if the rate of interest were conceived of as being determined by the demand for loans and the supply of loans. (Cf. chap. v.)

[29] That is, the function relating consumption to a simultaneous income.

transformed, the system may be used conveniently for a discussion of movements along the coördinates of figure 1 (p. 10) and also of figure 3 (p. 27). Dynamic analysis in general should be concerned with the entire range covered by these figures.

Without these changes, the Keynesian system postulates the equality of expected and realized magnitudes. Otherwise income could not determine simultaneous consumption as it does according to the Keynesian consumption function. This means that without the changes just discussed the system relates *ex hypothesi* to a condition of monetary equilibrium, that is, to an intersection point of the Y curve with the 45° line of figures 1 and 3. But although in this sense it is an "equilibrium system," and although it is useful in the sense in which monetary equilibrium theories are useful, it does not relate to an equilibrium level of output and of employment. Instead it relates to an unstable and changing level of output. This expresses itself in the fact that the basic functions of the system are unstable. The Keynesian system always applies to an intersection point in figures 1 and 3 (monetary equilibrium), but the basic functions of these figures, and with them the intersection point, shift incessantly and they cannot be said to oscillate around some "normal" level. The Keynesian system is in equilibrium so far as movements along its functions are concerned. But the Keynesian system itself is not in equilibrium so far as shifts of its functions are concerned. This, of course, means that it does not determine an equilibrium level of output and of employment. It does not determine the position which the economy would assume "in the absence of cyclical disturbances."

Consequently, the theory should not claim to have established a tendency toward underemployment equilibrium for mature economies in which extensive growth has slowed down. In the Keynesian analytical framework, and in reality, any level could be an equilibrium level if expectations were such as to stabilize the basic functions there (allowing for the gradual shifts discussed in connection with fig. 3, p. 27). This is true within the limits set by the available resources regardless of whether extensive growth does or does not take place. In reality, of course, no position actually assumed by the shifting functions satisfies the conditions of equilibrium.

This criticism, however, leaves open the question of whether declining population growth, the ending of territorial expansion, and changes in the character of technological progress actually lower the range within which the dynamic process causes the economy to fluctuate. If changes such as these lead to the lowering of either the upper or the lower limit, or of both limits, of the range of fluctuations, or if they aggravate the problem of underutilization by lengthening the periods of low utilization as compared to those of high activity, a dynamic version of the Keynesian theory ceases to be "merely" a useful analytical framework. In this event it may be made into a device expressing "stagnationist" assumptions with respect to the range and the nature of economic fluctuations. Yet such a theory expressing the assumption that recent changes exert an adverse influence on the range and on the nature of fluctuations is different in many ways from a theory of underemployment *equilibrium*. A priori analysis gives no conclusive answer to the question of whether the decline in population growth, the ending of territorial expansion, or the present "character" of technological progress are likely to lower the range of fluctuations or to lengthen periods of low activity as compared to periods of high activity. The problem of the inferences to be drawn from factual analysis will be considered in the next chapter.

Those underemployment equilibrium theories explaining the failure to accomplish full utilization by the existence of monopoly also suffer from the weakness that they are unable to explain why the amount of investment for further investment should tend to a normal level. Whatever the temporary level may be, consistent willingness on the part of the economic community to raise the level would actually result in its increase. Consistent unwillingness to maintain the level would actually result in its decline. Again, the monopoly theory of underemployment equilibrium may be translated into a dynamic device expressing the lowering of the range of fluctuations by the existence of monopoly (or possibly the lengthening of period of low utilization by the same circumstance). The merits and the limitations of such an approach will be considered later in some detail.

It follows from what has been said that the factual analysis of the subsequent sections will not attempt to test or to establish equilibrium theories. Sometimes it will be unavoidable to make the simplifying assumption that, in the long run, statistically observable (i.e., *ex post*) relationships contain indications as to the nature of planned relationships between economic variables. This, however, does not imply that the economy behaves as if it moved in dynamic equilibrium. The method merely implies that errors tend to cancel out in the long run. This may or may not be true, but even if it were true, this would not mean that in the absence of errors the same results would be obtained. The public may overestimate its income in one period and underestimate it by the same margin in the next, but this does not imply that in the absence of uncertainty the output of the two periods taken together would have been what it actually was. It may be taken for granted that both the expected and the realized income would have been different.

Part Two

HYPOTHESES

CHAPTER III

Protracted Depression in the Mature American Economy

THE PROBLEM

THE PRESENT and the subsequent chapter examine, in the light of the available American materials, certain hypotheses concerning the causes of "stagnant trends" and of "protracted depressions" in mature economies. It is not essential here to discuss in detail the problem of the limitations of time-series analysis. Economic time series do not relate to homogeneous universes, and, consequently, statistical generalizations derived from them are, strictly speaking, always "invalid." Nevertheless, the study of factual material is helpful in the same sense as that in which experience is helpful in everyday life. What the "correct" conclusions are that should be read from given factual material frequently is as controversial a question as is that concerning the "correct" behavior on the basis of a given experience in everyday life. Yet experience in both realms is of value.

The problem here is not that of finding the determinants of some observable economic equilibrium, but rather that of forming an opinion on the likelihood of certain influences raising or lowering the range of fluctuations, and of certain processes changing the duration of periods of low activity in relation to periods of high activity.

Considering the significant trend toward rising output per man-hour, the achievement of a high level of employment in the long run requires a substantially rising trend in physical output. The avoidance of severe *cyclical* unemployment requires that the range within which output fluctuates should be high, or, if this range reaches down to low levels, that the periods during which output remains low should be brief. It is a fact that in certain stages of economic development these conditions were not satisfied and that consequently the problem of unemployment became severe. The period between 1929 and about 1940 was undoubtedly of this character in the United States; and shorter periods following 1929 were of this character in many other countries.[1] In some of the earlier periods, in the nineteenth century, "unusually" long depressions existed, and they were accompanied by "unusually" severe unemployment. These periods, just like the 1930's, fell in longer intervals marked by a downward trend in prices and interest rates (i.e., in "Kondratieff downgrades") and they also consistently fell in downgrades of the building cycle. Lack of data stands in the way of a more detailed comparison of the 1930's with these earlier periods of stagnation; that is, mainly with the 1870's, possibly also with the late 1830's, and with the 1890's.

The task of "explaining," in any rigorous sense, why these periods have occurred—and more particularly the task of explaining the severeness of the depression of 1929–1933 and the incompleteness of the subsequent recovery—is obviously a hopeless one. Hypotheses relating to contributing causes are at best partial explanations. They can be tested at best for plausibility. Some of the hypotheses most frequently considered have not been rendered sufficiently plausible. However, there is ample room for legitimate differences of opinion in that matter and there should be no room for rigid interpretations and for obstinacy at the present stage.

The propositions which will now be discussed are partly those advocated by the Keynes-Hansen school. The following sections contain a discussion of the hypotheses maintaining that declining population growth, the ending of territorial expansion, and the lack of capital-deepening innovations produce chronic insufficiency of investment. However, the effect of monopoly and of wage changes on investment will also be considered.

---

[1] Such statistics as are available for the United States do not suggest that the unemployed percentage of the labor force was subject to a markedly rising trend during the first three decades of the present century (cf. Paul H. Douglas, *Real Wages in the United States, 1890–1926*, Boston and New York, Houghton Mifflin, 1930, pp. 458–460). In Great Britain, however, unemployment was considerably higher in the 1920's than before. The British economy was of course adversely affected by structural changes that took place in the world economy after the war, and the difficulties probably were accentuated by the "overvaluation" of the pound.

THE CONSUMPTION FUNCTION AND POPULATION GROWTH

The hypothesis that population growth stimulates production depends for plausibility partly on the character of the income-consumption relationship. Population growth might be expected to provide a stimulus if it resulted in an increased marginal or average propensity to consume.[2] If, however, the economy had to move to the right along the same over-all historical consumption function regardless of the rate of population growth, it is not obvious why the entrepreneurial decisions leading to expansion should depend on the growth of the population. Any given output would have to consist of consumers' goods, of investment for consumption, and of investment for further investment, in proportions that are not affected by the rate of population growth.

The conclusion is subject to a qualification which should be mentioned now. Even if the *over-all* consumption function should be completely unaffected by population growth, it still might be true that an upward movement along the consumption function materializes more readily with than without population growth, considering that for a growing population entrepreneurs may find it easier to forecast the *composition* of the additional consumption occurring when investment takes place and income rises. The addition to the population may be expected to consume more of the goods which the original stock has been consuming. This can be forecast more safely than the composition of the additional consumption of a given population. Waiving this qualification for the moment, we shall however concentrate now on the over-all effect (as distinct from the effect on the composition of output). In over-all terms, the available evidence does not point to any substantial stimulating influence of population growth.

The most obvious characteristic of the historical consumption function, as calculated from Professor Kuznets' estimates,[3] is that it does not show a tendency to flatten out. It tends to linearity regardless

---

[2] Assuming that—owing to the uncertainty considerations previously presented—investment for further investment cannot be relied upon to maintain a high level of aggregate output if the propensity to consume is too low.

[3] Cf. Simon Kuznets, *Uses of National Income in Peace and War*, Occasional Paper 6 (National Bureau of Economic Research, March, 1942), p. 31.

of the varying population growth of the subsequent historical sub-periods. In figure 11 aggregate consumption in constant prices is plotted against national income in constant prices. The data plotted are average values for overlapping ten-year periods, starting with the decade 1879–1888 and ending with the decade 1929–1938. The

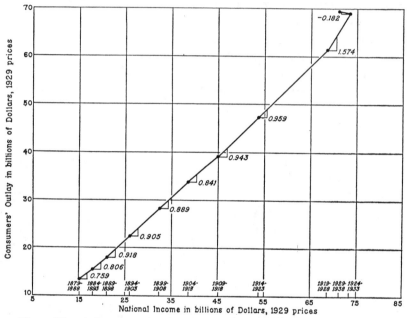

Fig. 11. Historical consumption function for overlapping decades (1929 prices). The figures beside each point express $\Delta C/\Delta Y$ from the decade in question to the next overlapping decade. Data from Kuznets, *Uses of National Income*, p. 31.

slope of this historical consumption function from the decade 1919–1928 to the next overlapping decade, 1924–1933, and its slope from the decade 1924–1933 to the next overlapping decade 1929–1938 are so largely affected by subperiods of declining output that it seems preferable to disregard the corresponding section of the curve for the moment, and to consider separately the problems appearing in this section of the curve. The technical reason for this separation of problems is that for periods with four years of sharp depression the method of overlapping decades does not perform the smoothing that is accomplished by the same method for the other periods considered. Consequently the data for 1924–1933 and for 1929–1938 are not comparable with the earlier ones; 1919–1928 is the last "comparable" decade.

If income and consumption in the decade 1879–1888 were compared with income and consumption in the decade 1919–1928, and if the intermediate decades were disregarded, a marginal propensity to consume of 0.904 would result. The average propensity to consume is very nearly the same in the two decades, respectively, namely 0.882 in the first and 0.899 in the last.[4] If the decades lying between these two are inserted, the deviations of the consumption function from linearity are found to be small. These deviations do not follow any regular pattern: in the early decades the slope of the historical consumption function; that is, the historical marginal propensity to consume, rises somewhat, then it declines and rises again. Inclusion of the rate of population growth or of the rate of change of income as third variables would not seem to lead to any profitable result. (For the data on population growth, cf. figs. 16 and 17.) On the whole, it may perhaps be said that the historical marginal propensity to consume showed a rising tendency over time, disregarding the meaningless figure of 1.574 for the comparison of 1924–1933 with 1919–1928 and the equally meaningless figure of –0.182 for the comparison of 1929–1938 with 1924–1933.[5] But from 1894–1903 through 1909–1918 the rising tendency was interrupted and thereafter it was slight.

The behavior of the marginal propensity to consume is similar if income and consumption are corrected not merely for price changes but also for the number of consuming units in the economy (cf. fig. 12).[6] Correcting for the average number of consuming units during the ten-year periods would seem to be the most appropriate of the available methods of "correcting for population." The number of consuming units corresponding to a given age distribution is taken from Warren S. Thompson's and P. K. Whelpton's *Popula-*

---

[4] The equation of the line of best fit is $C = -0.890 + 0.904\,C$ (in billions of 1929 dollars). The standard error of estimate is 0.370.

[5] These two figures are "meaningless" in the sense that they do not express any ten-year tendency or any change in ten-year tendencies. What they really express is that in the subperiods of declining income within each decade, consumption declined less than income.

[6] In figure 12 the two meaningless data pertaining to the last two decades are omitted.

tion *Trends in the United States.*[7] The weights attached to consumers belonging in different age classes is made to vary here with their assumed consumption characteristics.

The direct comparison of 1879–1888 with 1919–1928 (omitting the intermediate decades) yields for the corrected data a marginal propensity to consume of 0.945, which is somewhat higher than

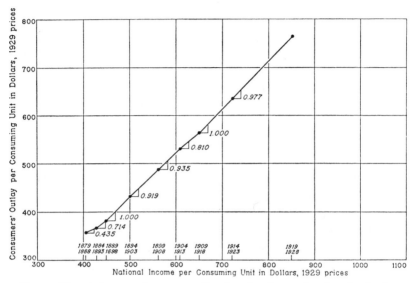

Fig. 12. Historical per capita consumption function for overlapping decades (1929 prices). The figures beside each point express Δ C/Δ Y from the decade in question to the next overlapping decade. Data from Kuznets, *Uses of National Income*, pp. 31, 39.

the figure obtained for the data uncorrected for population. If the intermediate decades are now inserted, it is again found that the historical marginal propensity to consume tends to rise up to the decade 1894–1903 and that only slight variation occurs thereafter. The rising tendency for the first three decades is more pronounced for the data corrected for population than for those uncorrected; and from 1894–1903 on it is scarcely appropriate to speak even of a slight tendency to rise. But in both cases the behavior of the marginal propensity to consume is adequately described by the statement that there existed a rising tendency up to about the last decade

---

[7] (New York and London, McGraw-Hill, 1933); cf. p. 169. Cf. also Kuznets, *op. cit.*, pp. 31, 39.

of the nineteenth century and that the oscillations from the 1890's on are small.

From the point of view of the present discussion it is important to note that five of the eight values for the marginal propensity to consume that can be read from figure 12 (corrected for population) are higher than the corresponding values in figure 11 (uncorrected for population). Only in three instances (two of which are those lying farthest back in history and one of which immediately precedes the First World War), did the growing American population have a higher historical marginal propensity to consume than the individual consuming unit, and in the last of these three instances, the difference is very small. In the other five instances the individual consuming unit had a higher historical marginal propensity to consume than did the aggregate (growing) population.[8] In other words, in five out of eight instances, the marginal propensity to consume of the initial population (i.e., of the old stock) was greater than the average propensity to consume of additional consuming units, and therefore it was greater than the marginal propensity to consume of the aggregate growing population. This surely contradicts the thesis that population growth, in general, tends to raise the marginal propensity to consume. This assumption is contradicted also by the circumstance that the consumption function for the aggregate population tends toward linearity with minor oscillations that seem to be unrelated to changes in population growth.[9]

The behavior of the marginal propensity to consume, as just discussed, is quite different from that to be read from household budget

---

[8] This is a consequence of the fact that in the five instances under consideration the individual consuming unit had a smaller average than marginal propensity to consume. If the additional income had been earned by a constant population, the marginal propensity to consume of the population would have been identical with that of the individual consuming unit. If the entire additional income had been earned by new consumers whose individual consumption functions were identical with those of the old, then the historical marginal propensity to consume of the growing aggregate population would have been identical with the *average* propensity to consume of the individual consuming unit. Therefore, it would be expected that the historical marginal propensity to consume of a growing population should be smaller than the historical marginal propensity to consume of the individual consuming unit whenever the average propensity to consume of the individual consuming unit is smaller than its historical marginal propensity to consume, and vice versa. This relationship actually holds in all eight instances considered

[9] For the changes in population growth, cf. figure 16, p. 73.

TABLE 1

AVERAGE AND MARGINAL PROPENSITY TO CONSUME FOR FAMILIES, SINGLE MEN, AND SINGLE WOMEN*

Income class	American families				Single men				Single women			
	Average propensity		Marginal† propensity		Average propensity		Marginal propensity		Average propensity		Marginal propensity	
	I‡	E§	I	E	I	E	I	E	I	E	I	E
dollars												
Under 500	1.519	1.494	.....	.....	1.188	1.188	.....	.....	1.130	1.095	.....	.....
500–750	1.148	1.128	0.778	0.765	1.029	0.986	0.893	0.814	1.026	0.965	0.918	0.830
750–1,000	1.066	1.046	0.862	0.838	1.017	0.949	0.988	0.855	0.985	0.908	0.880	0.764
1,000–1,250	1.028	1.006	0.890	0.865	0.991	0.909	0.900	0.772	0.947	0.859	0.814	0.688
1,250–1,500	0.990	0.965	0.816	0.775	0.965	0.875	0.846	0.720	0.912	0.817	0.762	0.633
1,500–1,750	0.965	0.938	0.831	0.790	0.941	0.845	0.806	0.681	0.882	0.782	0.719	0.590
1,750–2,000	0.950	0.921	0.834	0.793	0.918	0.819	0.772	0.648	0.857	0.752	0.697	0.563
2,000–2,500	0.918	0.886	0.770	0.724	0.889	0.787	0.737	0.617	0.827	0.717	0.666	0.530
2,500–3,000	0.884	0.848	0.731	0.676	0.857	0.751	0.710	0.589	0.794	0.679	0.642	0.503
3,000–4,000	0.844	0.804	0.685	0.629	0.819	0.711	0.671	0.552	0.753	0.632	0.604	0.464
4,000–5,000	0.794	0.746	0.624	0.549	0.773	0.662	0.636	0.519	0.715	0.590	0.578	0.436
5,000–10,000	0.705	0.648	0.547	0.474	} 0.612	0.494	0.518	0.394	0.547	0.394	0.469	0.304
10,000–15,000	0.611	0.537	0.467	0.367								
15,000–20,000	0.601	0.527	0.582	0.508								
20,000 and over	0.493	0.354	0.417	0.232								

* Data from U. S. National Resources Committee, *Consumer Expenditure in the United States, Estimates for 1935–36* (Washington, D.C., U. S. Government Printing Office. 1939), pp. 20, 81, 82.
† The marginal propensity to consume in a given income bracket column expresses $\Delta C / \Delta Y$ from the preceding income bracket to the one in question.
‡ I = inclusive of gifts and personal taxes.
§ E = exclusive of gifts and personal taxes.

statistics. Table 1 exhibits a comparison of the marginal and of the average propensities to consume for families of average size, for single men, and for single women. The data are calculated from the material collected by the National Resources Committee concerning household budgets. The average and marginal propensities to consume were computed both including and excluding gifts and personal taxes. The marginal propensity to consume declines here markedly after an income level of about $1,000 is reached (for single women it declines from the outset). If the relationship reflected by table 1 had *historical* validity, it would be expected that a substantial rise in the standard of living of the community as a whole, such as has occurred since 1879, would be associated with a very significant rise of the saving ratio out of income.

This divergence of the historical consumption function from the simultaneous consumption function may be explained in several ways. It has been suggested that the primary relationship might be conceived of as being in the nature of that reflected by table 1, and that the historical behavior of the function could be interpreted as being produced in the passage of time by continuous upward shifts of the household budget function.[10] The trendlike upward shift suggested by this hypothesis might be the result of technological innovations, which place new products on the market, or of other impacts producing a continuous decline in thriftiness. It is conceivable that technological changes and the increasing sales effort on the part of producers and retailers tend to produce an upward shift of the consumption function. Yet it is not necessarily legitimate to conceive of the historical behavior of the function as being produced by the interaction of a primary relationship, such as reflected by household budget statistics, plus shifts over time.

The reaction of income recipients to an increase in their incomes may well depend on whether the notions of the community on the "standard of living" are given or whether they are changing. Household budget statistics express at best the reaction of income recipients to a rise in income on the assumption that the community's conception of what is "poverty" or a "decent standard of

[10] Cf. Paul A. Samuelson, "Full Employment after the War," *Postwar Economic Problems,* ed. Seymour E. Harris (New York and London, McGraw-Hill, 1943), pp. 27–53. Cf. also p. 93, n. 1.

living" or "luxury" is given.[11] It is very likely, however, that consumption and saving habits are distinctly influenced by the prevailing notions of what constitutes a decent standard of living. For this reason, the marginal propensity to consume is likely to exhibit an entirely different behavior for a simultaneous comparison of various income groups on the one hand, and for an historical comparison of various periods on the other. For income exceeding the so-called standards of decency, the average and the marginal propensities to save are likely to be high, as long as the standards in question are "given." For incomes falling short of these standards, the average and the marginal propensities to save are likely to be low. This is likely to produce the substantial rise in the saving ratio actually observed in household budget statistics. Yet, the phenomenon leading to this increase in the saving ratio is meaningless in terms of historical analysis, because the standards of decency are substantially influenced by what the bulk of the population can afford.

It would oversimplify the thesis to say that the normal standards are determined by the average income or the modal income in any simple or clear-cut manner. Both the mean income and the modal income are statistical conceptions which are not necessarily significant for social psychology. Moreover, progressive opinion will always tend to define standards of decency so as to include more than has already been achieved by the bulk of the population. Nevertheless, it would be a grave mistake to dissociate these standards from what could at best be accomplished for a substantial portion of the population in a predictable future. Consequently, the standards tend to move upward whenever the mean income and the modal income rise.

It seems understandable, therefore, on purely a priori grounds that a person whose income rises beyond "normal incomes" in the community saves a relatively higher portion of the addition to his income, whereas no such stimulus to thrift arises when everybody's income rises. The second of these two situations is as different from the first as is a change of the general price level from relative price

---

[11] Household budget statistics express this *at best;* for even this reaction is expressed only with the qualification that income recipients moving from one category to another must be assumed to behave in the same way as the income recipients who formerly belonged in the second category.

changes. It seems somewhat artificial to argue that the historical behavior of the marginal propensity to consume results from upward shifts of household budget functions in the passage of time. It might be expected that household budget statistics would show low propensities to save for what are considered substandard incomes and high and increasing propensities to save for what are considered high incomes. This is what household statistics actually show. The phenomenon producing this behavior has no counterpart in a historical analysis, that is, for a general rise in incomes. This of itself provides a satisfactory explanation of a significant difference in the shape of the two types of consumption functions.[12] The long-run historical consumption function could probably be interpreted as resulting from shifts in the short-run historical consumption functions, but the latter are not identical with the consumption functions derived from household budget statistics. The statistical analysis of short-run consumption functions is subject to certain additional qualifications, considering that *ex post* findings are less characteristic of true propensities in the short run than in the historical perspective. It is interesting to note, however, that the year-to-year (or the quarter-to-quarter) income-consumption relationship during the 1920's and the 1930's in the United States does not bear out the assumption that the marginal propensity to consume declined with rising income. Only household budget "propensities" show a distinct tendency to decline; but not even in the short run do these have historical validity.[13]

---

[12] The implication of the contrary hypothesis (i.e., of Samuelson's hypothesis concerning shifts) is well brought out by E. A. Goldenweiser and E. E. Hagen in the following statement: "Such estimates as are available indicate that as income increased in the United States during the 50 years preceding the depression of the 1930's, consumption habits followed along. *People purchased more in a given year than they would have out of the same total income 10 years earlier.*" ("Jobs After the War," *Federal Reserve Bulletin* [May 1944], 426. Italics mine.) That part of the statement which I have italicized is a* non sequitur. There are no data available which would show that ten years earlier people would have bought fewer consumer goods out of a given income if everybody's income had been at the level actually reached ten years later. What data are available give an indication that a family spends more out of a given income if the incomes of other families are higher than if they are lower.

[13] In the comparison of household budget consumption functions with historical consumption functions, it is of course also necessary to take into account that the population of the different income classes changes, as income rises. This, however, could scarcely explain the existing differences.

In this connection the reader may be referred back to figure 10 (chap. ii) from which the conclusion was derived that the consumption function for the period 1919–1929 is well represented by a straight line, and that the function pertaining to the period 1930–

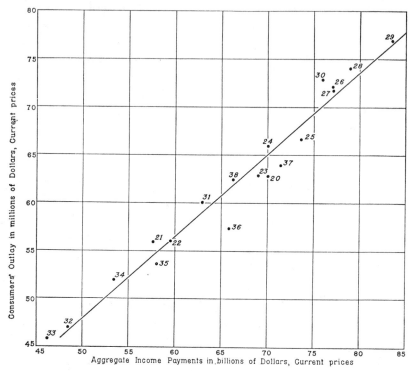

Fig. 13. Consumers' outlay—aggregate income payments relation, 1920–1938 (current prices). Regression equation: 1920–1938, C = 5.20 + 0.857 Y ± 1.655 (plotted) where C and Y are expressed in billions of dollars. For long-run material the equation is C = 0.04 + 0.889 Y ± 0.13. Data from Kuznets, *National Income and Its Composition*, I, 147.

1938 may be represented by a straight line of smaller slope (cf. above, p. 40). It was seen, however, that for the last years of the recovery period of the 1930's, the marginal propensity to consume again reached the level of the 1930's. Figure 10 contains consumption data plotted against national income, both in constant prices. If consumption is plotted against national income in current prices from Kuznets' yearly data or from Barger's quarterly data, the universe of the 'thirties lies closer to that of the 'twenties, but it still remains true that the line of best fit for the 'thirties has a smaller slope than that for the 'twenties. It also remains true that toward the end of the recovery period of the 'thirties the marginal propensity to consume reaches approximately the average level of the 'twenties. Plotting yearly consumption against aggregate income payments (instead of national income) in constant prices results in two lines, the slopes of which are less different from those of the national income regression lines. Finally, when consumption is plotted against income payments in current prices, as in figure 13, a single line results for the universe 1920–1938 (and dividing into two universes does not seem justified even if 1919 is included). Certain statistical tests may be better satisfied by non-linear functions including "time" as a variable but "time" being a catch-all, such "improvements" can always be accomplished and their logical value is doubtful.

The difference between the character of the national income *versus* consumption regressions on the one hand, and that of figure 13 on the other, seems to be mainly a consequence of the fact that the corporate plus the government dissavings of the depression period contributed to the maintenance of consumer expenditures.[14] Consequently, if consumers' outlay is plotted against national income (which does not include the corporate plus the government dissavings) the consumption function is shifted to the left rather considerably for the first years of the 'thirties, and, to a smaller extent, for the subsequent years in which the corporate plus the government dissavings still existed but were smaller. Therefore, the single universe appearing when consumption is plotted against income payments (from which the corporate plus the government dissavings are not deducted) is divided in two universes when consumption is plotted against national income. The period of high, but gradually decreasing, corporate plus government dissavings branches off to the left, as in figure 10. There exists a corresponding tendency for years with high corporate plus government savings to be shifted to the right when consumption is plotted against national income instead of aggregate income payments.

---

[14] The effects of this circumstance on the consumption function were first discussed by Paul A. Samuelson in the appendix to chapter xi of Alvin H. Hansen, *Fiscal Policy and Business Cycles.*

In conclusion, it may be stated that the historical marginal propensity to consume for the growing American population did *not* tend to exceed the historical marginal propensity to consume of the individual American consuming unit. Furthermore, the income-consumption relationship tends to linearity, if community income is set against community consumption. This is true for shorter time intervals and also for longer ones during which the rate of population growth has changed markedly. Mordecai Ezekiel argued that the linear relationship can be improved by the introduction of further variables if uncorrected yearly data are analyzed for the period 1920–1940, and if these are treated as a single universe.[15] Furthermore, it was pointed out in the preceding pages that two linear functions, rather than a single one should be applied to the period between the two wars if consumption is plotted against national income (not income payments) and if no further variables are introduced. It was also pointed out that the slope of the long-run historical consumption function arose in the last quarter of the nineteenth century (cf. figs. 11 and 12). Consequently, the statement that the community consumption functions are linear would oversimplify the facts. Nevertheless, it seems distinctly more appropriate to describe the community income-consumption relationship in terms of linear functions than in any other simple way. Between community consumption functions applying to shorter periods on the one hand, and longer ones on the other, there does not exist a difference comparable to that existing between the household budget consumption functions on the one hand, and the community functions, on the other. It should even be pointed out that the slope of the line of best fit for the income payments-consumption scatter applying to the period 1919–1938 (which may be treated as a single universe without introducing further variables) is close to the slope of the long-run historical consumption function derived from the "overlapping decades" material contained in Kuznets' *Uses of National Income in Peace and War.* If the data are corrected for prices, the line of best fit is $C = -0.890 + 0.904Y \pm 0.370$ for the long period and $C = 2.32 + 0.905Y \pm 2.032$ for the interwar period; with no price

---

[15] Mordecai Ezekiel, "Statistical Investigations of Saving, Consumption and Investment," *American Economic Review* (March, 1942), 22–49, and (June, 1942), 272–307.

correction the equations are $C = -0.04 + 0.889Y \pm 0.127$ and $C = 4.42 + 0.864Y \pm 2.153$, respectively.[16]

The reader's attention may be called briefly to the fact that Colin Clark's estimates, to be found in his *National Income and Outlay*[17] and in *The Conditions of Economic Progress*,[18] on British national income and consumption in certain noncontiguous periods and years, suggest that the British historical income-consumption relationship also exhibits some of the properties observed in the American data. Clark's estimates relate to the period 1860–1869 (average figure) and to the single years 1907, 1924, 1929, 1930, 1931, 1932, 1933, 1934, 1935, and 1937; they are corrected neither for price changes nor for population. The data are plotted in figure 14. A straight line could be drawn almost precisely through the points relating to 1860–1869, 1907, 1924, 1929, 1935, and 1937; at the same time a line possessing a smaller slope could be fitted to the data relating to the years 1930, 1931, 1932, 1933, 1934, 1935, and 1937. Just as in the United States, the drift of the entire material can be better described in terms of a linear equation than in any other simple terms; and just as in the United States, the early part of the 1930's tends to "branch off" to the left if consumption is plotted against national income. A difference is found in the long-run behavior of the average propensity to consume in the two countries, respectively. The line of best fit for the American long-run material intersects with the ordinate almost precisely at the origin, which is another way of saying that the average propensity to consume does not change significantly along the line of best fit. The British line of best fit[19] for the entire material intersects with the ordinate considerably below the origin and this expresses an increasing average propensity to consume.

It has been shown that, so far as the American material is concerned, there is no evidence that the minor deviation from linear trends are related to population growth or that the slope of the consumption function is greater for a rising population than for the individual consuming unit. The marginal thrift of the existing population has not tended to be greater than the average thrift of additional consuming units. It still might be true, however, that the

---

[16] The unit of measurement for the uncorrected American consumption functions is "billions of dollars" in all cases; for the American consumption functions in constant prices it is "billions of 1929 dollars" in all cases. The numbers appearing after the plus-minus sign indicate the standard error of estimate.

[17] Colin Clark, *National Income and Outlay* (London, Macmillan, 1937), pp. 88, 185.

[18] *Idem, The Conditions of Economic Progress* (London, Macmillan, 1940), p. 397.

[19] $C = -99.19 + 0.972 \, Y \pm 112$, in millions of pounds.

costs of raising children shift the consumption function, and with it the *average* propensity to consume, upward by a margin depending on the rate of population growth. (It might even be true that, as a consequence of the costs of raising children, an *increasing rate* of population growth would increase the *slope* of the historical consumption function, whereas a decreasing rate of population growth would decrease its slope.) Such an argument would be based on the

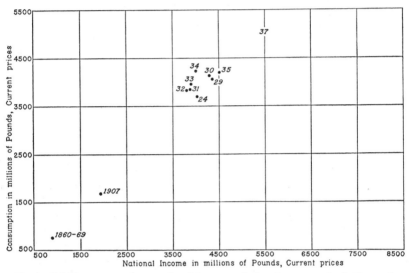

Fig. 14. British consumption—national income relation (current prices). Regression equation: $C = -99.1 + 0.972\,Y \pm 112$, where C and Y are expressed in millions of pounds. Data from Colin Clark, *National Income and Outlay* (London, Macmillan, 1937), pp. 88, 185; and *idem, The Conditions of Economic Progress* (London, Macmillan, 1940), p. 397.

costs of maintaining large families rather than on the assumption that the marginal thrift of the existing population is greater than the average thrift of additional consuming units. Yet the force of this more limited argument depends on whether the costs of raising children are allowed to cut mainly into the savings or into the consumption of the parents. The desire to provide for the future of the children might induce parents not to decrease their savings ratio.

Table 2 is based on material collected by the National Resources Committee. It shows, for four income classes, a comparison of the average propensities to consume of families including two persons, with those of "average-sized" families (consisting of approximately four persons) and also with those of families including seven or more persons.[20] On the whole, the table suggests that the addition of two children to a two-person family might raise the average propensity to consume by less than 5 per cent and that the addition of three more children might have a further effect of roughly similar

TABLE 2

AVERAGE PROPENSITY TO CONSUME FOR FAMILIES OF DIFFERENT SIZE*

Income class	Size of family					
	Two persons, average propensity		All families, average propensity		Seven or more persons, average propensity	
dollars	I†	E‡	I	E	I	E
750–1,000.	1.033	1.007	1.066	1.046	1.077	1.065
1,500–1,750.	0.924	0.890	0.965	0.938	1.007	0.988
2,500–3,000.	0.838	0.789	0.884	0.848	0.919	0.894
5,000–10,000.	0.698	0.622	0.705	0.648	0.804	0.759

* Data from U. S. National Resources Committee, *Family Expenditures in the United States* (Washington, D.C., U. S. Government Printing Office, 1941), p. 20.
† I = inclusive of gifts and personal tax.
‡ E = exclusive of gifts and personal tax.

magnitude (except that in the highest of the four income groups the second "addition" seems to have a considerably greater effect, whereas the first addition seems to produce a very low one). The conclusion is suggested that, in the range in which the size of the average family has changed in the countries of western civilization, the effect of the change on the average propensity to consume probably was small.

It may be concluded that the population growth of the earlier decades probably did not raise the over-all marginal propensity to consume and that it probably did not raise significantly the over-all

[20] Although it was argued earlier that the marginal propensities to consume which can be read from household budget statistics are entirely inconclusive so far as the slope of the community consumption function is concerned, the same is obviously not true of the average propensities to consume. The marginal transition means something different from the community as a whole, with changing community income, from what it means for an individual household, with a given community income. However, given the aggregate income and its distribution, the average propensity to consume of the community should be directly derivable from the average propensities to consume of the single units of which the community consists.

average ·propensity to consume. As was mentioned earlier, it is possible, however, that population growth has a favorable effect on investment (regardless of the over-all consumption function) because the composition of the consumption of additional consuming units can be forecast more easily (with less uncertainty) than the composition of additional consumption of a given population. Yet this qualification is weakened—although not destroyed—by the fact that even in periods of rapid population growth a large fraction of the total increase in consumption is reflected in a *per capita* increase.

As for the effect of population growth on investment (regardless of its effects on the over-all consumption function), it is impossible to verify or to refute statistically a hypothesis that would postulate a significant relationship between the two. It does seem legitimate, however, to conclude that the statistical material at best neither adds to, nor subtracts from, the a priori plausibility of the argument postulating a causal relationship between the decline in the rate of population growth and the weakness of the inducement to invest after 1929. And, the a priori force of the argument is substantially reduced, if the effect of population growth on the shape and on the position of the over-all consumption function is of no great significance. In this event an economy with a stagnant population could expand along an over-all consumption function which is no less favorable than that applying to an economy with rising population.

The discussion will now be concerned with the statistical relationship between new capital formation in constant prices, on the one hand, and population growth, on the other. Figure 15 shows that during the period covered by the Kuznets' statistics there was a negative relationship between the amount of investment and percentage population growth.[21] The years of high percentage population growth tended to be years of low investment, and vice versa. This tendency, of course, cannot logically be interpreted to mean that a high percentage population growth has the effect of decreasing the amount of investment. What the relationship really means

_____

[21] The capital formation during a decade was plotted against the *average* of the population growth from the preceding decade to the decade in question and of the population growth from the decade in question to the next decade. This is the closest approximation (available from Kuznets' published data) to the population growth *during* any decade.

trends. The percentage growth of population was declining with slight and unimportant interruptions during the period considered; absolute population growth, that is, population growth in millions of consuming units, was increasing on the whole, although not in each period. Figure 16 indicates the relationship between absolute population growth in consuming units, and investment. Up to the period affected by the developments following 1929 (i.e., including the decade 1919–1928 but not including 1924–1933), the scatter shows that capital formation rose consistently from decade to decade when the rate of absolute population growth was increasing or remained unchanged, yet the scatter fails to show a decline in capital formation in the only instance in which the rate of absolute population growth was declining appreciably. Absolute population growth was smaller in 1909–1918 than in 1904–1913, but net capital formation was greater. So far as the experience prior to 1929 is concerned, there seems to be an indication that parallel changes between the two variables merely reflect the existence of a secular upward trend for both the absolute population growth and the amount of real investment. When the absolute rate of population declined or remained unchanged (contrary to its long-run trend), the amount of real capital formation failed to react as it would have had there been a direct causal relationship between the two variables. This is shown—up to the Great Depression—by the existence of a positive slope in the scatter for periods of rising absolute population growth, by an infinite slope for periods of constant population growth, and by a negative slope for the one period of declining population growth. It is true that in the 1930's the absolute rate of population growth and real investment declined simultaneously,[23] just as it is true that the percentage rate of population growth and real investment declined simultaneously. Yet, the question of whether the simultaneous decline of population growth and of investment in the 'thirties should be interpreted "causally" or as "mere coincidence" depends partly on whether the causal interpretation can be

[23] Figure 16 merely shows that this is true for the decade 1924–1933 as compared to the previous decade (1919–1928), but the statement clearly continues to be true for the decade 1929–1938 as compared to 1924–1933. The method applied in deriving the data for population growth does not allow a precise evaluation of the figure for the decade 1929–1938 and therefore the corresponding point was omitted both in figure 15 and in figure 16. (As for the method, see above, p. 70, n. 21.)

substantiated by previous experience. Previous experience does not substantiate the causal nexus. It is true that in the period of declining population growth in which capital formation rose (1909–1918) there existed an "abnormal" inducement to invest. However, this could scarcely be maintained of the two instances in which population growth remained the same and capital formation rose considerably.

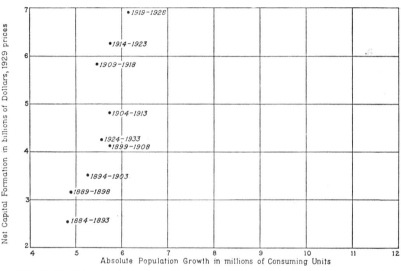

Fig. 16. Absolute population growth—net capital formation relation (1929 prices). Data from Kuznets, *Uses of National Income,* pp. 31, 39.

The last part of the analysis again is subject to certain qualifications arising from the fact that it relates to over-all magnitudes. There may well exist a significant relationship between population growth and specific fields of investment, such as residential construction. In consequence of immobilities specific disturbances may tend to become generalized. This may result in depressions ("normal" or "protracted") but scarcely in secular stagnation.

IMPROVEMENT AND NEW RESOURCES

Aggregate output and aggregate employment may rise or decline in consequence of technological or organizational innovations. Since the production of a given output typically requires a reduced labor

Monetary Policies and Full Employment

input after the innovation,[24] real output has to rise at least in the proportion of the labor saving, if employment is to be maintained. Consequently, the innovation will raise the level of employment only if it calls forth a rise in real output that outweighs the labor saving per unit of output. Propositions maintaining on a priori grounds that innovations in general do or do not produce the necessary expansion of output, would clearly be unjustified. Innovations might even diminish output, if their effect on investment for further investment or on the consumption function should be adverse. A rise in output requires that prices be reduced and also that the increased expenditure at the reduced prices should be enough to offset the increased savings.

One of the negative propositions that can be deduced on a priori grounds is worthy of emphasis, however. Whether an innovation does or does not raise the level of employment cannot be assumed to depend on the "deepening" or "widening" character of the innovation. In this regard the reasoning of the American stagnation school[25] can be disproved on purely logical grounds. The stimulus derived from the necessity to increase the capital stock per unit of

---

[24] This statement does not imply that innovations are typically "labor-saving" in the different senses suggested by various authors. Cf. J. R. Hicks, *The Theory of Wages* (London, Macmillan, 1932), chap. vi; A. C. Pigou, *The Economics of Welfare* (4th ed.; London, Macmillan, 1933), Part iv, chap. iv; R. F. Harrod's review of Joan Robinson's *Essays in the Theory of Employment,* in the *Economic Journal* (1937); Oscar Lange, "A Note on Innovations," *Review of Economic Statistics* (February, 1943). These definitions of labor-saving innovations—including Pigou's definition—do not make the "Labor-saving" quality of an innovation dependent on whether it reduces labor input per unit of output. Yet Pigou (cf. *loc. cit.*) says that the common use of the term *would* imply that innovations should be considered labor saving if they reduce the labor input per unit of output. This is true and there does not seem to exist any valid reason for deviating from the "common use." Why not call innovations labor saving (or spending) if they reduce (increase) labor input per unit of output and why not call them capital saving (or spending) if they reduce (increase) the capital input per unit of output? This would accord well with the common use of these terms. In this event it would have to be added that innovation might be both labor and capital saving and that they typically have been labor saving. Furthermore, it would have to be added that the labor- or capital-saving character of the innovations does not of itself determine their effects on the aggregate or on the relative share of the factors of production; nor their effect on the aggregate demand for the factors.

[25] Cf. mainly Alvin H. Hansen, *Full Recovery or Stagnation* (New York, W. W. Norton, 1938), pp. 314 ff.; "Economic Progress and Declining Population Growth," *American Economic Review* (March, 1939), 1–15; *Fiscal Policy and the Business Cycle* (New York, W. W. Norton, 1941), chap. xvii.

Hypotheses

output (i.e., from "deepening")[26] is, at best, of a temporary character, and it must by necessity be followed by an adverse effect of greater magnitude. The "innovation" would be no innovation if costs per unit of output did not decline. Consequently the rise in aggregate outlays (including new investment outlays) per unit of output, occurring if the innovation "deepens" capital, must be followed, for an indefinite period, by a reduction of unit operating costs, including maintenance, to a level *lower than the one that prevailed prior to the innovation.* Moreover, even the temporary stimulus derived from the necessity to "deepen" the capital stock must be disregarded if the concern is with a historical epoch during which "deepening innovations" are flowing continuously. The introduction of the successive deepening innovations will in this case require a continuous flow of new capital goods and this will keep at a constant level, *but not increase,* the output of a specific section of the capital goods industries.[27] On the other hand, the unit operating costs, including capital maintenance, of the innovating industries will *decline* continually. The total effect on output must be adverse, unless indeed the innovating industries increase their output. It is true that on strict *ceteris paribus* assumptions the output of the downward sliding economy would, at any given moment of time, be even lower with "merely widening" innovations than with "deepening innovations" because the demand for capital goods is lower in the first than in the second case. But in both cases, the economy would be involved in a cumulative downward process. The difference merely is that between (*a*) having a constant amount of investment which is being increasingly outweighed by ever-growing savings and (*b*) not even having the constant amount of investments. In a secular theory this difference is negligible. The difference consists of a time lag.

The deepening "stimulus" necessarily becomes more and more submerged in the cost-saving effect. Both are "per unit of output"

---

[26] Following R. G. Hawtrey, *Capital and Employment* (London, Longmans, Green, 1937), deepening of capital is defined as growth of the real capital per unit of real output, and widening of capital occurs when capital grows in the aggregate but not by per unit of output.

[27] Of the section producing the equipment used for introducing the "deepening" innovations.

effects, and the "per unit of output" effect of innovations must by necessity be unfavorable on balance, so far as the level of employment is concerned. Regardless of whether the innovation necessitates an increase in capital per unit of output (i.e., is "deepening") or requires an unchanging stock of capital per unit of output (i.e., is "merely widening"), costs and employment per unit of output will decline.[28] The deflationary "per unit of output" effect can be offset, or outweighed automatically—so far as aggregate output, or even as employment, is concerned—by increased consumption attributable to cheaper costs and prices, or by increased investment for further investment attributable to the same factors. In the unfavorable instances in which offsetting through these factors does not occur, a deflationary impact must develop. This is true of widening, as well as of deepening, innovations.

It should be added that the deepening effect is no different from that which arises when an innovation requires mere substitution of new equipment for the old. On the assumptions on which deepening innovations would stimulate economic activity, obsolescence would have the same stimulating effect. When processes involving obsolescence start, there is a temporary rise in producers' expenditures per unit of output. Yet this must be followed by a reduction of current expenditures per unit of output below the original level. If processes involving obsolescence are being introduced continuously, the continuous expenditures on new equipment merely maintain (but do not increase) output in certain sections of the capital goods industries. At the same time, the cost-saving effect of the innovations reduces continuously the demand for productive services per unit of output. The balance of these two phenomena (i.e., the per unit of output effect as a whole) is adverse rather than stimulating. Here, too, a stimulus can originate only from an increased demand for the cheapened products of the innovating industries. Technological progress is not rendered expansionary by deepening or by obsolescence. Whether aggregate demand will increase as a consequence of improvement and, if so, whether the rise in demand will be sufficient to maintain or even to increase employment depends

---

[28] *Cf.* my article, "The Technological Argument of the Stagnation Thesis," *Quarterly Journal of Economics* (August, 1941), 638–651.

partly on how the consumption function is affected and partly on how investment for further investment reacts to the change of production functions. The crucial question is whether the cost-saving industries increase their output at reduced prices.[29]

Historically it seems legitimate to argue that the conspicuous cases of stimuli provided by innovations are those in which innovations were organic parts of long-run processes of growth affecting, primarily, specific segments within economic systems. These processes of specific growth may have been started by innovations or the main innovations may simply have occurred in the course of these processes; at any rate these processes as a whole lead to significant decline in the prices of certain goods and services and to a significant rise in their consumption. They also created the expectation that a secular trend favored investment in specific fields and that investment activity in these fields was going to continue. In our terminology, the processes in question created a high inducement to invest for further investment. The dramatic instances of stimulating innovations were organic parts of such processes. In addition, innovations may have been partly responsible for preventing a long-run decline of the over-all marginal propensity to consume. Yet this latter hypothesis should not be carried too far considering that the marginal propensity to consume seems to have been maintained in the United States (and probably also in Great Britain) at an approximately constant level throughout many decades during which the relative significance of innovations must have varied considerably.

The acquisition of new and better resources by territorial expansion is substantially a specific type of improvement. New resources, like improved techniques, counteract the tendency toward diminishing returns by making it possible to increase output without the necessity of changing the proportions in which the factors of production are applied; at the same time costs per unit of output are reduced. Consequently, it would be expected that the effect on aggregate output and employment of the acquisition of new resources (e.g., by means of territorial expansion) should be subject to the same indeterminateness as is the effect of technological im-

---

[29] With new goods, the price cut is from infinite to finite and the increase in output from zero to finite.

provement. If full employment could be taken for granted, the acquisition of new resources, like technological improvement, would necessarily increase real output. Given the lack of reliability of the necessary "adjustments" it is true of both these phenomena that they may reduce employment. In fact, a reduction of employment is unavoidable in both cases if, as a consequence of improved resources, employment per unit of output declines and output does not increase sufficiently to offset this circumstance. Whether output does or does not increase sufficiently depends on how the consumption function, on one hand, and investment for further investment, on the other, is affected.

It is somewhat unusual to think of the acquisition of new resources as having even potentially depressive effects. It is not thought of in this way because the "dramatic" instances of territorial expansion are those in which the consumption function as well as investment for further investment were affected favorably and significantly. That depressing effects are conceivable becomes clear, however, if account is taken of that fact that a shift toward free trade is in the same nature as territorial expansion. If two isolated economic communities become interrelated through foreign trade, the situation is then one of mutual territorial expansion so far as economic considerations are concerned. It is obvious that, in "rigid" economies, processes such as these might lead to a reduction of employment and even of output, although a rise in real output could be taken for granted if a smooth process of adjustment were assumed or actually enforced.

As was stated above, valid objections may be raised to the deepening argument of the American stagnation school on a priori grounds. In spite of this, it seems worth while to examine the actual behavior of the capital-output ratio over the decades covered by the Kuznets' statistics.

Estimates of the magnitude of the capital stock are, for obvious reasons, very unprecise. The best available method of arriving at estimates of the capital-stock output ratio would seem to be the following. The Federal Trade Commission has published estimates of the American national wealth as of December 21, 1922.[30] These

---

[30] *National Wealth and Income* (Washington, D. C., U. S. Government Printing Office, 1926).

estimates can be made roughly comparable with Professor Kuznets' estimates of new capital formation[31] by deducting from the national wealth estimates the value of unimproved land and of the stock in the hands of ultimate consumers, which are not included in Kuznets' capital formation estimates. Furthermore, in order to arrive at more meaningful figures concerning the stock-output ratio, it seems advisable to deduct monetary metals and claims against foreign countries from the national wealth and also from capital formation. After these adjustments, the capital stock estimate for 1922 can be rolled backward and forward to earlier and later periods respectively, by subtracting or adding Kuznets' estimates of new capital formation for various periods prior to and after 1922. The stock estimates thus derived can be compared with the output estimates of the identical periods. The Kuznets' estimates of capital formation are given in 1929 prices, whereas the wealth estimates of the Federal Trade Commission are expressed in prices of 1922. The price levels of these two years were so closely similar, however, that data expressed in the prices of the two years respectively may be considered roughly comparable.[32] The figures concerning real capital and real output arrived at by this procedure are given in table 3.

The comparison of the capital stock with the output flow of the single decades would lead to the conclusion that a considerable deepening process occurred between the early part of the 1880's and the end of the nineteenth century. From that period on the stock-output ratio has changed but slightly. It should be pointed out that the stock-output ratio indicated in table 3 for the decades 1924–1933 and 1929–1938 are too high for a meaningful comparison with earlier decades. The existence of a substantial stock of unemployed resources tends to raise this ratio, because in periods of underutilization part of the stock is idle (i.e., does not "participate" in the production of output). As was stated earlier, the method of overlapping decades does not smooth out the depression of 1929–

---

[31] To be found in Simon Kuznets', *National Income and its Composition, 1919–1938* (New York, National Bureau of Economic Research, 1941); and *idem, Uses of National Income in Peace and War*, Occasional Paper 6 (New York, National Bureau of Economic Research, March, 1942).

[32] Cf. Simon Kuznets, "Capital Formation in the United States, 1919–1935," *Capital Formation and Its Elements* (New York, National Industrial Conference Board, 1939), p. 46.

1933 effectively. Consequently, the ratio figures for 1924–1933 and for 1929–1938 are not comparable with the preceding figures.

The data in table 3 would lead to the belief that if the degree of deepening were an important determinant of aggregate investment

TABLE 3

THE CAPITAL-OUTPUT RATIO*

Decade	Average yearly real output 1922 *or* 1929 prices	Real capital stock at center point of decade 1922 *or* 1929 prices	Ratio of real stock to real output (3) = (2) ÷ (1)
	1	2	3
	billions of dollars	*billions of dollars*	
1879–1888................	15.2	39.17	2.58
1884–1893................	18.1	50.27	2.77
1889–1898................	21.2	64.47	3.04
1894–1903................	26.1	81.22	3.11
1899–1908................	32.4	100.67	3.11
1904–1913................	38.7	123.37	3.19
1909–1918................	45.0	147.22	3.27
1914–1923................	53.8	170.32	3.17
1919–1928................	68.6	197.12	2.87
1924–1933................	73.3	222.02	3.03
1929–1938................	71.1	235.02	3.31

* The yearly figures for output and net capital formation in 1929 prices were taken from Simon Kuznets, *National Income and Its Composition*, Vol. I, table 37, p. 269; the adjustment of the net capital formation figures for change in the claims against foreign countries were taken from *ibid.*, table 38, p. 272. The national wealth estimate of the Federal Trade Commission, amounting to 353 billion dollars for the end of 1922, becomes 183.7 billion dollars after subtracting the value of land and goods in the hands of consumers and the value of the stock of monetary metals.

The decade figures for average output and average net capital formation in 1929 prices were taken from Kuznets, *Uses of National Income in Peace and War*, Occasional Paper 6 (New York, National Bureau of Economic Research, March, 1942), table 2, p. 31; the adjustment of the net capital formation figures for changes in the claims against foreign countries were taken from *ibid.*, table 5, p. 34.

The real capital stock figures for the single years 1919 to 1928 were found by adding or subtracting the net capital formation figures for successive years to the 1922 figure of 183.7 billion dollars. After this, the average real capital stock was found for the decade 1919–1928 and this was interpreted to be interchangeable with the stock of the center point of the decade, that is, of 1923–1924. The stock at the center points of the other "overlapping decades" (which is interpreted as standing for the average stock during the decade in question) was derived from the stock of 1923–1934 by a method of averaging exemplified by the following: To arrive from the center point, 1923–1924, to the next earlier center point, 1918–1919, we estimated and then deducted the capital formation of the five years between 1918–1919 and 1923–1924; this was done by assuming that in those five years capital formation proceeded at a rate corresponding to the average of the rate prevailing during the decade 1914–1923 and the decade 1919–1928. Kuznets' figures are available only for *decades* such as these.

and output, some of the difficulties of the 1930's should have manifested themselves around the turn of the century. No one knows, of course, whether deepening did or did not occur in the early years of the nineteenth century, since the "revolutionary innovations of early capitalism" increased not merely the capital stock but also the flow of output in a very high proportion. It is not clear on a priori grounds whether the proportion in which real capital was increased in those years was greater or smaller than the proportion in which real output rose.[33] But to the extent to which it is possible to rely on the data in table 3, it seems warranted to conclude that deepening did occur at a substantial rate in the last quarter of the nineteenth century, whereas the process of deepening seems to have stopped or to have become quite insignificant thereafter. Later on, even some decrease in the stock-output ratio seems to have taken place. Yet this decline seems to have occurred between the center date of the decade 1914–1923 and that of the decade 1919–1928, and yearly figures not given here, indicate that in the later years of the 1920's there again was probably a slight rise.

In the usual presentation of the stagnation thesis, the substantial expansion of output experienced during the 1920's is explained away with reference to certain "accidental" developments which are assumed to have postponed the appearance of the stagnant trend for about one decade. It is realized that most of the criteria of "maturity" were observable already in the decade after the First World War; hence if maturity is responsible for the stagnant trend of the 1930's, it is necessary to formulate specific hypotheses about why stagnation did not appear at least one decade prior to the Great Depression. This usually is done by interpreting the 1920's as a prolonged postwar expansion and by stressing certain additional "specific" features of the period. However, if it is concluded from study of table 3 that the deepening process came substantially to an end around the turn of the century, it becomes necessary, so far as the deepening argument is concerned, to explain away about thirty years, instead of merely one decade. In consequence of the high degree of underutilization during the 1930's there are no comparable data for that decade in which, according to stagnationists, the lack of deepening innovation was partly responsible for stagnation. But, whatever the situation may have been during the 1930's, a significant change in the trend of the capital-output ratio does seem to have taken place thirty years earlier and this does not seem to have affected the general economic trend at that time. The first half

---

[33] It is, of course, necessary to bear in mind that estimates of "real" magnitudes have little meaning when the composition of the magnitudes in question changes significantly.

of this thirty-year interval could not be considered "exceptional" or "abnormal" in the same sense as that in which the First World War and its aftermath could conceivably be so considered.

From a purely technical point of view, a similar statement could be made with respect to the stagnationist argument emphasizing the cessation of territorial expansion. Yet the analogous criticism of the territorial expansion argument must be qualified with reference to broader sociological considerations. The frontier "disappeared" several decades prior to the stagnation of the 'thirties and this did not produce any break in the continuity of economic development at that time. Thus the territorial expansion argument shares one of the weaknesses of the deepening argument. On the basis of Kuznets' estimates and the data in table 3, improvement seems to have been adequate to offset diminishing returns (not merely in the average but also in the marginal sense) even after the ending of territorial expansion. During the first three decades of the century, subsequent additions of equal absolute size to the capital stock do not seem to have been associated with decreasing additions to aggregate output;[34] and equal absolute additions to the population seem to have been associated with distinctly increasing additions to output. Not even the logarithmic trend line for aggregate output seems to have flattened out until the Great Depression, as may be seen from figure 17 which is plotted from Kuznets' data. Yet, by analyzing marginal output for rising factor inputs, or average output per unit of input, or trends in aggregate output, the potentially significant aspects of territorial expansion and of its cessation are not exhausted. It is likely that certain types of internal friction develop less rapidly in an extensively growing economy than in a system with a given economic area. Additions to the economic area frequently remain relatively free from institutional rigidities, at least for some time. The cessation of extensive growth may therefore result in a more rapid emergence of rigidities and of internal frictions, which, in turn, may with a time lag result in adverse economic trends. Consequently, the available material comes much closer to contradicting the deepening argument than to refuting the argument relating to the growth of the economic area.

---

[34] Compare columns 1 and 2 of table 3.

It should be repeated that the hypotheses so far considered cannot be disproved by statistical analysis. It is possible merely to test these hypotheses for "plausibility," in the light of factual material. The matter of plausibility depends, of course, on the judgment of the individual who has to express an opinion on the problems of economics. In our judgment the material considered in this chapter

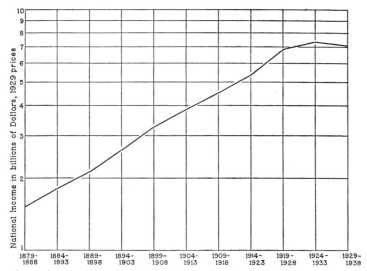

Fig. 17. National income or output for overlapping decades (1929 prices). Data from Kuznets, *Uses of National Income,* p. 31.

fails to lend plausibility to the population growth argument and to the technological argument of the stagnationist schools of thought. Other material may not; and untried multiple correlation hypotheses may yield different results to some ingenious investigator.

THE MONOPOLY POWER OF FIRMS AND MONOPOLISTIC RESTRICTION

The "degree of [producers'] monopoly power" is an ambiguous concept. In recent theoretical discussion various measures of monopoly power have been suggested. These relate to different aspects of the monopoly problem. Thus Professor Lerner's measure—the difference between price and marginal cost divided by price—has the significance of "measuring" the malallocation of resources caused by monopoly.[35] As is well known, Lerner's measure of monopoly power becomes the reciprocal of demand elasticity, if equality of marginal revenue and of marginal cost is postulated. The concept possesses an important bearing on the allocation of resources, but it has no direct bearing on the aggregate level of activity which is the main concern in the present context.

K. W. Rothschild made the interesting suggestion that monopoly power should be measured by the ratio of the slopes of Professor Chamberlin's dd′ and DD′ demand curves.[36] These two curves had been christened earlier, by Morris Copeland, the species demand curve and the apportioned genus demand curve.[37] The first of the two relates the demand for the product of a monopolistically competitive firm to the price charged by the firm, on the assumption that the prices charged by the other firms of the monopolistically competitive industry—that is, of the "group"—remain unchanged. The second curve relates the same demand to the same price, on the assumption, however, that the prices charged by the other firms are identical with those charged by the firm to which the demand curve relates. The first curve (dd′) obviously slopes downward less steeply than the second (DD′). The ratio of the slopes expresses, in a sense (i.e., with the appropriate *ceteris paribus* clause) the relative significance of the firm in question within the group in which it belongs. If, in a given range, the dd′ curve has a very much smaller slope than the DD′ curve, then the relative significance of the firm is likely to be small, because it is in a position to increase its sales very considerably by acquiring the buyers of competing firms. If, in the neighborhood of the actual price, the slope of the dd′ curve is but little smaller than that of the DD′ curve, the relative significance of the firm in the industry is likely to be great because the impingement on the markets of competing firms increases the sales of the firm

---

[35] A. P. Lerner, "The Concept of Monopoly and the Measurement of Monopoly Power," *Review of Economic Studies* (June, 1934), 157–175.

[36] Cf. K. W. Rothschild, "The Degree of Monopoly," *Economica* (February, 1942), 24–39; for the definition of the two demand functions, see Edward Chamberlin, *The Theory of Monopolistic Competition* (3d ed.; Cambridge, Harvard University Press, 1938), pp. 90–91; see also Joe S. Bain, "Measurements of the Degree of Monopoly: A Note," *Economica* (February, 1943), 66–68.

[37] Morris A. Copeland, "Competing Products and Monopolistic Competition," *Quarterly Journal of Economics* (November, 1940), 1–36.

only by a small margin. By comparing the two slopes there is measured, in a sense, the *relative significance* of the firm within the group, since the slope of the DD′ curve is approximately that of the demand curve for the product of the industry,[38] whereas the slope of the dd′ curve is determined by this very same factor *plus* the increase in sales realized by the firm in question through underbidding the other firms of the group. The ratio of these two slopes therefore isolates the second of the two factors.

It should be added, however, that something like a *pure* measure of relative significance could be derived this way only on the assumption that the firms in each Chamberlinian group (i.e., in each "industry") are arrayed in a distinct manner so far as substitutability is concerned. The constellation would have to be analogous to that existing in spatial competition if all firms were of equal size and if they were situated at equal distances from their neighbors (for example, in a circle of given radius). In this case, the quantity by which a firm may increase its sales through underbidding others by a given margin depends exclusively on the number of firms in the industry, that is, on the share of the "industry output" produced by any one firm.[39] If, however, conditions such as these are not satisfied the rise in sales through impingement on others depends on the distance between the competitors of different sizes as well as on relative significance.

Yet even if Rothschild's measure of monopoly power did constitute a pure measure of the relative significance of single firms within Chamberlinian groups, this measure would still not be directly relevant to the problem of aggregate output and employment. The relative significance of the single firms constituting an "industry" (that is, a Chamberlinian group) ceases to be a factor determining the degree of monopolistic restriction of output, once it is taken for granted that the single firms are aware of exerting an influence on the price of their product. The degree of monopolistic restriction does not in these circumstances depend on the relative significance of the individual firms or on the slopes or the elasticities of the nega-

---

[38] Provided that the relative share of the different firms is approximately the same at different prices of the "product" in the broader sense.

[39] Given the transportation costs.

tively inclined individual demand curves, but on other factors which will be considered presently.

The relative significance of single firms within an industry may be, however, of importance in studying the question of the likelihood of single firms becoming aware of their influence on price and of the likelihood of single firms colluding. This question led several investigators to compute so-called "concentration ratios" for a number of industries, that is, to compute figures expressing the share in industry output of the x largest (typically of the four largest) producers; or to compute the percentage of all establishments employing x per cent (e.g., one-half) of the labor force of the industry.[40] On the appropriate *ceteris paribus* assumption it might be argued that higher concentration ratios (reflecting higher "relative" significance of the x largest firms) mean greater likelihood of the emergence of monopolistic constellations. Unfortunately, the appropriate *ceteris paribus* conditions are not satisfied in reality. The following seem to be the most important reasons why the concentration ratios do not of themselves contain a satisfactory indication of the likelihood of the emergence of monopoly power. (*a*) The closeness of the substitutes produced by other ("neighboring") industries is very different for the different industries compared, and this factor changes also over time. (*b*) The size of the market for which the industry is producing is different for different industries. (*c*) The distribution of relative significance within the aggregate of firms not belonging in the group of the x largest may be very different. (*d*) Foreign competition is disregarded in the concentration ratios actually computed for American industries.[41]

It has been seen that Lerner's measure of monopoly power relates to the problem of the relative malallocation of specific resources, given the aggregate output of the economy. Concentration ratios on the one hand, and the slopes considered by Rothschild, on the other, bear on the likelihood of the emergence of monopoly. Yet

[40] Cf. mainly *The Structure of the American Economy, Part I*, National Resources Committee, 1939; and *The Structure of Industry*, T. N. E. C. Monograph No. 27, 1941. The second of the two measures is, of course, inversely related to the degree of concentration.

[41] Cf. George J. Stigler, "The Extent and Bases of Monopoly," Supplement to the *American Economic Review* (June, 1942), 6–8.

the concern here is with monopolistic restriction of output; and once monopoly power *has* emerged, the degree of restriction does not depend on the degree of concentration or on the slopes of the market curves. Joan Robinson has shown that, given the emergence of monopoly, the degree of monopolistic restriction, as compared to perfectly competitive conditions, depends on the *curvature* of the demand curve and on that of the competitive supply curve, assuming that the cost curves remain unaffected by monopolization, and that the individual demand curve faced by the monopoly is identical with what previously was the market demand curve for the product of the competitive industry.[42] In these conditions monopolization always leads to output restriction and the percentage reduction of output will be the greater, the more concave the demand curve is, as viewed from above, and the more convex the supply curve is, equally as viewed from above. If these two functions are linear, monopoly output will be one-half the competitive output regardless of the slope and of the elasticity of the functions; if the demand curve is convex and the supply curve concave, it will be more than one-half the competitive output; if the demand curve is concave and the supply curve convex, the output under monopoly will be less than one-half of what it was prior to the monopolization.

The analysis seems to point to the conclusion that, although the factors determining the degree of monopolistic restriction are not statistically measureable, an all-around tendency toward monopoly does lead to a restriction of aggregate output (income).[43] Monopoly output is smaller than competitive output in each individual industry, and, therefore, also in the aggregate economy. The conclusion does not, however, follow by logical necessity, although it very likely is more often correct than incorrect. In the first place, monopolization may be associated with a lowering of the cost functions in the specific industries in which it occurs.[44] Second, *expected* demand

---

[42] Joan Robinson, *The Economics of Imperfect Competition* (London, Macmillan, 1934); cf. chap. xi.

[43] The price-elasticity effects (repercussion) arising when the relative price changes occur will be considered in chapter v.

[44] If reversible external economies exist in a competitive industry, then the competitive supply curve is necessarily higher than the curve that becomes the monopolist's marginal cost curve, provided the monopolist pays no rent to the owners of scarce factors. If the monopolist pays rent, his (relevant) marginal cost curve may lie above

curves may shift to the right, as compared to their previous competitive positions; and this, by leading to increased output, may
shift *actual* demand curves to the right, thereby restoring aggregate
output, even in the long run.

Neither of these offsetting forces comes into play by necessity:
both are undependable. Some lowering of cost functions in the
industries subject to monopolization may perhaps be rather common. It is true that a monopoly will introduce an innovation only
if total costs with the new method are lower than are prime costs
with the old, whereas innovations will be adopted by competitive
industries if total costs with the new methods are lower than total
costs with the old. This, considered by itself, would lead to the belief
that competitive costs tend to become lower than monopoly costs
because competitive industries are more ready to adopt innovations.
Yet, on the other hand, inventions would presumably be made at
a much lower rate if large-scale enterprise with its research facilities
was eliminated. On balance, the "concentration of economic power"
may well be associated with some lowering of the cost functions for
the methods actually applied. However, even if this should be so,
the degree of lowering may be insufficient to offset the restrictive
effect of output-determination by functions *marginal* to the competitive determinants. Consequently, the first potential offset to the
restrictive impact of monopoly, namely, the lowering of potential
or of actual cost functions, may frequently be weaker than the restrictive influence itself (even in cases in which the offsetting force
does develop).

Needless to say, the second potential offsetting factor, namely, the
shift-to-the-right of expected demand curves as compared to their
competitive positions, equally is not a necessary phenomenon, although it may occur in certain instances for the following reason.
In conditions of full employment an upward shift of expected demand curves is self-defeating, assuming that the monetary authority
is prepared to intervene if inflationary developments get under way.

---

or below the competitive supply curve depending on the relative significance of the
marginal rent as compared with the external economies (i.e., with the economies that
used to be external in competition). Much more important than this, however, is the
fact that monopolistic tendencies may be associated with a downward shift of cost
curves in consequence of the "setting up of new production functions."

In conditions of substantial underemployment expectations of shifts to the right justify themselves *ex post*, if they are consistently maintained. In an all-round monopolistic, underemployed economy, random causes producing the shift may lead to a higher level output which may be maintained over a considerable period. It is true, of course, that random causes may also cause a downward shift of expectations which justifies itself *ex post*, if it remains consistent over time. But in an economy that initially is fully employed *only* this latter statement is true; the upward shift is self-defeating if inflationary developments are counteracted by the monetary authority.[45] The likelihood of shifts depends largely on how the degree of uncertainty is affected by the changes in the degree of competition.

On the whole, the forces which may offset the restrictive effect of monopolization, are not dependable. They may or may not come into play and if they do, they may act as merely partial offsets. Complete and consistent offsetting would have to rest on an unlikely coincidence of circumstances.

Finally, it should be pointed out that monopoly may result in a restriction of output also through its effects on income distribution. Professor Bain's measure of monopoly power is concerned with this aspect of the problem. Bain's measure consists of the average profit rate, that is, of the difference between price and average cost, where, however, average cost is defined so as to include interest (plus risk premium) merely on the assets that would also exist in a competitive economy.[46] In other words, such capitalized quasi rents as flow from artificial scarcities (that is, scarcities other than those inherent in "nature") are excluded from asset valuation and the excess of price over average cost thus derived is conceived of as a measure of monopoly power. What is measured here in a direct sense, is an important aspect of the monopolistic distortion of income distribution. The measure becomes significant for other considerations only to the extent to which income distribution has a bearing on them.

[45] The statement implies that it is substantially easier to counteract inflationary than deflationary tendencies. This point will be discussed at some length in the later course of the argument.

[46] Joe S. Bain, "The Profit Rate as a Measure of Monopoly Power," *Quarterly Journal of Economics* (February, 1941), 271–293; and *idem*, "The Normative Problem in Industrial Regulation," supplement to the *American Economic Review* (March, 1943), 54–70.

Bain's emphasis on the concept in question is to be attributed only partly to the significance of income distribution per se; his analysis rests in a large measure on the notion that redistributing incomes at the expense of noncompetitive profits is likely to raise the level of output and of employment through increasing the propensity to consume. Whether this actually is so depends on circumstances discussed in the earlier sections of this volume. Correctness of the assumption depends on whether entrepreneurs are so much more willing to produce for a more stable consumer market than for a more volatile producer market, that they produce more for the former than for the latter even at lower profit rates. This is taken for granted in Bain's argument. The assumption does not seem to me to be of *general* validity. The lower the propensity to consume and the higher the average profit rate, the greater the likelihood that the assumption is valid.

To summarize, although monopolistic tendencies always lead to a malallocation of resources, it is conceivable that their restrictive effect on the aggregate level of output and of employment could be offset by simultaneous changes which, indirectly, also are produced by monopolization. However, it seems very unlikely that this would occur consistently.

A discussion of output restriction attributable to monopoly should not be concluded without pointing to an important qualification. Monopoly output frequently is incomparable with competitive output. Whenever a commodity can be produced only with cost functions that exclude competition (because the optimum size of the firm is large in relation to the market), the question of the effect of monopoly on the size of output loses much of its meaning. The perfectly competitive output would have to be a different kind of output. The fact that in a different world with different techniques and commodities the amount of employment also would be different possesses little significance for an inquiry concerned with the actual world. Of course, not all features of the actual world can be assumed as given: a useful analytical system must contain variables as well as parameters. But it should take the existence of many commodities for granted which, given the present cost and demand functions, could not be produced in pure competition.

The Trend Toward Monopoly

The statistical approach is not very helpful in testing the plausibility of the hypothesis according to which the trend toward monopoly is responsible for the protracted depression after 1929. As has been shown, a priori analysis leads to the conclusion that awareness of influence on price, (i.e., monopoly), results in a curtailment of output if market demand curves and industry cost curves remain unchanged when competitive conditions are replaced by monopoly. In this event, the degree of output reduction depends on the curvature of the market curves, rather than on the various measures of monopolistic intensity advocated in recent literature. The statistical approach would, therefore, first have to devise a method by which the likelihood of awareness of price influence could be traced; and, second, it would have to trace the curvature of the market curves, as well as the shifts in these curves produced by monopolization (including the shifts due to repercussions, provided relative prices also change). The second of these tasks is obviously a hopeless one. As for the first, the so-called concentration ratios are measures computed by recent investigators with the intention of arriving at conclusions concerning the likelihood of the existence of competitive or monopolistic conditions in specific industries. It was pointed out in the preceding section that only with very serious qualifications can these concentration ratios be said to provide indications of the emergence of "monopoly" (i.e., of awareness of price influence).

In the present context it should be added that if "concentration ratios" could be interpreted to provide valuable information about monopolistic restrictions, the actual figures computed by Willard L. Thorp, Don D. Humphrey, and Martha H. Porter, would not indicate much change in this respect as between 1914 and 1937. Thorp, Humphrey, and Porter, on the one hand, and Walter F. Crowder, on the other, computed two different kinds of concentration ratios to be briefly considered here.[47] One type of concentration ratio (that computed by Thorp, Humphrey, and Porter) is based on the number of establishments which in 195 different industries

---

[47] *The Structure of Industry,* Temporary National Economic Committee, Monograph No. 27. Cf. parts i and v.

employ one-half of the labor force of the entire industry. The number of these establishments is then expressed as a percentage of all establishments in the industry. The other measure of concentration (that computed by Crowder) expresses for 1,807 manufactured products the proportion of output produced by the four largest producers. The *smaller* the percentage of establishments employing one-half of the labor force, the *greater* is the "concentration" in the first of these two senses (Thorp-Humphrey-Porter) and the *greater* the percentage of output produced by the four largest producers, the *greater* the "concentration" in the second sense (Crowder). If the limitations to which all reasoning in terms of "concentration ratios" is subject could be disregarded, it might be said that high concentration ratios in the first sense (i.e., the smallness of the proportion of establishments employing one-half of the labor force) reflect the coexistence of a few dominating establishments with a great number of relatively insignificant ones. High concentration ratios in the second sense (i.e., the highness of the proportion of output produced by the four largest producers) reflect the existence of powerful firms in the industry without indicating anything about their coexistence with a great number of weak firms. High concentration ratios in either sense might be interpreted, with the qualifcations already mentioned, to indicate the likelihood of the existence of monopoly power; that is, the likelihood of awareness of influence on market price on the part of significant producers. This, in turn, establishes the likelihood of monopolistic restriction of output, provided cost and demand curves remain as they would be in competition.

It was emphasized earlier that these qualifications are severe. In the present context it should be noted that the Thorp-Humphrey-Porter "concentration ratios" can be more adequately characterized as being very high than as having increased significantly since 1914. As of 1937, both kinds of concentration ratios are high for the two aggregate samples respectively.[48] Only the first kind of concentration

---

[48] In 1937, 2.9 per cent of all establishments employed one-half of the total labor force in the Thorp-Humphrey-Porter sample. In the same year it was true of 75 per cent of all products included in Crowder's sample that the four largest producers manufactured more than 50 per cent of total output, and it was true of more than 50 per cent of the products that the four largest were responsible for more than 70 per cent of output (cf. *The Structure of Industry*, p. 56 and 275).

ratio (that relating to the proportion of establishments employing one-half of the labor force) is computed for earlier dates as well, namely for 1914, 1919, 1921, 1923, 1929, 1933, and 1935. Concentration ratios for the sample as a whole rose but slightly from 1914 to 1937; and for a substantial number of industries the concentration ratios declined.[49] Reasoning in terms of concentration ratios is subject to too many qualifications to be of decisive significance; yet if these ratios are interpreted as containing some indication about monopoly power, the indication would seem to be that monopoly power was not much lower prior to the First World War than during the "stagnant" 1930's.

On the other hand, "concentration" in a different sense seems not merely to be high but also to have increased considerably since the early part of the present century. The largest 200 nonbanking corporations not merely own a very high percentage of the gross assets of all nonbanking corporations, but it also seems to be true that their gross assets have grown at a more rapid rate than those of the others.[50] It is possible to interpret this as suggesting the opposite of what is suggested by the approximate constancy of the Thorp-Humphrey-Porter concentration ratios for industrial establishments. In this event it would have to be argued that the "evidence" is inconsistent: some data (those relating to the concentration of corporate *wealth*) indicate that the likelihood of monopolistic collusion has increased considerably, whereas other findings (e.g., those relating to the concentration of *production* in the leading industrial

[49] The average concentration ratio, defined as the reciprocal of the proportion of establishments employing one-half of the labor force of the industry, rose by 17 per cent. This expresses the circumstance that from 1914 to 1937 the proportion of the establishments employing one-half of the labor force declined from 3.4 per cent to 2.9 per cent. However, for 97 of the 195 industries, the concentration ratio declined. (Cf. *ibid.*, p. 57 and pp. 88–93.)

[50] According to Berle and Means, the annual compound rate of increase was 5.4 per cent for the 200 largest nonbanking corporations and 3.6 per cent for the more than 300,000 remaining nonbanking corporations, during the period 1909–1928. In 1930 the 200 largest corporations owned 49.2 per cent of the gross assets of all nonbanking corporations. (Adolf A. Berle and Gardiner C. Means, *The Modern Corporation and Private Property*, New York, Chicago and Washington, Commerce Clearing House, 1932. Cf. pp. 28 and 36.) According to the Natural Resources Committee, a further substantial increase has taken place in this kind of "concentration ratio" during the first half of the 1930's (*The Structure of the American Economy*, Washington, 1939, I, 107).

establishments) indicate the opposite. It could also be argued, how-ever, that the two types of evidence are not inconsistent because: (*a*) it is conceivable that the largest producing units have become wealthier in relation to the others without having increased their share in production; (*b*) or, it is conceivable that the largest corpo-rations have operated an increasing number of establishments with the result that their share in wealth and in production has increased significantly in spite of the fact that the share of the largest industrial establishments has remained approximately constant. In the first case (*a*) concentration may not have increased in the sense relevant for monopoly trends, in the second case (*b*) it may well have. Even if the various data relating to concentration could be accepted as expressing precisely what they intend to express, it still would re-main questionable whether in recent decades, and particularly in the stagnant 'thirties, concentration in the here relevant sense has or has not increased significantly. Many economists (including the author) feel that it probably has, but it is not possible to "justify" this view adequately in terms of statistical material.

As for the monopoly power of labor organizations, there cannot be much doubt that this increased significantly during the 1930's. The rise in the power of labor organizations has been an important contributing cause of the rise in money wage rates. But the problem of changes in the wage level requires special analysis. It is not iden-tical with the problem of changes in the monopoly power of firms.

THE EFFECT OF GENERAL WAGE CHANGES ON OUTPUT AND EMPLOYMENT

In "orthodox" economics it was frequently taken for granted that unemployment was caused by high wages and that it could be remedied by the lowering of money wage rates. Economists whose orientation is influenced by the underconsumption theories typi-cally are "unorthodox" in their views concerning the effects of autonomous changes in the general wage level. Some argue that a general reduction of money wage rates will neither diminish nor increase unemployment, others that the lowering of wage rates is even likely to reduce the level of employment. The latter of these two positions might lead to the belief that employment would be increased by a general raise in wages. Actually, a raise in wages has rarely been recommended by professional economists as a means to increase employment. But, in recent times, refraining from general wage reductions has been recommended frequently and it has been maintained that general wage changes would have no effect on employment, except indirectly via liquidity preference. This view implies, of course (as does the subsequent discussion), that after a change the new wage level is expected to remain stable. It is obvious that the expectation of an impending fall in the wage level affects employment adversely and that the expectations of an impending rise exerts a favorable influence.

The view that a change in the money wage level would presumably not alter the amount of employment, and that consequently the lowering of the wage level would not reduce unemployment, implies, however, also certain propositions with respect to investment for further investment (i.e., with respect to that amount of net capital formation in each period which results in such additional output as represents a further increase in net capital formation during the subsequent period).[51] These implications will not be accepted uncritically in the following discussion.

The view that employment remains unaffected is correct if it is assumed that the share of real output going into investment for further investment is independent of the level of money wage rates (which means that the amount of investment per unit of expected consumer demand is not affected by wage changes). For this special case it can be shown that the real output flow cannot become smaller nor greater as a consequence of the change in money wage rates, except possibly for a transitional period during which incorrect decisions will be reversed. A change in the ratio of commodity prices to money wage rates for a given range of output is associated with a change in the average and marginal propensity to consume for the entire range in question. If either the average or the marginal propensity to consume changes the share of output going into investment for further investment also changes. Consequently, a change of prices in relation to money wage rates involves a change

---

[51] This amount equals the aggregate net investment multiplied by one minus the marginal propensity to consume.

in the ratio of aggregate output to investment for further invest-
'ment, that is, a change in the aggregate amount of investment
undertaken per unit of expected consumer demand. Postulating
that no such change occurs means assuming that prices will increase
or decrease in the same proportion as that in which money wage
rates do and in this event the change in money wage rates has no
effect on real output or on employment.

The conclusion corresponds closely to Professor Lerner's interpretation of the Keynesian position.[52] It is not clear, however, from
that interpretation that the conclusion rests on the assumption that
the share of output absorbed by investment for further investment
remains unchanged. It follows from the argument here presented
that the conclusion could not be maintained if the relative significance of real investment for further investment was assumed to
change as a consequence of a change in the level of money wages.
If a reduction of the level of money wage rates increases the share
of output which producers are willing to allocate to investment for
further investment, and if a rise of the money wage level decreases
this share, then a rise in money wage rates will not be associated
with a proportionate rise in prices, and a decline in money wage
rates will not be associated with a proportionate price decline. It
seems plausible to assume that the level of money wage rates is
inversely related to the share of output allocated to investment for
further investment because, although wages influence the costs of
investment for further investment, they are not direct determinants
of the demand for the products of this activity. The products in
question remain in a sphere of circulation restricted to producers,
although the process of course raises incomes and, therefore, also
aggregate consumer demand.

The assumption may be made that, in consequence of a decline in
money wage rates, producers are willing to allocate an increased
share of real output to investment for further investment (which

[52] Cf. A. P. Lerner, "Mr. Keynes' 'General Theory of Employment,'" *International Labor Review* (October, 1936), 435–454; see mainly pp. 440–442. The doctrine is quali-
fied by Keynes in chapter xix of the *General Theory of Employment, Interest and Money*. In Lerner's interpretation the qualifications appear on page 442, *op. cit.* These, however, relate to such changes in the interest rate as are brought about by changes in the money wage rate. The qualifications in question are on lines different from those suggested in the text above; they will be considered later, on page 100, n. 59.

means that they are willing to undertake more net investment in relation to consumer demand.) In this event the aggregate expenditure on goods tends to rise in relation to the aggregate wage bill. This is a result of the fact that the total expenditure that producers are willing to undertake exceeds the expected consumer demand by a greater margin after the decline of money wage rates than before.[53] Consequently the total producers' expenditure that, to entrepreneurs, seems to be justified tends to exceed the expected consumption spending, and thereby the wage bill,[54] by a greater margin than before. This is another way of saying that a decline in money wage rates *increases the ratio of nonwage incomes to wage incomes and thereby decreases real wage rates,*[55] and that a rise in money wage rates has the opposite effect. In this context changes in real wage rates mean changes in "product wage rates"; that is to say, changes in money wage rates corrected for the selling prices of the industries paying the wages. The conclusion concerning the effect of changes in money wage rates on changes in real wage rates follows from the assumption that the share of output allocated to investment for further investment is inversely related to the level of money wage rates. This assumption seems justified because wages are cost factors but not (in any direct way) demand-influencing factors for this type of economic activity.

If the share of output allocated to investment for further investment would be uninfluenced by changes in money wage rates, then real wage rates and the flow of real output would also remain unaffected. On (probably) more realistic assumptions, such as those outlined in the preceding paragraph, it seems appropriate to conclude that autonomous changes in money wage rates are likely to be associated with changes in real wage rates in the same direction. From this it follows that a decline in money wage rates is likely to produce a primary tendency toward an increase of aggregate real output and of employment, and vice versa. Such a tendency *may,*

[53] As must be so if producers are willing to allocate an increased share of output to investment for further investment.

[54] The wage bill stands, in the first approximation, for consumption expenditure to be expected out of wage income. The average propensity to consume obviously is higher for wage income than for profits.

[55] Given the man-hour output.

however, be subsequently reversed; or it may even be simultaneously submerged in an opposite, secondary tendency. This point must be examined in some detail.

As was already stated, the argument rests on the notion that a rise in the general level of money wage rates reduces the share of output which producers are willing to allocate to investment for further investment, and that a reduction of the money wage level increases this share. In other words, investment expenditure per unit of consumption tends to vary inversely with money wage rates. This produces a tendency for money and real wage rates to move in the same direction and it also produces a primary tendency for output to move in the opposite direction. Yet, the primary tendency for aggregate output and employment to rise when money and real wage rates are reduced (and vice versa), may or may not stay final. Whether it stays final or is reversed depends on whether the stimulating effect of lower real wage rates is or is not offset by the increased instability and increased uncertainty attending the lowering of the average propensity to consume. As was pointed out earlier, the sensitiveness of consumer demand to consumer income and to income expectations is smaller than is the sensitiveness of producer demand to producer income and to income expectations. Consequently the market for consumer goods is more stable, more "dependable," than is the market for investment goods. Circumstances are conceivable in which total output declines when costs of production are reduced in a manner involving a decrease in the relative significance of consumer demand as compared to producer demand. The degree of instability and, therefore, the average degree of uncertainty, is increased when such a change occurs. The final outcome depends on whether the stimulus provided by the lower average and marginal wage costs per unit of output is more or less potent than the adverse effect produced by the increased uncertainty.[56] The prop-

---

[56] Even abstracting from technological progress, it should not be overlooked that man-hour output changes as output increases or decreases, unless the average product per unit of input should remain constant. If, for example, the average productivity of labor decreases with rising output, the rise in profit margins, and also the decrease in the average propensity to consume, is smaller after an increase in output (or is greater after a decrease in output) than how great the change in profit margins and in the average propensity to consume would be at the original output with reduced wage rates. These considerations enter into a quantitative appraisal of the effect discussed in the text.

osition is symmetrical with respect to wage changes. A rise in money and real wage rates leads to a primary tendency toward a decline in aggregate output and employment, but this tendency may also be followed by, or simultaneously submerged in, an opposite tendency attributable to a decline in the average degree of instability and thereby of uncertainty.[57]

The conclusion may be summarized in the following four points. (1) If no definite assumptions are made with respect to the effect of changes in money wage rates on the share of output allocated to investment for further investment, the relationship between changes in money wage rates, on the one hand, and changes in real wage rates and in output, on the other, is indeterminate. (2) If the share of output allocated to investment for further investment is assumed to remain unaffected by changes in money wage rates, then real wage rates and aggregate output also remain unaffected. (3) It seems probable, however, that the share of output allocated to investment for further investment should rise when money wage rates decline and that this share should decline when money wage rates rise. If this assumption is made, real wage rates (from the standpoint of the entrepreneur—i.e., product wage rates) tend to rise and to decline along with money wage rates. (4) Aggregate output rises or declines with declining real wage rates depending on whether, in the relevant range, the lowering of wage costs (i.e., the increase in most probable average and marginal profit rates) coupled with an increase in uncertainty exerts, on balance, a favorable or an adverse effect on the willingness to produce.[58] If in some definite range, aggregate output rises with declining real wage rates, then it should be expected to decline with rising real wage rates and vice versa.

Therefore, the element of truth behind the reasoning of the underconsumption theories possesses a bearing on the problem of the effects of equalitarian tendencies. Constellations may very well exist in which real wage rates can be increased at the expense of profit rates, with favorable effects on output and employment, and

---

[57] It probably is correct to say that this idea underlies the conclusions reached by J. M. Clark in *Strategic Factors in Business Cycles* (New York, National Bureau of Economic Resarch, 1935), pp. 140–142, 212.

[58] The increase in uncertainty is a consequence of a decrease in the average propensity to consume.

in which a reduction of real wages creates more unemployment. This is true because, for any given output, the average degree of uncertainty attaching to profit expectations is smaller if the average propensity to consume is high than if it is low, and because lower wage costs (i.e., higher most probable profits for a given output) plus higher uncertainty may, in certain circumstances, call forth a lower output than higher wage costs plus lower uncertainty. The "unorthodox" effect under consideration will, however, always be limited to a certain range. In general, the likelihood of its occurrence is the greater, the lower the average propensity to consume and the higher the profit rate is in a specific economy during a specific period. In the industrially advanced economies, the likelihood of the "unorthodox" effect is comparatively small in depressed, or stagnant, periods because these are characterized by an "abnormally" high average propensity to consume and by low profit margins. Moreover, in the long run, the unorthodox effect in question would tend to be somewhat weaker on employment than on output because a rise in real wages stimulates the substitution of assets for labor and vice versa.[59]

The preceding analysis led to the conclusion that a rise in money wage rates will tend to be associated with a rise in real wage rates, if, as seems likely, the proportion of output allocated to investment for further investment (and therefore the amount of investment per unit of consumption) declines in consequence of the wage raise. A rise in money and real wage rates may affect output favorably or adversely.

---

[59] In the foregoing paragraphs I have disregarded the increase in liquidity attending a general reduction in money wages and the corresponding decline in liquidity when money wages are increased. In the Keynesian reasoning this circumstance supplies the main qualification to the thesis that changes in the general money wage level do not influence the level of real output. The change in liquidity might affect the level of output only through changing the rate of interest. The process under consideration is therefore subject to the general limitations of interest rate policies. It will be argued later that these limitations are substantial so far as stimulating output by lowering interest rates is concerned, and this is the reason why the effect of wage reductions via liquidity can hardly be expected to become significant. It is true that the limitations of interest-rate policies are less severe so far as stopping a boom by raising interest rates is concerned. Consequently an increase in money wages might actually have a depressing influence through decreasing the liquidity of producers and increasing the structure of interest rates. This effect, however, can be counteracted by monetary action whenever expansion seems desirable. Therefore, neither of the two halves of the liquidity argument seems particularly significant, although both halves are theoretically valid.

The outcome depends on whether, in the given range, the reduction of uncertainty (attributable to the increased propensity to consume) coupled with an increase in wage costs (and thereby with a decrease of most probable profit rates for a given output) has favorable or adverse effects on balance. This reasoning implies, however, given man-hour output. The assumption of given man-hour output is justified in the analysis of instantaneous changes, and the preceding analysis was of such character. If, however, man-hour output changes simultaneously with wage rates, as is historically always true, both the potential stimulating effect and the potential adverse effect derive not from the change in the real wage rate itself, but from the change in unit labor cost. In other words, the change in money wage rates must be corrected not merely for changes in selling prices but also for changes in man-hour output. In the event of rising wages both the adverse effect on the profit rate and the favorable effect on the average propensity to consume become diminished to the extent of the rise in man-hour output, whereas with falling wages both the favorable effect on the profit rate and the adverse effect on the propensity to consume effects become reinforced by the same circumstance. There has existed a significant trend toward a rise in man-hour output, and this trend continued through the 'thirties.

The factual material expressed in diagrammatical form in figure 18 is consistent with the assumption that the favorable effects of rising unit wage costs outweigh the unfavorable ones more frequently when business activity is high than when it is low. This assumption possesses a certain amount of a priori plausibility because, when business activity is high, profit expectations are usually favorable, whereas the less stable and less dependable investment demand for goods accounts for a relatively high share of the total demand. Consequently a range within which the greater dependability of consumer markets may be substituted with favorable results for a certain portion of the profit margins, is more likely to exist in these circumstances than in the advanced stages of depressions and in periods of stagnation, which are characterized by low profit margins and a high average propensity to consume.

The data expressed in figure 18 are not inconsistent with this reasoning. Perhaps they may even be said to add some amount of plausibility to the a priori reasoning of the preceding paragraph. For manufacturing as a whole it seems to have been consistently true during the entire forty-year period 1899–1939 (with a single exception applying to a highly "abnormal" subperiod), that upturns occurred in yearly intervals of declining unit labor costs. At the same time, it is not consistently true that downturns occurred in

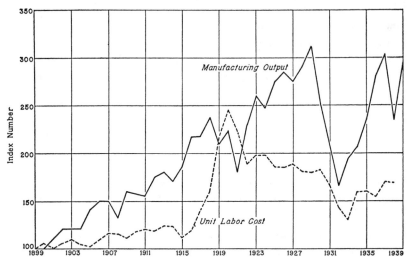

Fig. 18. Manufacturing output and unit labor cost, 1899–1939 (1899 = 100). Secular trend equation: 1899–1929, y = 92.660 + 6.518 x, origin 1899. Data for the index of manufacturing output for the years 1899–1926 is from Paul H. Douglas, *Theory of Wages*, table 1, appendix; for the years 1927–1939 (converted to an 1899 base) from Irving H. Siegel, "Hourly Earnings and Unit Labor Cost in Manufacturing," *Journal of the American Statistical Association*, vol. 35, no. 211 (September, 1940), 458, table 2. The index of unit labor cost for 1899–1926 was derived from the data in Douglas, *op. cit.*, appendix, by dividing the index of physical production (table 1) by the index of employment (table 5) and by dividing this quotient into the index of money wages (table 7). For the period 1927–1939, the index of unit labor cost is that found in Siegel, *op. cit.*, p. 458, table 2, converted to an 1899 base.

yearly intervals of rising unit labor costs. On the contrary, they occurred more frequently in years of declining or constant labor costs per unit of output than in periods of rising costs.[60] This does

[60] The following were first years of expansion (revival): 1908 to 1909, 1914 to 1915, 1919 to 1920, 1921 to 1922, 1924 to 1925, 1927 to 1928, 1932 to 1933, 1938 to 1939. Unit labor costs declined markedly in all cases except from 1919 to 1920. The following were first years of contraction: 1907 to 1908, 1913 to 1914, 1918 to 1919, 1920 to 1921, 1923 to 1924, 1926 to 1927, 1929 to 1930, 1937 to 1938. Unit labor costs failed to rise (i.e., they declined or remained constant) in all years except from 1918 to 1919, from 1926 to 1927, and from 1929 to 1930.

not of itself prove that declining unit labor costs contributed to ending periods of contraction (i.e., that they had a favorable effect in periods of low activity). Nor do these facts of themselves prove the hypothesis that rising unit labor costs failed to exert an adverse influence in the upswing. The same facts could be fitted into a great many different types of reasoning. But the facts are not at variance with the tentative hypothesis here expressed on the effects of changing unit labor costs in expansion and contraction. This tentative hypothesis can be explained with the help of the notions previously developed concerning the effects of changing real wage rates on profit margins, on uncertainty, and thereby on aggregate output.

Whether autonomous changes in money wage rates actually tend to be accompanied by movements of real wages in the same direction[61] cannot be tested, because there is no way of distinguishing between autonomous and induced wage changes for longer periods. However, in certain critical subperiods during the "stagnant 'thirties," when a rise in money wages was in a large measure clearly attributable to government attitudes and to the effective organization of labor, real wage rates did rise along with money wage rates. Unit labor costs also rose, in spite of the simultaneous rise in man-hour output. The period was, of course, characterized by a high average propensity to consume and by comparatively low profit margins. Consequently, in the period under consideration there was less likelihood of favorable effects from rising unit labor costs than would have been the case in a period with the opposite characteristics.

APPENDIX TO CHAPTER III

A Note on the Determination of Wage Rates under Bilateral Monopoly

THREE WAGE LEVELS FOR SPECIFIC FIRMS AND FOR THE REPRESENTATIVE ENTERPRISE

THE CONCEPT OF autonomous wage changes should be made somewhat more precise than has so far been the case. This requires in the first place an explanation of the determination of money wage rates in tolerably

---

[61] This was maintained on a priori grounds in chapter ii.

realistic conditions which typically contain elements of bilateral monopoly. The model portrayed in figure 19 might serve as a sketchy framework for a wage theory.[1] The model could, of course, be considerably refined, if applied to markets the specific characteristics of which were known.

The figure relates to an individual firm. The expected average value product function (AVP) and the expected marginal value product function (MVP) indicate the average and the marginal net value product for the quantities of labor service measured along the abscissa, on the assumption that the quantity of the other factors employed is adjusted optimally for profit maximization to each potential quantity of labor

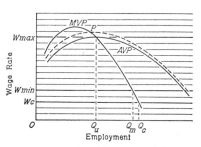

Fig. 19. Money wage rate under bilateral monopoly.

service (except for the marginal variation which of course assumes at each level a constant quantity of other factors). These value products are net in the sense that the total costs of employing the optimal quantities of the other factors of production are deducted; and also in the sense that the reward for uncertainty, required to call forth the output in question, is deducted. The broken curve should be disregarded for the moment. The horizontal lines express successively higher indifference levels, as viewed from the angle of the labor union. For these indifference curves, the ordinate measures the money wage rate, and the abscissa, as before, the quantity of labor service employed. It is implied, for the time being, that any given wage rate gives the same "satisfaction," regardless of the quantity of employment. This assumption will be modified later so as to take account of two special problems (pp. 106 and 109).

In these circumstances maximum bargaining power for the union could be defined as the ability to enforce the wage rate W_{max}. The corresponding quantity of employment is Q_u. Assuming that there exists a minimum wage level below which the union is "truly" not willing to go (W_{min} in the figure), a possible way of defining the upper limit of the bargaining power of the management is with reference to this wage level. For the wage rate W_{min}, which, here, expresses the maximum bargaining power of the management, the quantity of employment is Q_m. This definition of maximum bargaining power for the management (or of minimum bargaining power for the union) implies that the level of the

---

[1] The model makes use of the indifference curve technique. An approach to the problems of wage theory with the aid of this technique is found in an article by John T. Dunlop and Benjamin Higgins. " 'Bargaining Power' and Market Structures," *Journal of Political Economy* (February, 1942), 1–26.

minimum wage rate "acceptable" to the union (W_{min}) is *ex ante* to bargaining power. This in turn implies that the wage level W_{min} reflects partly objective and partly psychological circumstances that can be distinguished from "bargaining power." It seems reasonable to make this distinction, and it may perhaps be suggested that the wage level W_{min} can be derived from the wage rate W_c, which the labor stock in question believes it could earn if it were not organized, by adding a margin by which the union must make its members fare better in order not to lose their support. The "expectations of the labor stock" is, however, obviously a very vague concept, and consequently the foregoing sentence merely expresses that a substantial portion of the employed labor stock must feel that it gains through being organized. In these circumstances the wage rate paid by the firm lies between W_{max} and W_{min}, and the employment supplied by the firm lies between Q_u and Q_m, at levels depending on the "bargaining power" of the two parties concerned.

In terms of these concepts the closeness of substitutes is not a determinant of bargaining power but a determinant of the distance between the upper and the lower limit of the bargaining range, within which the wage rate is determined by bargaining power. The greater the number of close substitutes on the demand side of the labor market (i.e., the more firms are buyers of labor in similar conditions), the more is the lower limit of the bargaining range elevated, given the substitutability conditions on the supply side. On the other hand, the closer the substitutes on the supply side of the labor market, the more is the lower limit lowered, given the substitutability conditions on the demand side. Therefore, substitutability on the supply side tends to increase the range, whereas substitutability on the demand side tends to reduce it. The reducing effect of substitutability on the demand side may typically be even greater than indicated, if the firms hiring labor in similar conditions also produce similar products, thereby lowering one another's AVP and MVP curves. The range left for bargaining, but not the bargaining power, is determined by substitutability conditions. Bargaining power decides the outcome of the bargain within the bargaining range. It depends mainly on the loss that would be caused by work stoppage, to the two parties respectively, on public policies, and on what may be called genuine negotiating ability. Public policies, however, do not merely affect bargaining power; they may also influence substitutability conditions and thereby the position of the upper and of the lower limit of the bargaining range.

Should the firm be confronted with a competitive labor supply, the wage rate would presumably be lower than W_{min} by a certain margin. For the union, in order to be recognized as "effective," must keep the wage rate beyond the level at which it would be if the labor stock in question were unorganized. This statement is subject, however, to the qualification that "public opinion" in the ranks of labor may misjudge the relationship existing between actual wage rates and the would-be wage rate W_c. The employment corresponding to W_c is Q_c.

This leaves the question open as to what would determine wage rates if the labor supply to the firm was unorganized. One way of answering this question is to say that the earnings, in other occupations, of similar labor (i.e., of labor belonging in the same Cairnesian group) determine W_c. Correction must be made for the expenses and the inconvenience of transferring from one occupation to the other, and also for differences in inconvenience between jobs, for costs of acquiring skills, and so on *á la* Adam Smith. Such an answer is correct but incomplete for two reasons. In the first place, it takes the wage rate in other occupations as given, and second, it leaves a high margin of indeterminateness if the costs of transferring from one occupation to the other are significant. The following may, therefore, he added to an opportunity wage rate theory (as interpreted with Adam Smith's and Cairnes' amendments). The general level of the wage rate, that is, W_c for the economy as a whole (or for the "representative" enterprise) , could not decline below the level at which the pressure of public opinion for government regulation would become irresistible. For high levels of employment (i.e., in the right-hand segment of the figure) the level of W_c could, however, be substantially in excess of this modern equivalent of the subsistence level. This is a consequence of rising transfer costs if the model relates to an individual firm and it is the consequence of the increasing disutility of working "beyond normal" if the figure relates to the economy as a whole (or to the "representative" enterprise). Consequently Q_c and all indifference curves should properly be so drawn as to slope upward in (but only in) the region of very high employment. In the figure they actually are not so drawn—only the horizontal segment is drawn—because this discussion leads up to the problem of the effects of general wage changes on unemployment, and, therefore, it implies that employment usually is within the limits set by "normal" hours for the "normal" labor force.

ANALYTICAL SHORT RUN AND CLOCK-TIME LONG RUN

Nothing has been said so far about whether the curves of the figure should be interpreted as pertaining analytically to the "long run" or to the "short run." If by the "analytical long run" a condition is meant in which no costs whatsoever are considered fixed (or sunk), the relevant functions must certainly not be interpreted in the long-run sense. Analytically it will always be true—and therefore it will be true in the clock-time long run as well as in the clock-time short run—that certain costs are sunk before wage decisions are made. In this sense the relevant functions are always "analytically" short run (even in the clock-time long run!), although the type of function relevant to a particular situation may be more or less "short run"—i.e., it may be more or less different from the long-run type analytically—depending on whether certain changes in plant, equipment, and other long-term commitments are or are not contemplated for the relevant range of potential outputs. It should be realized, however, that this does not necessarily imply the possibility of forcing the enterprise to operate in conditions in which only average *variable* costs are covered.

Considering that the AVP and the MVP function of the figure are short-run functions in the sense that certain costs of future output had been sunk before these curves were drawn, it is possible to draw an alternative curve to AVP in such a manner as to deduct from the gross value product of labor merely the variable costs of employing the coöperating factors. Essentially this new function—the broken line of the figure— bears the same kind of relation to AVP as does the traditional average variable unit cost curve to the average total unit cost curve. The MVP function has no such "broken" alternative since fixed costs do not enter into marginal costs, and if AVP were to be interpreted in the long-run sense, then no such alternative would exist even for this latter function. Since, however, it is true of any moment of time in which wage decisions are made that certain costs of future output had been sunk before, and since, therefore, analytically the relevant functions are not of the purely "long-run" variety, the "broken" alternative is a legitimate alternative of the AVP curve. This raises the question of whether the solution corresponding to the maximum bargaining power of the union (minimum bargaining power of the management) should not be expressed by the maximum point of the broken curve (P) instead of the maximum point of AVP. The solution suggested for the other two cases (minimum bargaining power of the union and competitive labor supply to the firm) remains unaffected by the answer since the AVP curve does not enter into the determination of the corresponding wage rates and of the corresponding amounts of employment.

As was indicated above, the "short-run" character of AVP does *not* necessarily imply that the broken curve should be substituted for AVP in the solution corresponding to maximum union bargaining power. Although it is true that some costs will always be sunk, regardless of what moment of a clock-time long run is taken, it is not true that a firm may be induced to stay in business in the clock-time long run if it is compelled to write off at regular intervals such investments as have been "sunk" during these intervals. Sooner or later such a firm would cease to "sink" any costs, and this means that the expiring portion of long-term commitments will not be renewed. It should be remembered in this connection that replacement is never truly "current." Replacement is lumpy and consequently always creates "sunk" costs for subsequent periods. In addition, the legal long-term commitments also expire gradually and these, too, must be renewed if the firm is to stay in business. Firms always operate in "short-run" conditions analytically, because part of the costs of future production is already sunk; yet firms do not continue to operate for more than a limited period if there does not exist an adequate inducement for the further "sinking" of costs. In the clock-time short run it may be possible to force an enterprise into paying wages at a rate corresponding to point P in figure 19. In the clock-time long run it is not possible to push a firm beyond the maximum point of the AVP function, even if its "bargaining power" on the labor market is zero. However, the AVP function is never of a truly "long-run" character analytically, because there exists no moment in the life of an enterprise in which all costs would be variable.

AN AMENDMENT

Nevertheless, the short-run character (in the analytical sense) of the relevant curves does make it necessary to modify the conclusions to be derived from figure 19 in one respect. The likelihood of discontinuities in the AVP and MVP functions is substantially increased if part of the costs is fixed, because in these circumstances the production functions are likely to have discontinuities. Furthermore, it should be remembered that the expected demand curves for the products of the firms in question also enter into the determination of the functions portrayed in figure 19; therefore, if these have kinks, and the corresponding marginal revenue functions have discontinuities, ranges of discontinuity might appear in the AVP and MVP functions, regardless of the production functions. The case for the assumption of discontinuities on the demand side of commodity markets was argued convincingly by Professor Sweezy,[2] for oligopolistic markets. Discontinuities in the functions shown in figure 19 may render employment insensitive to the wage rate within certain ranges. If the figure relates to the economy as a whole (or to the "representative" enterprise), the ranges of discontinuity are much smaller than if it relates to an individual firm. Possibilities of substitution are much less limited for the economy as a whole, even in the analytical short run.

ANOTHER AMENDMENT

Would it not be more realistic to assume that the indifference curves of unions are concave, as viewed from above, rather than horizontal? At first sight, this might seem a realistic assumption because an excessive amount of unemployment in the ranks of any union endangers the position of the leadership, just as low wages do. It is preferable, however, to take account of this circumstance in a different way. Concave indifference curves would suggest a direct functional relationship between wage rate and unemployment on any given level of satisfaction, and they would suggest that this relationship could be expressed *ex ante* in the

---

[2] Paul M. Sweezy, "Demand Under Conditions of Oligopoly," *Journal of Political Economy* (June, 1939), 565–573.

curves determining the behavior of the union. The relationship between wage rates and the amount of unemployment is, however, at best very imperfectly foreseen by a union; and so is the pressure, or the degree of dissatisfaction, resulting from any given amount of unemployment. It seems preferable, therefore, to conceive of the indifference curves as being horizontal *ex ante*,[3] and to point out separately that the upper limit of the bargaining power of the union may, in certain circumstances, be lower than was indicated in the figure. In the clock-time short run the maximum level indicated in the figure does not require modification. In the clock-time long run it may require modification, if at this level a reduction of unemployment yields more "satisfaction" to the leadership of the union than does the failure to reduce wages. In this latter case, the subsequent horizontal indifference curves, from the origin upward, cease to express monotonously increasing levels of satisfaction. Instead, in the clock-time long run, they may express increasing levels of satisfaction up to a certain point along the ordinate, and decreasing levels from there on. The maximum level may lie below the horizontal line tangential to AVP, and the wage and employment for the maximum bargaining power of the union may in this case be determined by the intersection of the lower horizontal line in question with the MVP function.

THE RELATIONSHIP BETWEEN THE DEMAND SIDE AND THE SUPPLY SIDE OF THE LABOR MARKET

It is possible now to express in terms of the model the difficulty brought out by the Keynesian controversy. The essence of the difficulty is that if wage rates change throughout an economy, or change even only in a significant segment of an economy, the AVP and MVP functions do not remain unchanged. Consequently a theory of wages is not obtainable (except on specific equilibrium assumptions) without introducing definite hypotheses on how the value product functions react to such general changes of the wage level as do not stem from primary changes of the value product functions. In the preceding discussion these changes were termed *autonomous* wage changes.

Professor Lerner's interpretation of the Keynesian theory would lead to the conclusion that a rise or a decline in the money wage level throughout the economy calls forth a corresponding rise or decline in the value product functions (in such a manner that prices change in the same proportion and employment remains unchanged).[4] If, on the other hand, it should be true that a rise in the money wage level reduces, and a decline increases, the share of output allocated to investment for further investment, prices must be assumed to increase or to decline in a smaller

---

[3] Except for ranges of very high employment, where they slope upward.
[4] Except for roundabout effects via the interest rate.

proportion than money wage rates. (Cf. above, pp. 94–100.) In these circumstances, output and employment will tend to decline with rising money wages, and to rise with declining money wages, provided the entrepreneurial charge for uncertainty, per unit of output, remains unchanged. When money wages rise, the upward shift of the value product functions of the "representative" entrepreneur would be smaller than is required for the maintenance of output and employment. When money wages decline, the downward shift of the value product functions would be smaller than that which would prevent output and employment from rising. Yet if, within a certain range, the entrepreneurial charge for uncertainty declines considerably when money and real wage rates rise and if, within the same range, the charge for uncertainty increases with declining money and real wage rates,[5] then, in the range under consideration, output and employment may vary positively with the wage level. Under these conditions, the value product functions rise more than "correspondingly" (i.e., more than is required to maintain output and employment) when money wages rise, and they decline less than correspondingly when money wages decline because, although prices rise less than correspondingly with a rise in money wages and decline more than correspondingly with a fall in money wages, the change in the charge for uncertainty outweighs the effect of the incompleteness of the price adjustment. It should be remembered that decreasing uncertainty shifts the value product functions upward, and that increasing uncertainty shifts them downward, because the functions are defined to be "net"; they are derived from the gross value product functions by subtracting the costs of the coöperating factors and of uncertainty.

Changes on the Supply Side of the Labor Market

A brief comment may be added here on the involved problem of changes on the supply side of the labor market which, instead of being autonomous, are induced by primary changes in the value product functions. A rise in the value product functions tends to raise the minimum money wage level acceptable to unions, the maximum money wage level acceptable to managements, and probably also the bargaining power of unions. The minimum wage level acceptable to unions tends to rise because, with the rise in prices, the money wage level below which public pressure would not allow wage rates to decline, increases.[6] The maximum level acceptable to managements rises for obvious reasons, and the bargaining power of unions should be expected to rise because if the margin between the shifted lower and upper limits of the bargaining ranges were divided in the same proportions as before, the rise in profits would render work

---

[5] In consequence of changes in the average propensity to consume, which affect the average degree of uncertainty due to the high stability of consumer demand as compared with producers' demand.

[6] W_c is shifted upward.

stoppages more costly to firms. Moreover, the decline in unemployment also tends to increase the bargaining power of labor organizations. For analogous reasons, a decline in the value product functions lowers both the upper and the lower limits of the bargaining range and it should be expected to diminish the relative bargaining power of labor.

It might be concluded that wage rates are likely to be more flexible than prices in expansions as well as in contractions. Experience, however, seems to indicate that money wage rates tend to be more flexible than prices only *upward;* when the change occurs *downward,* money wage rates tend to be less flexible than prices.[7] It seems that the instances of downward inflexibility are consequences of the existence of a long-run social trend which—like most social trends of the subsequent historical epochs—becomes accelerated whenever the system is exposed to a shock. The trend toward "economic democracy" raises the lower limit of the bargaining range in terms of money and real wage rates, although it does not necessarily bring the lower limit closer to the upper since, at the same time, technological trends have the effect of raising the upper limit. Yet when the system is exposed to a shock, the current social trends usually gain momentum and in these short-run periods[8] the pressure of public opinion may well bring the lower limit (W_c and W_{min}) closer to the upper. If "bargaining power" is defined to relate merely to the proportion in which the margin between the two limits is divided (rather than to the position of the limits themselves), it may then be said that in recent decades the trend sometimes prevented the lower limit of the bargaining range from declining in periods of contraction in a measure equal to that in which prices and the upper limit of the bargaining range declined. The result has been that even the reduced "bargaining power" of labor in depressions sometimes yielded money wage rates that corresponded to increased real wage rates.

---

[7] This statement is based on a comparison of changes in money wage rates in manufacturing industries with changes in the selling prices of manufacturing industries. The data are found partly in Paul H. Douglas, *Real Wages in the United States* (Boston and New York, Houghton Mifflin, 1900), p. 108, table 24, and partly in *idem, The Theory of Wages* (New York, Macmillan, 1934), p. 506, Statistical Appendix, Table II. There exists no contradiction between the statement of the text and the thesis maintaining that although real wage rates tend to *rise* along with money wage rates there exists no uniform tendency downward; nor does there exist any contradiction between the statement of the text and the thesis maintaining that money and real wage rates tend to rise and also to decline together. The first of these two theses is deduced from British material by John T. Dunlop, "The Movement of Real and Money Wage Rates," *Economic Journal* (September 1938), 413–434; the second is deduced from American material by Lorie Tarshis, "Changes in Real and Money Wages," *Economic Journal* (March 1939), 150–153. However, for Dr. Dunlop and for Dr. Tarshis real wages means "money wages corrected for the cost of living," whereas in the text above changes in money wage rates were compared with changes in the prices charged by the industries paying the wages in question.

[8] "Short run" in the sense of clock time.

CHAPTER IV

Generalized Expansion

Surproduction Généralisée and Its Logical Counterpart

THE FOLLOWING pages present a hypothesis concerning factors contributing to a high inducement to invest in extended periods of economic expansion. It is recognized, of course, that any one hypothesis can at best claim to be taken into account in conjunction with many others when an interpretation of economic reality is attempted.

In business cycle theory it has been frequently maintained that the phenomenon appearing as general overproduction should be interpreted as *surproduction généralisée* rather than *générale*.[1] Essentially this view represents an attempt to reconcile facts with Say's law: There exists no such thing as general overproduction, but partial overproduction may become "generalized" by giving rise to processes temporarily conveying the impression of general overproduction. Assume that there exists partial overproduction of Commodity A, and that this, in accordance with Say's law, is tantamount to partial underproduction of Commodity B. Resources should now be shifted from Section A to Section B of the economy. This takes time, however, and consequently production and employment as a whole will be curtailed for a period that should not be long, if the initiating causes themselves determined the entire

---

[1] For the literature on this topic, cf. the references to be found in Albert Aftalion, *Des Crises Périodiques de Surproduction* (Paris, Marcel Rivière, 1913), Vol. I, Book IV, chap. i; see also Jean Lescures, *Des Crises Générales et Périodiques de Surproduction* ([1st ed., 1906], 4th ed.; Paris, Donat-Montchrestien, 1932), pp. 488–492. Of the advocates of the doctrine listed by Professor Aftalion, Tugan-Baranowsky is the earliest. Cf. Michael von Tugan-Baranowsky, *Studien zur Theorie und Geschichte der Handelskrisen in England* (Jena, Gustav Fischer, 1901),.pp. 10–12, and Part I, chap. viii. Tugan-Baranowsky pointed out (*op. cit.*, p. 250), that his theory had appeared in 1894 in the first Russian edition of his book. As will be seen presently, the theory is implicit in numerous cycle theories.

process. Yet during the period required to conduct the unemployed resources into another section of the economy and to expand production in other fields, the demand for goods as a whole may decline, and this would give rise to a downward spiral. In other words, the contractionary half of the adjustment to partial overproduction may not be followed by the expansionary half with the lag determined by physical factors alone, because a cumulative process of contraction may start during the period constituting the lag. Moreover, quite aside from lag considerations, the adverse psychology created by overproduction in specific sections of the economy may spread and become "generalized." This may occur initially with no "objective" justification, but it may create its own justification by generating a depression.

Elements of this doctrine of generalized overproduction are found in a great many business cycle theories. In fact, they are found in most business cycle theories with the exception of the typical—or pure—underconsumption theories. The underconsumption theories give a different answer to the question of "what is wrong" with orthodox versions of Say's law. Their answer is that, given the distribution of income, all goods may be overproduced relative to effective demand because part of "disposable income" (in the Robertsonian sense) may give rise to a demand for idle balances instead of a demand for goods. But other theories, those explaining the demand for higher liquidity as a consequence rather than as the originating cause of depression tendencies, in most cases argue from specific disturbances to general ones. They usually have certain elements in common with the theory of generalized overproduction.

Generalized overproduction may, in fact, easily grow out of partial overproduction whenever the contractionary half of the adjustment starts the entire process. If that section of the economy which is hit by overproduction shrinks before investment can start in the section earmarked for expansion, the partial depression tendency may easily become generalized. This assumes that the expansion in certain sections, that is, the expansionary half of the adjustment is dependent on adjustments induced by the contractionary half.

The results may be radically different if the process is started by the positive (expansionary) half of the adjustment. The term "generalized expansion" is more suitable to express the development to be expected in this event. It is possible to interpret significant periods of economic expansion as having been initiated by shifts from certain sections of economic activity to others with the positive (expansionary) half of the adjustment acting as the "starter." The negative (contractionary) half then frequently becomes submerged in the "generalized" process of expansion, just as the positive half of the adjustment may become submerged in the deflationary spiral when overproduction "generalizes" itself. The hypothesis is the precise counterpart of the doctrine of *surproduction généralisée*.

What does it mean to assume that the positive half of the adjustment acts as the "starter" in a situation characterized by partial overproduction and partial underproduction? The meaning of this assumption is that, given the level of aggregate income, the physical composition of output would tend to change, and that the shift away from certain sections would be induced by the growth of other sections, rather than the other way around. It is, of course, very unrealistic to assume lags away. On realistic assumptions either the positive half or the negative half of the adjustment leads in time as well as in the causal sequence. Yet, conceptually, the distinction between these two contrasting processes does not rest on time lags—but rather on which half of the process is a consequence of the other. Conceptually, this distinction turns on whether the shift away from Commodity A presupposes increased expenditures on Commodity B or whether the shift away from Commodity A would take place even if expenditures on Commodity B did not increase. In the latter case (in which the negative half acts as the "starter") adjustments *may* result in a rise in expenditures on, and in the output of, Commodity B, so that the partial overproduction *may* fail to become generalized. Yet even if this should be true for a certain period, the potentiality of generalized overproduction is always present and a deflationary spiral may easily develop. In the former case, that is, if the shift away from Commodity A presupposes increased expenditures on B, there exists a strong likelihood of generalized expansion, regardless of whether the positive half of the adjustment, in addition to being the "starter" in a causal sense, also leads in time by an appreciable lag. Even if the lead in time is negligible it still remains true that the new investment activity in Section B of the economy will usually outweigh the disinvestment in Section A. Consequently, what starts as a shift from A to B tends to become general growth, frequently extending to Section A itself. This occurs principally because the time rate of undermaintenance in Section A is smaller than the time rate of new investment in Section B (unless the stock of real capital required to produce a unit of Commodity A should be a high multiple of the capital required to produce that quantity of Commodity B which is being substituted for a unit of Commodity A).[2]

Such a theory of generalized expansion is but an elaboration on the innovation theories of economic development, *if* the primary shifts in the composition of output are interpreted as being induced by the setting up of new production functions. In this event, the circumstances here considered merely explain how the impact originating from innovations spreads over the economy via shifts in the composition of output. We feel, however, that the case in which the primary shifts in the composition of output are induced by innovations, that is by the setting up of a new production functions, is only a special (although significant) case among a great many possible ones. The innovations themselves may frequently be induced by such generalized expansion as is initiated by shifts in relative demands which in turn may be produced by institutional factors, population movements, the depletion of natural resources, and so on.

In fact, for rapidly growing industries the distinction between movements along given production functions and the setting up of new production functions cannot be drawn sharply. Logically, this distinction rests on the difference between adopting methods of production that have been known but have not been used, and methods of production that have not even been known before. If the growth of the market, or relative price changes, result in the adoption of methods previously known, the situation is that of a movement along given production functions. Only if methods previ-

---

[2] Cf. J. M. Clark, *op. cit.*, p. 175; Alan Sweezy, "Wages and Investment," *Journal of Political Economy* (February, 1942), 117–129.

ously unknown—and not merely unused—are introduced, is there a setting up of a new production function, that is, an "innovation." This distinction is of doubtful significance for a rapidly growing industry because entrepreneurs and their engineers are not usually concerned with the technological yield of such alternative input combinations as might result in many times the output actually produced. The question of whether Henry Ford, in the main, discovered unknown methods of producing automobiles or whether he "simply" foresaw that the demand functions of automobiles were such as to make it profitable to apply previously "available" but unused methods cannot be answered satisfactorily. He obviously did both. It is equally obvious that it is impossible to attribute a clearcut supremacy to one of these factors over the other.

Innovation theories of economic development necessarily imply the distinction just considered because they shrink to a tautology once it is maintained that movements into previously unused portions of given production functions are identical in character with the setting up of new production functions. Economic growth cannot be said to be *caused* by "innovations" if innovations are so defined as to include movements into previously unused portions of given production functions, as well as the setting up of new production functions: Economic growth *by definition* consists either of a movement into previously unused portions of given production functions or of the setting up of new production functions. Innovation theories of growth lose their content if there is a failure to distinguish between these two processes, and the theories in question must be interpreted as stressing the setting up of new functions as against "mere" movements along given functions. This distinction, however, lacks precision in cases in which no one had previously given serious thought to producing the amount of output now under consideration.

Distinctions such as these are not entirely meaningless, however, because there exists something like an unprecise common-sense line between certain changes falling in the first category and others falling in the second, with a very broad margin of indeterminateness or ambiguity between the two. Yet, although on common-sense grounds it may be meaningful to say that the first decision to produce Watt engines or steamboats represented the setting up of new production functions, doubts of where the emphasis should be placed arise precisely in cases such as these. Growth to economic significance usually did not occur until several decades after the "first decisions" were made—if it came at all. The entrepreneurs of the period of growth to economic significance usually were different from those who made the "first decisions." For the economically critical period, which frequently came after the period in which novelties were "first produced," decisions to make substantial movements along given production functions and decisions to make first movements along new production functions cannot readily be disentangled.

Professor Schumpeter correctly points out that, on the plane of logic, there exists no necessary contradictions between the causal model of the innovation theories, on the one hand, and those models, on the other, which suggest that innovations are produced by preceding historical changes.[3] Nor does there necessarily exist a logical contradiction between the model of the innovation theories and the doctrine that the so-called innovations typically are historical processes of long duration consisting of numerous, roughly discernible phases.[4] After all, persons suggesting that eggs should be looked upon as coming from hens cannot properly be interpreted as denying that hens come from eggs; and, generally speaking, persons calling attention to certain phases of a historical process need not be interpreted as denying the continuity of historical processes. Yet there does exist a substantial difference in emphasis between the model of the innovation theories and a conceivable alternative model in which the *truly important entrepreneurial decisions* (those lending economic significance to previously unimportant processes) would be viewed as being made under the immediate impact of institutional changes and of changes in demand, considerably later than the time of the "first introduction" of the corresponding production functions. The difference in emphasis remains even if it is added that these "truly important" entrepreneurial

[3] Cf. e.g., S. C. Gilfillan, *The Sociology of Invention* (Chicago, Follett, 1935).
[4] Cf. e.g., Abbott Payson Usher, *A History of Mechanical Inventions* (New York, McGraw-Hill, 1929).

decisions, in turn, are associated with, and lead to, further improvements. There also exists a substantial difference in emphasis between the causal model of the innovation theories and another conceivable alternative model in which the innovations themselves would be viewed as being induced by preceding changes in demand, and in which the primary significance of these preceding changes would be stressed.[5] It may well be that certain specific historical processes lend themselves more readily to interpretation in terms of one of these alternative models, whereas others are more readily described with the well-known and significant Schumpeterian apparatus.

Incompleteness of agreement with the innovation theories should not, however, be given the appearance of disagreement. What matters in the present context is that the innovation theories fit into a broader framework that may include other theories as well. Large-scale substitution of certain products for others tends to increase the vigor of the expansion phase of the cycle. The same process tends to shorten depressions.

During the expansion the stimulating effect of shifts in the composition of output derives from the fact that new investment proceeds more rapidly than undermaintenance. New investment in certain industries is incompletely offset by the undermaintenance of real capital in others. In the industries that are adversely affected by the shifts it is impossible to disinvest in any sense other than that of abstaining from current maintenance expenditure, and "mainte-

---

[5] The following figures and dates are taken from Professor Knowles' book on the industrial and commercial revolutions; they show a significant rise in the imports of cotton wool in Great Britain preceding the famous inventions in the manufacture of cotton. Imports of cotton wool: 1746, 1,645,031 lbs.; 1751, 2,976,610 lbs.; 1764, 3,870,392 lbs.; invention of the spinning "jenny" by Hargreaves, 1767; of the water frame by Arkwright, 1768; of the "mule" by Crompton, 1775; of the power loom by Cartwright, 1784. Mrs. Knowles considers the preceding rise in imports as "not very rapid." It was not very rapid in comparison with the rise that followed, yet it undoubtedly reflects a change of considerable magnitude that may have "induced" inventions. The decade of the 1740's was preceded by institutional changes and by changes in preferences that may be viewed as having prepared the ground for the development during the later part of the century. It must be admitted, however, that the period in question also was preceded by earlier inventions which also were significant. Only a historian could undertake to appraise the relative significance of these two types of antecedents. Cf. L. C. A. Knowles, *The Industrial and Commercial Revolutions in Great Britain during the Nineteenth Century* (London, Routledge, 1926), p. 45, n. 2; and pp. 47–49.

nance with a negative sign" does not offset "new investment with a positive sign." The reasoning is analogous to that underlying the Acceleration Principle. The Acceleration Principle expresses the fact that the gross capital formation required for the maintenance of an output flow of x units plus for the increase of output flow by further x units is more than twice the capital formation required for maintenance alone, because the entire capital to be used in the production of the additional output must be formed and not merely the depreciation quota of this capital. The reasoning ordinarily subsumed under the heading "Acceleration Principle" turns on this single point. The principle of generalized expansion turns on precisely the same point. Yet, the reasoning of the Acceleration Principle proceeds vertically, from direct to derived demand, whereas the principle of generalized expansion applies to horizontal shifts in the structure of production. What is created by the industries in favor of which the shifts take place is "the entire capital." What is suppressed in the industries at the expense of which the shifts occur is "merely the depreciation quota" or some proportion thereof. This gives a positive net balance, and the generalized expansion in which this positive net balance results may cancel the negative tendencies even in the industries that, in the initial stage, were adversely affected by the substitution process.

Trends toward large-scale substitution of certain commodities for others may also be expected to exert a mitigating influence in periods of depression. During depressions the crucial aspect of the trend away from certain products toward others is that such a trend creates fields of investment which are not commonly judged to share the fate of the "economy as a whole." The vicious circle of cumulative deflation is more easily split if the economy is unbalanced in this sense than if it is balanced in the composition of output. An economy in which the composition of output tends to remain unchanged rolls downward once the general trend is assumed to be unfavorable, and the forces tending to halt this process of shrinkage may not become effective before a very low level of business activity is reached. The existence of specific fields to which the Wicksellian cumulative psychology does not apply creates a presumption, however, that the recovery may set in at an earlier stage.

When the general economic tendency is unfavorable, it clearly is advantageous to have specific fields which, in the typical entrepreneurial psychology, are dissociated from the general economic tendency. A trend toward large-scale substitution creates fields that become dissociated from over-all tendencies and the recovery may start to spread from these fields at a stage in which expectations for over-all tendencies have not yet hit a bottom.

In a depression, too, there is a lack of symmetry between the favorable effects of the expansionary half of the substitution process, on the one hand, and the adverse effects of the contractionary half, on the other. The industries adversely affected by the shifts in the composition of output merely share the fate of "the economy as a whole" in a somewhat more accentuated form: the degree of under-maintenance may be greater in these industries than is true in other segments of the economy. This addition to the deflationary impact amounts to less than the expansionary effect developing in the industries favored by the substitution process, provided that the optimism concerning the specific trend of the industries favored leads to a revival of new investment in these fields after a brief interruption.

Obviously, the same inducement as that derived from shifts in composition of output would also be provided, if the historical processes in question started from the outset as net additions to output rather than as processes of substitution of commodities or services for others. In this case the initial stimulus would even be stronger because not even an incomplete offsetting item would appear on the other side of the scale. Yet, it is likely that the investment plans of entrepreneurs are frequently based on the assumption that individual saving habits of the public will not alter significantly and that aggregate income will not change appreciably in consequence of the investment decisions themselves. This means that the planned investment processes must largely be expected to pay on a given aggregate output (income) level, that is, that initially there must exist a strong presumption that buyers would be willing to substitute the goods in question for other goods. Consequently it seems appropriate to view a great many processes that have resulted in a net growth of the economy, as having been largely substitution processes *in statu nascendi,* although in certain cases some rise in aggregate buyers' expenditures and thereby, implicitly, in aggregate income may also have been anticipated from the outset.

SHIFTS IN COMPOSITION: DIFFERENT CONSTITUENTS OF MANUFACTURING OUTPUT

In an attempt to test whether American economic developments of recent decades lend support to the hypothesis here developed, the relative significance of the manufacturing industries growing at a rate exceeding the average rate of growth of manufacturing industry as a whole was investigated.[6] With the (unfortunately important) qualifications arising from the imperfections of the method applied, it may be concluded that the relative significance of the groups growing at a substantially higher rate than the average, increased to some considerable extent from the turn of the present century to the early 1920's, and that the relative significance of these groups declined considerably during the 1920's. This can be seen from table 5, on page 125. The table will be explained later in some detail, but the general character of the findings may be observed at this point. Business trends in general were distinctly satisfactory throughout the period under consideration (1899–1929). Table 5 may be interpreted as indicating that the relative composition of output changed significantly during the early part of this period but ceased to change significantly in the later part. The facts could therefore be interpreted in terms of the hypothesis under consideration without being strained. This interpretation would maintain that certain processes resulting in significant changes in the composition of output contributed in a large measure to the upward trend of aggregate output. The generalized expansion produced by these shifts in composition may have rendered the upswings of the period more vigorous,[7] and the depressions of the period may have been shortened by the existence of specific fields of investment about which entrepreneurs were optimistic, regardless of their forecasts for the "general situation." The generalized expansion outlasted the

---

[6] The relative significance of the rapidly growing industries was measured by their share in total value added and in gross value product.

[7] In consequence of the lack of symmetry between new investment and undermaintenance, which was discussed in the earlier part of this chapter.

period during which the relative weight of the industries growing at a substantially greater than average rate was rising. It extended into the period in which the weight of the group in question was declining (that is, it extended into the middle and late 'twenties). But the first major depression occurring at a time when the weight of the "substantially higher than average" group was already small, and was still declining, turned out to be an extraordinarily long and severe depression. The subsequent recovery did not possess much momentum.

This may be offered tentatively as a partial explanation of economic trends in the recent past. Yet, it should be emphasized that the possibilities of "verification" are limited indeed. The general limitations of verifying hypotheses in economics are valid in this case as in others. In addition, there exist numerous specific limitations. The remaining part of the present section substantiates the foregoing propositions with the aid of data relating to American manufacturing production. This part of the discussion, ending on page 129, should be read only by readers interested in the details of the factual analysis.

The data to be used in the present section relate to the manufacturing industries alone and they cover a fairly large, but not necessarily representative, sample of these industries. The sample is derived from that used by Professor Mills in his study on *Economic Tendencies in the United States.*[8] Mills' sample is, of course, limited by the fact that physical production indexes are available only for commodities that are reasonably homogeneous physically so that it is possible to express output in terms other than dollars.[9] The data relate to three successive subperiods within the interval 1899–1929, namely to 1899–1914, 1914–1923, and 1923–1929. The number of items included in the sample increases from the first subperiod to the second, and then again from the second to the third. The percentage of value added by manufacturing covered by the sample in-

[8] Frederick C. Mills, *Economic Tendencies in the United States: Aspects of Pre-War and Post-War Changes* (New York, National Bureau of Economic Research, 1932). Cf. tables 10, 76, and 123.

[9] As regards trends for manufacturing series satisfying this test, see also Solomon Fabricant, *The Output of Manufacturing Industries, 1899–1937* (New York, National Bureau of Economic Research, 1940).

creases from the end of the first subperiod to that of the second, and declines slightly thereafter.[10]

The subperiods distinguished in tables 5 and 6 of this chapter are somewhat different, however, from those distinguished in Mills' book. This is because it is essential to the purposes here that the beginning and closing years of the subperiods fall in similar stages of cyclical development. The years, 1899, 1909, 1923, and 1929 (all of which are census years) may, with certain qualifications, be considered cyclically similar, whereas the beginning and closing years of Mills' periods, namely 1899, *1914*, 1923, and 1929, cannot be so considered. Hence 1899–1909, 1909–1923, and 1923–1929 have been chosen as the subperiods here. The procedure has the disadvantage of rendering the specific industry data from which the changes *during* the second subperiod are calculated less comparable over time (i.e., from census year to census year). Mills made his specific industry figures within each of the subperiods distinguished by him (1899–1914, 1914–1923, and 1923–1929) as nearly comparable over time as he could. Undertaking the first break in 1909 instead of in 1914, unfortunately undoes for the second subperiod some of what Mills did. This modification also reduces the coverage of the sample for the second subperiod to somewhat less than the size of that for the first.[11] Consequently, instead of the coverage of the Mills' sample,[12] there is obtained for the subperiods chosen here the coverage indicated in table 4. It is felt, however, that for the present analysis the

---

[10] It can be seen from tables 15, 80, and 130 on pages 40, 199, and 307, respectively, in Professor Mills' *Economic Tendencies in the United States* ... that the representativeness of the sample cannot be taken for granted. This also is emphasized by the author. The percentage *growth of the "values added"* included in the sample was somewhat different from the percentage growth of the value added by all American manufacturing for the first two subperiods (92.2 per cent as against 104.5 per cent, and 193.3 per cent as against 166.2 per cent) and it was markedly different for the third subperiod (13.7 per cent as against 23.2 per cent). It does not follow by necessity from this that the sample lacks representativeness so far as physical growth is concerned. The representativeness of the sample for physical growth can of course not be tested satisfactorily because the industries excluded from the sample are those for which physical growth figures are not available.

[11] Industries first appearing in Mills' 1914–1923 period cannot be included in the 1909–1923 period considered here; and those industries of Mills' 1899–1914 period which are not continued for his 1914–1923 period can also not be included in the 1909–1923 period here. Consequently, the size of the 1909–1923 sample is smaller than that of Mills' 1914–1923 sample and smaller also than his 1899–1914 sample.

[12] Cf. Mills, *op. cit.*, tables 10, 76, and 124 on pp. 30, 194–195, and 292–293.

complete cyclical dissimilarity of 1914 with the other critical years of Mills' study would be an even graver disadvantage. In fact, complete cyclical dissimilarity would be a prohibitive disadvantage for the present purpose. Moreover, lack of comparability of specific industry figures over time gives rise to conceptual difficulties in all events. Even if the difficulty is largely excluded for the census years of one and the same subperiod, as is so for Mills' subperiods, the

TABLE 4

COVERAGE OF THE SAMPLE FOR THE THREE SUBPERIODS

Subperiod	Number of industries included in the sample	Percentage accounted for by the sample	
		Of total value added by all manufacturing	Of total gross value product of all manufacturing
1899–1909.	34	29.87	38.39
1909–1923.	29	28.51	36.23
1923–1929.	59	35.62	44.83

difficulty still enters with full force wherever the subperiods are compared with one another. These comparisons constitute the main objective of the present analysis.

To summarize, caution is required because the data relate merely to manufacturing industries[13] (as represented by a sample that is not necessarily representative), and also because the comparability of the data is incomplete. With the rather serious concession to practicability involved in disregarding these difficulties, it is possible, however, to argue that the relative weight of the industries growing at a substantially higher than average rate increased from the end of the first to the end of the second subperiod. It also is possible to argue that the relative weight of these industries declined from the end of the second to the end of the third subperiod (i.e., in the six years preceding the depression of 1929–1933). As was pointed out, the upward trend for physical output as a whole, and for aggregate employment in the American economy, did not change its general character until 1929 but was interrupted for an unusually long period during and after the first major depression that found the economy

---

[13] See, however, below, pp. 129–133.

"well balanced" in the foregoing sense (i.e., without a strong tendency toward shifts in composition). Obviously, it is not implied that "balance" in this undesirable sense has been established secularly.

Table 5 includes data for the manufacturing industries the rate of growth of which, during any of the subperiods, *exceeded* the average rate of growth of physical output for manufacturing as a whole. The average rate of growth for manufacturing output as a whole was calculated from index numbers used also in other contexts in the present study. These were published by Professor Douglas, and they are based on the Day-Thomas index so far as census years are concerned. For 1929 (a year lying beyond the period covered by Douglas' statistics) the index numbers published by Irving H. Siegel were used which also are largely based on the Day-Thomas index.[14] The industries growing at a more than average rate in any one of the subperiods were divided in seven groups in the following manner. The first group includes all industries growing at more than the average rate; the second group includes merely those growing at a rate higher than 150 per cent of the average; the third group contains the industries growing at a rate higher than 200 per cent of the average. For the fourth, fifth, sixth, and seventh groups the rate of growth which is *exceeded* by the industries belonging in the group becomes 300 per cent, 400 per cent, 500 per cent, and 1,000 per cent of the average, respectively.

The relative weight of the industries belonging in each group is expressed in four different ways. The four measures of relative significance used are: (1) the percentage of total value added by American manufacturing, accounted for by the industries belonging in each group; (2) the percentage of the value added by the industries included in the sample,[15] accounted for by the industries belonging

[14] Paul H. Douglas, *The Theory of Wages*, Appendix, Table I, Cf. the manufacturing index weighted according to value added; and Irving H. Siegel, "Hourly Earnings and Unit Labor Cost in Manufacturing," *Journal of the American Statistical Association* (September, 1940), 458, table 2. We have compared the change in the Douglas index with that in the Day-Thomas index for 1909 as against 1899 and for 1923 as against 1909; and we have compared the change in the Siegel index with that in the Day-Thomas index for 1929 as against 1923. The correspondence is close in all cases. This means at the same time that the comparability of the Siegel index for 1929 with the Douglas index for 1923, 1909, and 1899 seems satisfactory.
[15] That is, in Mills' sample as adjusted to the subperiods used here, cf. pp. 123–124.

TABLE 5

RELATIVE SIGNIFICANCE OF MANUFACTURING INDUSTRIES GROWING IN EXCESS OF THE
AVERAGE RATE OF GROWTH OF PHYSICAL OUTPUT FOR MANUFACTURING AS A WHOLE

	Subperiods		
	1899–1909	1909–1923	1923–1929
Average rate of growth of American manufacturing in per cent...	60.3	62.4	17.6

INDUSTRIES GROUPED ACCORDING TO RATE OF GROWTH IN RELATION
TO AVERAGE RATE FOR MANUFACTURING

More than Average			
Relative significance measured by percentage share of industries in value added:			
By American manufacturing.....................	14.35	17.46	22.56
By industries of sample........................	48.04	61.24	63.34
Measured by percentage share in gross value product:			
Of American manufacturing.....................	16.40	21.40	26.36
Of industries of sample..........................	42.72	59.07	58.80
More than 150 per cent of average			
Relative significance measured by percentage share of industries in value added:			
By American manufacturing.....................	4.43	10.08	8.68
By industries of sample.........................	14.83	35.37	24.36
Measured by percentage share in gross value product:			
Of American manufacturing.....................	3.78	12.63	11.44
Of industries of sample..........................	9.85	34.86	25.52
More than 200 per cent of average			
Relative significance measured by percentage share of industries in value added:			
By American manufacturing.....................	3.58	8.39	8.25
By industries of sample.........................	11.99	29.43	23.16
Measured by percentage share in gross value product:			
Of American manufacturing.....................	2.76	10.98	10.78
Of industries of sample..........................	7.19	30.31	24.05
More than 300 per cent of average			
Relative significance measured by percentage share of industries in value added:			
By American manufacturing.....................	2.20	7.10	2.11
By industries of sample.........................	7.37	24.90	5.92
Measured by percentage share in gross value product:			
Of American manufacturing.....................	1.84	9.86	3.97
Of industries of sample..........................	4.80	27.22	8.86
More than 400 per cent of average			
Relative significance measured by percentage share of industries in value added:			
By American manufacturing.....................	1.63	7.10	2.03
By industries of sample.........................	5.46	24.90	5.70
Measured by percentage share in gross value product:			
Of American manufacturing.....................	1.44	9.86	3.89
Of industries of sample..........................	3.75	27.22	8.68

TABLE 5—*Continued*

	Subperiods		
	1899–1909	1909–1923	1923–1929
More than 500 per cent of average			
Relative significance measured by percentage share of industries in value added:			
By American manufacturing	1.63	7.10	0.12
By industries of sample	5.46	24.90	0.34
Measured by percentage share in gross value product:			
Of American manufacturing	1.44	9.86	0.14
Of industries of sample	3.75	27.22	0.31
More than 1,000 per cent of average			
Relative significance measured by percentage share of industries in value added:			
By American manufacturing	1.38	5.67	....
By industries of sample	4.62	19.89	....
Measured by percentage share in gross value product:			
Of American manufacturing	1.21	6.90	....
Of industries of sample	3.15	19.04	....

in each group; (3) the percentage of the total gross value product of American manufacturing, accounted for by the industries of each group; (4) the percentage of the gross value product of the industries included in the sample, accounted for by the industries of each group. The relative significance is measured for the last year of each subperiod, although the classification is made dependent on the rate of growth from the first to the last year of the same subperiod. For example, the figures of table 5 indicate that the industries in which the output grew at a rate exceeding the average rate of growth of manufacturing output as a whole from 1899 to 1909, accounted in 1909 for 14.35 per cent of the value added by American manufacturing, for 48.04 per cent of the value added by the industries included in the sample, for 16.04 per cent of the gross value product of American manufacturing, and for 42.72 per cent of the gross value product of the industries included in the sample. The figures for value added and for gross value product were taken from the census of manufactures of the closing year of each subperiod (e.g., of 1909).

Table 5 shows that the relative significance of the industries growing substantially in excess of the average rate of growth, increased considerably from the first to the second subperiod. There was some increase in the relative significance of the more-than-average group as a whole. Yet, this increase is much smaller for the groups that include the industries growing but slightly in excess of the average rate than for the groups that contain merely the industries growing very much more rapidly. From 1909–1923 to 1923–1929 the relative significance of the industries growing very much in excess of the average rate decreases significantly. The relative significance of the more-than-average group as a whole increases again,[16] but this is a consequence exclusively of the increased weight of such more-than-average industries as are in the neighborhood of the average. There is a decline in every single group except the one that includes the close-to-average industries. The decline becomes increasingly marked in the "higher" ranges of the table.

It is believed that this type of treatment of the material is more informative than would be an attempt to express the dispersion of the rate of growth around the mean rate by some single measure. In the first place, single measures have little meaning for the kind of universe dealt with here. Second, the data available for industries that are insignificant, and are becoming more so, are fewer and poorer than those applying to significant and growing industries. Third, there exists no presumption that the behavior of these two classes of industries should be analogous, so far as the dispersion around mean rates of change is concerned.

Indeed, it might be well to point out that the behavior of the industries growing at a less-than-average rate and that of the industries absolutely declining is not analogous to that of the more-than-average groups with respect to the shifts considered here. It is not true that the weight of the industries growing at a rate much smaller than the average, increased from the first to the second subperiod and that the weight decreased from the second to the third subperiod in relation to the close-to-average industries. Nor did the weight of industries absolutely declining increase from the first subperiod to the second and decrease from the second subperiod to the third, in relation to the stagnant and near-stagnant industries. This is the behavior that would be analogous to that of the more-than-average groups, yet the less-than-average groups do not exhibit

---

[16] Except in the last of the four senses distinguished.

this behavior. Considering the lack of symmetry between the process of new investment, on the one hand, and that of undermaintenance, on the other—and the general lack of symmetry between the positive and the negative "half" of shifts in composition—the foregoing discrepancy is not particularly astonishing.

Table 8 (Appendix II, p. 241), contains summary information on all industries of the sample, including the less-than-average and the declining industries. The table shows in what category each industry belonged during the various subperiods.[17] The categories are distinguished according to the rate of growth (or decline) of the industry.

SHIFTS IN COMPOSITION: MANUFACTURING VERSUS
OTHER ACTIVITIES

Shifts other than those that occurred within the field of manufacturing are not analyzed here. It is obvious, of course, that important shifts in composition of output took place in other sectors of the economy too. It also is obvious that the relative significance of the different fields in the production of output as a whole changed during the thirty years considered here. The significance of manufacturing, for example, increased at first and then, in the second half of the period, declined in relation to other activities. It has not been possible to compare the quantitative significance of shifts other than those in manufacturing for the various subperiods of the thirty-year interval under consideration. A limited number of these shifts could conceivably be traced back with methods more or less satisfactory, but data are not available for a quantitative appraisal of the problem as a whole, outside the manufacturing industries. It may be called to the reader's attention, however, that the three-year period immediately preceding the breakdown of 1929 was one of "balance" (i.e., of the absence of significant relative shifts) also in the sense that the weight of manufacturing as a whole remained approximately constant in relation to other output yielding activities. This is shown in table 6.

It seems, moreover, that the material with which Professor A. F. Burns worked in his study of American production trends, at least

---

[17] More precisely, during the subperiods for which data are available concerning the industry in question.

tentatively supports the assumption that, even if a universe more inclusive than that of manufacturing were analyzed, the production trends for different segments of the universe became more dissimilar

TABLE 6

RELATIVE SIGNIFICANCE OF MANUFACTURING IN THE PRODUCTION OF OUTPUT AS A WHOLE*

Successive overlapping decades compared with one another	Percentage change in total output from preceding period to period	Percentage change in manufacturing output from preceding period to period
1904–1913..........................	19.4	21.7
1909–1918..........................	16.3	21.7
1914–1923..........................	19.6	14.9
1919–1928..........................	27.5	16.0

Periods, for a comparison of first with last years	Percentage change in total output from first to last year	Percentage change in manufacturing output from first to last year
1919–1929..........................	52.8	44.9
1923–1929..........................	23.2	17.6
1926–1929..........................	10.3	9.9

* Data from Simon Kuznets, *Uses of National Income in Peace and War*, p. 31; and *idem. National Income and its Composition*, Vol. I, 269, for national income in 1929 prices. Paul H. Douglas, *The Theory of Wages*, Appendix, Table I, and Irving H. Siegel, "Hourly Earnings and Unit Labor Cost in Manufacturing," *Journal of the American Statistical Association* (September, 1940), 458, for index of manufacturing output.

in the first two decades of the present century, and more similar in the third decade.[18] This may be interpreted as expressing increasing shifts in the composition of output during the first two decades and a decreasing tendency toward these shifts in the third decade. In Burns' study, decils of trends are compared with one another for

[18] Arthur F. Burns, *Production Trends in the United States Since 1870* (New York, National Bureau of Economic Research, 1934): cf. chap. v in general and particularly chart 5 on p. 184, chart 21 (for "all series") on p. 243, and footnote 54 on pp. 242–243. Burns concludes that a rise in dispersion (i.e., in dissimilarities between production trends) preceded, and possibly was responsible for, major depressions. This thesis obviously contradicts the hypothesis expressed in the present study, so far as the Great Depression is concerned. Yet Burns obtains an increase in dispersion for the period preceding 1929 by eliminating a downward "secular trend" from the dispersion itself. The charts referred to in the first sentence of this footnote strongly suggest that without this manipulation the dispersion would show a marked decline for the period in question; and this would be consistent with the hypothesis expressed in the present study rather than with Burns' hypothesis. Moreover, for some of the earlier depressions falling in the period analyzed by Burns, his hypothesis (concerning a preceding rise in dispersion) is not fully supported by the material he used. Absence of supporting evidence is admitted by Burns for the depression of 1893–1894; yet such evidence is

overlapping ten-year periods, after elimination of the secular drift (the first decil being a trend value that is exceeded by nine-tenths of all items included in the sample, the second, a trend value that is exceeded by eight-tenths, etc.). These decils are plotted against time and the courses of the resulting "decil lines" are compared with one another. This makes possible an analysis of increasing or decreasing similarities as between different segments of Burns' sample. It follows from what has been said that the segments of the sample are distinguished from one another by the magnitude of the trend to which they were subject. However, the relative significance of the various segments can be calculated neither in terms of gross value product nor in terms of value added.

In the preceding pages it was emphasized that, so far as the behavior of manufacturing during the interval studied here is concerned, the rise in the relative weight of the industries growing very much in excess of the average rate was both accompanied and followed by a substantial upward trend of total physical production. This trend for physical production as a whole was interrupted at a time when the relative weight of the industries growing very much in excess of the average rates had already declined substantially. The relative weight of the industries in question declined during the subperiod 1923–1929, whereas the significant upward trend of total physical output was not interrupted before 1929. It should now be added that the rise in man-hour output also stayed very high during the subperiod following the rise in the relative weight of the rapidly growing industries. In fact the rise in man-hour output was higher in the subperiod 1923–1929 than in any of the preceding subperiods distinguished either by Mills or in the present study. According to

claimed for the depressions of 1882–1883, 1907, 1920–1921. However, two of these depressions, namely that of 1907 and that of 1920–1921, fall in decades in which the dispersion calculated by Burns was declining rather than increasing. It is true that these depressions follow decades of rising dispersion but such a situation is ambiguous when the question is considered of whether the dispersion was increasing or declining immediately prior to the depression in question. None of these depressions are comparable with that of 1929–1933 in depth or duration. Burns' study does not go back far enough for an analysis of the changes in dispersion prior to the depression of the 1870's (which perhaps is comparable with the Great Depression of 1929–1933). On the whole it seems that Burns' data come closer to supporting the hypothesis presented in this study than the contrary hypothesis presented by himself. But here again there is room for legitimate differences of opinion.

Professor Mills' estimates concerning his sample of the manufacturing industries, the rise in physical output *per wage earner* was 19.9 per cent for the subperiod 1899–1914 as a whole, 12.8 per cent for 1914–1923, and 17.8 per cent for 1923–1929.[19] The first two figures correspond approximately to the identical *yearly* rate of increase, whereas the last figure corresponds to more than twice this yearly rate. These estimates apply to output per wage earner rather than to output per man-hour, but the decline of the length of the working week was rather continuous and slow during the entire time interval discussed so that the conclusion for the trend in man-hour output would have to be quite similar. It does not necessarily follow, however, that the rate of technological progress became more rapid during the 'twenties than was the case before. The quantitative appraisal of other characteristics of technological progress cannot be undertaken as readily as that of changes in man-hour output. For example, the difficulties standing in the way of deriving an index for output per unit of raw material input are already severe enough to preclude, at the present time, any attempt to supplement man-hour-output analysis with its obvious counterpart.

It should also be remembered that in certain strategic industries the characteristics of the man-hour-output trend were different from its characteristics for manufacturing as a whole. In the automobile industry, for instance, the highest yearly rate of increase came in the beginning of the thirty-year interval covered by the Mills' statistics. The decline of the yearly rate of increase, from Mills' first subperiod to the second, is slight, but from the second to the third subperiod it is significant.

On the whole it may be stated that a sharp upward trend in aggregate output accompanied, and for a brief interval outlasted, the growth of the relative significance of the industries growing at a rate substantially exceeding the average. An appreciable decline in the relative significance of the "much higher than average" groups preceded the stagnant trend of the 1930's by several years. The hypothesis that substantial shifts in the composition of output may give rise to over-all growth and that the cessation of significant shifts may contribute to stagnant over-all trends is broadly supported by

[19] Cf. Mills, *op. cit.*, tables 11, 77, and 124, on pp. 33, 195–197, and 296–297.

these data. More is not claimed. The significance of other causal factors should not be denied or minimized. It is very likely, for example, that the temporary saturation in the field of residential construction belonged among the circumstances that, in the 1930's and also in the earlier "protracted depressions," aggravated the situation considerably.[20]

---

[20] Alvin H. Hansen, *Fiscal Policy and Business Cycles* (New York, Norton, 1941), cf. pp. 19–27.

Part Three

POLICIES

CHAPTER V

Interest Rates and the Problem of Cost Rigidities

PRICE AND WAGE RIGIDITIES VERSUS THE RIGIDITY OF THE INTEREST STRUCTURE

IN THE PAST, full employment was closely approximated in certain periods, except for brief intervals of "cyclical" depression, yet in other periods there existed a "chronic" tendency toward substantial underemployment. This, of course, means that the cost structure of capitalistic economies did not, in general, "adjust" instantaneously, in a manner which would restore a high level of employment when part of the available human resources became involuntarily unemployed; and that in certain periods the cost structure failed to "adjust" even with a considerable lag.

The failure of the cost structure to adjust is sometimes presented as a matter of price and wage rigidities. To make the rigidity of the commodity-price and of the wage-rate structure responsible for the failure of employment to return to a "full" level more or less promptly, means postulating that a downward adjustment of commodity prices and of wage rates would, in times of underutilization, increase the level of employment. The effects of price and wage changes on the level of activity, however, present a very involved problem—provided prices and wages are assumed to remain unchanged after the initial change. (Obviously, the expectation of future price and wage *reductions* would affect activity adversely and the expectation of future *increases* would have a favorable effect.)

The effects of a simultaneous proportional reduction of all commodity prices and of money wage rates are but partly distinct from those of expansionary credit policies. One of the effects of the simultaneous proportional reduction of commodity prices and of money wage rates is to increase the existing degree of liquidity in real terms. Such a rise of liquidity in real terms may induce a flow of idle funds into the loan market and the corresponding lowering of the interest-rate structure may produce new investment. This effect the measure has in common with credit policies aiming at the same objective. In addition, the policy of "proportional" deflation of prices and wages possesses the highly unwelcome effect of inflating past claims, as expressed in present "real" terms. The policy therefore brings the characteristic results of an expansionary credit policy, plus an unwelcome by-product.

It follows from the earlier discussion that a reduction of the general level of money wage rates, given the relative wage structure and in the absence of any interference with commodity prices, stimulates output and employment on balance if the stimulus provided by the lowering of real wage rates outweighs the consequences of the increase in uncertainty. (The increase in uncertainty is brought about by the reduction of the average propensity to consume.) The conditions under which a general reduction of money wage rates increases output are more likely to be satisfied in periods in which the average propensity to consume is high and in which profit margins are low than in the opposite circumstances. On the other hand, a reduction of the general level of commodity prices, given the relative price structure and in the absence of any interference with money wage rates, is more likely to have favorable effects in periods in which profit margins are high and in which the average propensity to consume is low. However, the favorable effects will always be limited to certain ranges of price or wage reductions and it is not, in general, possible to make dependable forecasts on the magnitude of these ranges.

This leaves open the question of the probable consequences of the lowering of specific commodity prices, without interfering with the other segments of the price structure. Such a measure, producing relative price changes by the lowering of the prices of specific goods, shares some of its effects with the shifting of the general level of commodity prices in relation to wage rates. Yet, in addition to these, relative price changes possess distinctive characteristics. The distinctive effect of the lowering of specific prices will be favorable initially, if the price elasticity of the demand for the goods in question proves to be greater than the price elasticity of the demand for the aggregate of other goods. In the opposite case the initial effect of the relative price change per se will be unfavorable. However, secondary effects are superimposed upon the initial impact since total money expenditures on the relatively cheapened goods and on the relatively more expensive goods respectively change by different amounts. A net rise in aggregate money expenditures tends to produce a multiplier effect, whereas a net decline of money spending tends to produce contraction in real terms.

To sum up, the effects of price changes which affect the general level as well as the relative structure of prices may typically be analyzed under four headings before a final appraisal is undertaken. (1) The shifting of the general price level changes the degree of liquidity in real terms and it also changes the value of past commitments in terms of present goods. (2) The shifting of the price level in relation to the wage level affects profit margins, and it also affects, through the average propensity to consume, the degree of uncertainty. (3) The shifting of price ratios tends initially to increase the output of certain goods and to diminish the output of other gods. (4) The two halves of the initial effect considered under (3) tend on balance to increase or to decrease aggregate money expenditures (depending on the magnitude of the price elasticities), and the change in money expenditures affects the level of real output.[1]

The conclusion suggests itself that in periods of underutilization the price structure of imperfectly competitive economics could always be "improved" from the standpoint of aggregate output and employment. It is practically always true that favorable results could be obtained either from the lowering of the general price level in relation to the general wage level or from the lowering of the general wage level in relation to the price level, or from the "relative" lowering of the prices of specific goods for which the demand elasticity is high, or from some combination of these policies. In this sense, the emphasis on price rigidities is fruitful, especially in view of the fact that investment opportunities in any specific field of activity are subject to oscillations and that therefore a permanently

---

[1] Points 3 and 4 relate to the changing position of specific prices in relation to the general price level. The shift of the latter is covered by points 1 and 2.

high level of aggregate investment requires the substitution of other fields for those temporarily exhausted. But, aside from the difficulties standing in the way of the "regulation" of the entire price structure in democratic communities, it must not be implied that by the appropriate manipulation of prices full employment could always be accomplished. In the "perfectly competitive equilibrium," full employment is produced not merely by the complete fluidity of prices but also by the absence of uncertainty. Moreover, it follows from the foregoing considerations that the inappropriate policies of combating price rigidities may increase, rather than diminish, unemployment and, on the basis of the available evidence, it may frequently be difficult to decide which of the possible lines of approach are appropriate to a specific situation. Such findings as that the frequency distribution of price changes is U-shaped, or that the frequently changing prices also tend to change with a greater amplitude, do not of themselves supply a guide to policy. But, as can be seen from the preceding remarks, there exists a presumption that in periods of low activity it would be advantageous to reduce the "sticky" prices of specific goods for which the demand is elastic. To be effective, such a policy would frequently require the simultaneous lowering of the prices of complementary producers' goods because an elastic response of the demand can scarcely be expected if merely one of several jointly needed goods is supplied at a lower price. The demand for building materials is an obvious example.

It is appropriate here to turn to the questions concerning the causes and the significance of interest-rate rigidities. Why do interest rates fail to adjust downward in periods of underutilization, and why is their downward adjustment insufficient to maintain output? What results could be expected from a lowering of interest rates by means of a deliberate policy?

ELASTIC VERSUS SHIFTING LIQUIDITY FUNCTIONS

In one respect, the reasons for the insufficiency of the downward adjustment of interest rates do not constitute a particularly controversial problem. It is generally accepted that, in periods of underutilization, the reduction of the demand for funds destined for investment is at least partly offset by an increase in the demand for funds destined for hoarding or for the repayment of bank loans. If, however, the question is raised why this increase occurs, the ground becomes more controversial. Furthermore, the question of how successful monetary policy could be in compensating for the increase in the demand for idle funds is also controversial.

According to one type of interest theory, the rise in the demand for liquidity is a consequence of a direct functional relationship between this demand and "the" rate of interest. This type of theory, of which Keynes' doctrines may be said to constitute the "basic version," maintains that the demand for liquidity rises when interest rates decline because (1) the likelihood of a rise in interest rates (i.e., of a decline in capital values) increases; and (2) at the same time, the compensation for bearing the risk of declining capital values is reduced. Consequently, if the supply of loanable funds[2] (S) is divided in two parts, namely, into "savings out of expected gross income" (Sg) and additions to the money supply (M), and if the demand for loanable funds (D) is also divided into two parts, namely into the demand for funds for planned gross investment (I), and the demand for funds for planned new hoarding (L), then the downward rigidity of interest rates becomes a matter of the negative slope and of the high elasticity of the second constituent on the demand side (i.e., of the L function). Figure 20 represents the determination of "the" interest rate (r) by the functions just described.[3] In the figure the Sg, S, I, and D functions are drawn as curves. The M function is

---

[2] Loanable funds are the funds actually exchanged for claims during the period, plus that part of the expected gross savings of the period which the savers themselves plan to use for investment or for hoarding.

[3] Cf. Gottfried Haberler, *Prosperity and Depression* (Geneva, League of Nations, 1941), p. 180 ff. Professor Haberler's illuminating presentation of the determination of the interest rate is based on Professor Lerner's exposition although the conclusions of these two authors are different. (Cf. Abba P. Lerner, "Alternative Formulations of the Theory of Interest," *Economic Journal* [1938], Vol. 48.) However, neither Lerner nor Haberler makes clear that L expresses *planned* hoarding and that I expresses *planned* investment and that these magnitudes differ from actual hoarding and from actual investment whenever expected income is different from realized income. The failure of some authors to make this clear may be attributed to the fact that they treat the Swedish period analysis as though it were interchangeable with the Robertsonian (cf. Haberler, *loc. cit.*). In the Robertsonian model it is true that savings plus new money equals actual investment plus actual hoarding. But the Robertsonian approach is equivalent to the Swedish only if expected income equals disposable income. This condition is not generally satisfied, and it is not generally true in the Swedish model that *ex ante* savings plus the increase in the money supply equals actual investment

expressed by the horizontal distance between the Sg and S curves, and the L function by the horizontal distance between the I and D curves.

Figure 20 is intended to express the Keynesian type of interest theory with the aid of the apparatus of the loanable funds approach.

To establish a link between this apparatus and the demand-for-money *versus* supply-of-money technique in interest theory, it may be useful to point out that the S function (or Sg + M) of figure 20

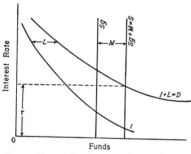

Fig. 20. Keynesian interest theory in terms of the loanable funds approach.

stands for that part of the money flow which is available for non-consumption purposes, and the D function (or I + L) stands for the demand for this money for non-consumption purposes.[4](This does not, however, mean that the effect of consumption loans is disregarded in the loanable funds theory. A person borrowing for consumption either dissaves or increases his investments or his hoarding correspondingly, and this reflects itself in the functions of figure 20.)

Furthermore, to establish a link between the loanable funds theory and the "classical" theory, it may be observed that if net hoarding is assumed away "in the long run," then the L function of figure 20 disappears from the corresponding long-run model. As for changes in the supply of money, these affect the interest rate directly only while these changes take place. This is true of the loanable funds theory considered here, as well as of the classical theory. But in the theory considered here, changes in the money supply may possess a permanent indirect effect because, when the money supply has ceased to change (so that M ceases to be a direct determinant

plus hoarding. The sum of the two constituents of the supply side equals the sum of planned investment and of planned hoarding. I am indebted to Miss Mona Dingle for a discussion of this point.

[4] That the price (in this case: the interest rate) equating demand for and supply of *flows* is the same as that equating demand for and supply of *existing stocks* is a generally valid and familiar proposition in price theory. In the Keynesian analytical framework the interest rate equates the demand for money with existing stock.

for the subsequent periods), I and Sg need not have changed by the identical amounts.[5] On the classical assumptions, I and S must have changed by the identical amounts so that changes in the supply of money possess no indirect aftereffects. This is true because, in the classical theory, changes in the supply of money affect neither the volume of trade nor relative prices in the long run. They affect merely the general price level: all money flows (such as Sg and I) change in the same proportion. Since, prior to the change in the money supply, S and I were equated by the interest rate, and since they change in the same proportion, they must also change by the identical amounts.

For the Keynesian type of interest theory, the significant property of the diagram is that the L function (which is expressed by the horizontal distance between the D and I curve) is negatively sloped and that the elasticity of the function becomes substantial for low interest rates. In fact it is assumed in the theory under discussion that at some sufficiently low (but positive) level of the interest rate the L function, and therefore also the D curve, become horizontal. On these assumptions it is then argued that a downward shift of the I curve, such as occurs in periods of contraction, is not accompanied by a decline in interest rates in any proportion corresponding to the downward shift itself, since at lower interest rates the other constituent of the demand, namely hoarding, is higher. The downward adjustment of interest rates will not restore output to its original level. Should the interest rate gradually decline to the level at which the L and D functions became perfectly elastic, further shifts to the left of the I function would leave the interest rate unchanged and they would merely result in increased hoarding and reduced investment at this floor level of interest.

The figure was drawn with two accidental properties in addition to the essential property just discussed. These are that, (1) the Sg curve is vertical, expressing the absence of any functional relationship between the rate of interest and "savings out of expected in-

---

[5] In the analytical framework used by Lord Keynes for the presentation of his own interest theory, these indirect aftereffects of a change in the supply of money become "direct" effects. Obviously, if the demand-for-money *versus* supply-of-money technique is used, it ceases to be true that changes in the supply of money affect the rate of interest directly only while they occur. The whole demand and supply affects the rate "directly."

come"; and (2) the M curve also is vertical, expressing that the addition to the quantity of money (including the addition to check deposits) also is "given" regardless of the level of interest rates.

If "savings out of expected income" should increase (or if they should decrease) with rising interest rates, the Sg function would acquire an upward slope (or a downward slope, respectively). The Sg function may very well be upward sloping or downward sloping. It is quite likely, however, that savings are not very sensitive to interest rates in the usual range of change: whereas some persons will increase their savings when interest rates rise, others will react in the opposite way and still others will save (or dissave) a constant fraction of their income irrespective of the change.

It should be added that the shape of the Sg function has no direct bearing on the validity of the time-preference theory, as developed by Professor Fisher. Even if the Sg function should be vertical, or approximately so, it may be maintained that the typical saver, unless he hoards money, decides to acquire future flows of goods instead of consuming a present stock. Therefore, he equates his marginal rate of time preference to the interest rate, in a fashion similar to that in which the consumer equates his marginal rates of substitution to price ratios. The phenomenon of hoarding merely requires adding that the marginal rate of liquidity preference also is equated with the interest rate. The indifference map underlying the time-preference theory (present goods *vs.* future flows of goods) may easily be drawn so that the line connecting the points of tangency (i.e., the optimum points) for different rates of interest will reflect the identical amount of present consumption for all conceivable rates of interest—just as the Allen-Hicks indifference map for two consumers' goods may be drawn so that the price-consumption line will reflect the identical amount of consumption for one of the two goods irrespective of the price ratios. The validity of the time-preference theory is not affected by the shape of the Sg function.[6]

The vertical shape of the Sg function is an accidental property of the graph and so is the vertical shape of the M function. The figure could have been drawn with an upward sloping M function so as to express the assumption that at lower interest rates the public not

---

[6] I am indebted to Mr. Henry J. Franck for a detailed discussion of this point.

merely hoards more but also repays more bank loans and borrows less. If the Keynesian assumption concerning the downward slope of the L curve is accepted, the upward slope of the M curve could be attributed to the same circumstances which lead to increased hoarding at lower interest rates. These circumstances are the increased likelihood of a rise in interest rates, that is, of a fall in capital values, when interest rates decline, and the reduction of the compensation obtained for bearing the risk of a fall in capital values. A vertical M curve expresses the somewhat doubtful assumption that the monetary authority has the stock of money (including check deposits) completely under control. On this assumption, there ceases to exist any functional relationship between M and the level of interest rates, since the conception of the monetary authority concerning the appropriate supply of money is not likely to depend on the interest level in any direct fashion. Yet this point too is of slight significance for the problems under consideration here. What really matters is the elasticity of the L function; in consequence of this, the effects of shifts of the I function will not be offset by changes of "the" interest rate. If the M curve slopes upward, instead of being vertical, the downward rigidity of interest rates is correspondingly increased.

It should be added that it is possible to analyze the entire interest structure, instead of "the" interest rate, with a similar apparatus. In this event I, L, Sg, and M must be represented as functions of all interest rates belonging in the structure, the equality of demand and supply must be postulated for all segments of the loan market, and a simultaneous solution must be sought, in a quasi-Walrasian fashion, for each single rate. Direct graphic presentation becomes impossible because the number of "dimensions" becomes high.

So far the Keynesian interest theory has merely been translated into the language of the loanable funds approach. It is convenient to deal with this "translated" version of the theory because a comparison with other theories can be undertaken more readily within the framework of the loanable funds technique, than within the original Keynesian framework.

The "generally acceptable" and "controversial" elements of what has been said so far can now be distinguished. As was pointed out earlier, it is a generally accepted proposition that the degree in which interest rates adjust in the face of shifting I curves is reduced by changes in the demand for idle balances. It also seems to be a generally accepted proposition that the determinants of interest rates can be expressed in terms of a model containing the four functions defined in the preceding paragraphs.[7] However, the Keynesian explanation of the increase in hoarding that takes place when the I curve shifts downward still is distinctly controversial. Keynes and some of the Keynesians maintain that the stock of idle balances is elastic to interest rates, or in terms of the loanable funds model, that the L function is negatively inclined, and that it flattens out. Alternative theories maintain that a rather inelastic L function typically shifts to the right when the I function shifts to the left (and vice versa). It should be realized that these are not alternative representations of one and the same fact. The type of hoarding reflecting itself in an elastic L function is different from that reflecting itself in an L function of small elasticity. The effectiveness of certain policies aimed at reducing the stock of idle balances also becomes different in the two cases, respectively. By raising interest rates, money hoards can be substantially reduced along an elastic L function; they cannot be so reduced along an L function of slight elasticity. There exists a very real and significant difference between the hypothesis of elastic L functions and that of inelastic but shifting L functions.

Speculative versus Contingency Hoarding

The theory that the L function is highly elastic is based on the notion that the idle balances are mainly those maintained for speculative purposes. Speculation is, of course, a very indistinct concept in economic theory. What is meant by calling the balances in question "speculative" can best be inferred from the fact that they are distinguished from contingency (or "precautionary") balances, and

---

[7] Some Keynesians would maintain that a presentation of the problem in terms of the loanable funds technique is inconvenient as compared with a presentation in terms of the demand-for-money and supply-of-money technique. Cf. A. P. Lerner, "Interest Theory—Supply and Demand for Loans or Supply and Demand for Money," *Review of Economic Statistics* (May 1944). However, my foregoing presentation would presumably not be considered incorrect by Keynesians.

that both the speculative and the contingency balances are distinguished from working balances (M_1). Now *working balances* (as distinct from contingency balances and from speculative balances) are clearly that part of the money stock which the public would continue to hold if it were certain that the prices of "perfectly safe" securities would not change. In these circumstances, money stocks would be maintained only because the costs and the inconvenience of buying and selling securities outweighs their yield unless they can be held continuously for at least a certain period of time. Balances held for this reason are generally considered working balances. Money stocks exceeding the stock of working balances—that is, "hoards" in the narrower sense, or "idle" balances, consisting of contingency and of speculative balances—would not be held if there existed securities the prices of which would necessarily remain unchanged. It is not a specific characteristic of speculative balances that they would not exist if the prices of perfectly safe securities would necessarily remain unchanged. Contingency balances would also not be held in these circumstances because institutions and individuals would prefer to maintain their contingency reserves in the form of securities.

The dividing line between contingency hoards and speculative hoards should therefore be drawn so as to leave in the one category (contingency hoards) the balances held because contingencies requiring money for producers' or consumers' expenditures may arise in the future *and* because security prices may decline between "now" and the future date in question. The other category (speculative hoards) should contain the balances held merely because security prices may decline and it may therefore be preferable to purchase them later at a lower price. Or, to express the same idea in different words, contingency balances are held because it is unsafe to buy securities (the prices of which may fall) for the entire stock of money that might be needed for "unexpected" producers' or consumers' expenditures. Speculative balances are held because it seems preferable to postpone the purchase of securities if their prices are likely to fall. The definitions corresponding to this distinction are as follows: The *speculative* money stock is that part of the idle (i.e., nonworking) balances which the public would continue to hold even if it were certain that its "most probable" expectations concerning future receipts from the sale of, and concerning future expenditures on the purchase of, commodities and services will come true; the remainder of the money hoards (i.e., of the nonworking balances) consists of *contingency* (or "precautionary") money.

The hypothesis that the interest elasticity of hoarding is substantial is based on the notion that "speculative" hoards constitute the strategically significant item within the aggregate of idle balances. It is a general belief among economists that contingency hoarding is likely to be rather insensitive to changes in interest rates within the usual range of these changes. Provisions for contingencies presumably depend mainly on the nature and on the likelihood of the contingencies for which allowance is made. It might be said that they depend mainly on how probable the "relatively improbable" is, and on what the consequences of the "relatively improbable" are if it should materialize. Once it is felt that provision should be made for contingencies, the nature and the magnitude of this provision is not likely to be greatly affected by a few per cent rise or decline in the interest cost of hoarding. Moreover, the occurrence of (unfavorable) contingencies itself may appear to be more probable if interest rates rise, and it may appear to be less probable if interest rates decline, because interest rates enter into the costs of enterprise. Consequently, it is not only true that the interest elasticity of contingency hoarding is likely to be small, but the algebraic sign of this elasticity could sometimes even be "inverse." The worsening of profit expectations occasioned *ceteris paribus* by rising interest rates may conceivably induce entrepreneurs to increase their hoards, and vice versa.

Whether, in periods of significant hoarding, the idle balances should be regarded as being mainly of the speculative (rather than contingency) variety, depends on whether, in these periods, the probability of a rise in net rates of interest typically seems high. It is not convincing to argue that at low interest rates a rise in these rates is expected and that these expectations are responsible for the increase in hoarding at low rates and for the incompleteness of the downward adjustment of the interest structure. If the decline in interest rates is assumed to be trend-like, a return to the previous level in the near future will not be expected, and hence speculative hoarding will not become significant. If the decline is regarded as cyclical, a return to the previous level will typically be expected but by the time these expectations might result in substantial hoarding of the speculative variety, the analogous expectations with respect to other variables of the economic system are likely to result in a shift to the right of the I curve. In other words, it is not convincing to argue that the expectation of a "return to normalcy" of interest rates produces substantially increased hoarding at lower-than-normal rates. If the expectation of a return to normalcy is strong enough to produce significant phenomena it is likely to produce a recovery to previous levels of the main economic variables, including the I function and thereby of the interest structure.

In periods of downward shifts of the I curve the demand for idle balances typically rises but this rise is more likely to reflect an increased desire to provide for contingencies than an increased propensity to speculate on a rise in net rates of interest. For the reasons indicated above it is not satisfactory to assume that the typical hoarder of cyclical depression periods and the typical hoarder of protracted periods of "stagnation" maintain idle balances *because* they believe that a postponed purchase of securities is likely to be more advantageous than an immediate purchase. They maintain idle balances because the likelihood of certain "unexpected" developments (which at all times is greater than zero) increases in the periods under consideration. It will be argued presently that the most important "unexpected" development of this character consists of the blocking of the credit market to individual firms as a consequence of unfavorable business results.[8] If this should take place, and if security prices should decline between now and the period in which the blocking of the credit market occurs, the individual firm is forced to "liquidate" in highly unfavorable circumstances unless it possesses a substantial contingency balance which it can use for purposes of self-financing. If the likelihood of the

---

[8] The view developed here on the risk of being cut off from the credit market, shares many features with the position taken by Professor A. G. Hart. Cf. the list of works cited below, p. 152, n. 10.

"relatively improbable" (i.e., of the "unexpected") increases significantly, contingency hoarding will increase even if the likelihood of a decline in security prices has become smaller, as long as the possibility of a decline in security prices is not completely excluded. Increased speculative hoarding presupposes an increased likelihood of a decline in the prices of "perfectly safe" securities; that is, an increased likelihood of a rise in net rates of interest. Increased contingency hoarding may occur even if the likelihood of a rise in net rates of interest has decreased—provided that the possibility of such a rise is not completely excluded and provided that the likelihood of producers' losses and of a subsequent blocking of the credit market to the individual firms has increased significantly. In this event the likelihood that "money will be needed" for producers' expenditures may increase sufficiently to induce increased money hoarding, in spite of the fact that the likelihood of losses on "safe" security portfolios (i.e., the likelihood of rising net rates) may not have risen or may even have decreased.[9]

It should be understood that the difference between speculative hoarding, on the one hand, and contingency hoarding, on the other, relates to intentions; that is, to processes in the minds of the owners of balances. Consequently, the amount of information that is obtainable on the relative significance of these two types of hoarding should not be overestimated. In a matter like this, all "evidence" is highly indirect. It does seem, however, very unconvincing to argue that in periods of protracted stagnation, characterized by a consistent downward trend in interest rates, a general belief in an upward trend should be one of the outstanding features of public psychology. It seems just as unconvincing to argue that a cyclical decline in net rates produces the expectation of a cyclical rise and thereby produces cyclical depression hoarding, whereas analogous expectations of a return to normalcy fail to materialize for other markets and therefore fail to bring about an actual return to normalcy. This

---

[9] If the possibility of losses on perfectly safe securities (i.e., the possibility of rising net rates of interest) were completely excluded, then no contingency balances would be maintained because all contingency reserves would be held in the form of securities. But if the likelihood of rising net rates remains unchanged, or if it declines without shrinking to zero, and if at the same time the likelihood of contingencies increases, contingency hoarding may increase considerably.

set of assumptions, underlying the speculative theory of hoarding, is highly artificial. The assumptions are not logically inconsistent but they lack plausibility because they imply that the public is consistently and obstinately wrong and that a certain type of "incorrect" behavior is limited to one market. It is considerably more plausible to assume that the likelihood of producers' contingencies, and also that of consumers' contingencies, seems to be high in periods in which contingencies requiring emergency money stocks actually occur frequently. Obviously, whenever producers have good reasons to hoard for emergencies, the same is true of individual income recipients, that is, of "consumers." The emergencies of producers tend to become emergencies of individual income recipients, too.

It will be argued later in this chapter that a shift to the left of the I curve in figure 20, typically is associated with an increased likelihood that individual firms will have to rely on their own resources to finance themselves, in order to avoid liquidation in highly unfavorable conditions. This should be expected to result in increased contingency hoarding on the part of firms and, for the reason just indicated, also in increased liquidity provisions on the part of individuals. As long as the possibility of a rise in net interest rates (i.e., of a decline in the prices of perfectly "safe" securities) is not completely excluded, a contingency reserve maintained in the form of a security portfolio will always be an imperfect substitute for a contingency money reserve.

Accepting the *communis opinio* of economists according to which contingency provisions are not likely to be very sensitive to changes in interest rates within the usual range of these changes, the foregoing assumption would permit the D curve in figure 20 to be drawn approximately parallel to the I curve, thereby making the L function inelastic. The incompleteness of the downward adjustment of interest rates in periods of downward shifted I curves must then be explained by the fact that a downward shift of the I curve typically is associated with an upward shift of the (rather inelastic) L function; that is, with an increase in the distance between the I and the D curve. The subsequent section is concerned with the problem of the effects of a downward shift of the I curve on the position of the L function and, thereby, of the D curve.

BUSINESS DECISIONS AND THE PROBABILITY CALCULUS

The relationship of business decisions to the probability calculus constitutes a logical problem that cannot be solved satisfactorily.[10] Yet, it is even more unsatisfactory to leave this problem completely out of account. The difficulties arising from this problem cannot be solved by implying that businessmen, whose expectations extend to a broad range of possible outcomes, act "as though" they maintained single-valued expectations. This, however, is the usual procedure. G. L. S. Shackle has made this time-honored procedure explicit by introducing the concept of the "certainty-equivalent" of expectations.[11] Businessmen, as Shackle rightly emphasizes, have several possible outcomes of their ventures in mind but he postulates that hypothetical definite expectations can be described on the basis of which precisely those decisions would be made which actually are made. These hypothetical definite expectations are the certainty equivalents of the actual expectations, where the latter are recognized as relating to a whole range of possible outcomes.

[10] This problem may be considered the central theme of Professor F. H. Knight's *Risk, Uncertainty, and Profit* (Boston, 1921; reprinted, London School of Economics). For further problems arising in this connection, see H. Makower and J. Marschak, "Assets, Prices and Monetary Theory," *Economica* (August, 1938), where, on p. 271 some of the earlier literature will be found listed; J. Marschak, "Money and the Theory of Assets," *Econometrica* (October, 1938); G. L. S. Shackle, *Expectations, Income and Investment* (Oxford, 1938), and *idem*, "The Nature of the Inducement to Invest," *Review of Economic Studies* (October, 1940); A. G. Hart, "Uncertainty and the Inducement to Invest," *Review of Economic Studies* (October 1940), *idem*, "Anticipations, Business Planning, and the Cycle," *Quarterly Journal of Economics* (February, 1937), *idem, Anticipations, Uncertainty and Dynamic Planning* (Chicago, 1940), and *idem*, "Risk, Uncertainty, and the Unprofitability of Compounding Probabilities," in *Studies in Mathematical Economics and Econometrics: In Memory of Henry Schultz* (Chicago, 1942); G. B. Sanderson, "A Note on the Theory of Investment," *Economica* (May, 1941); A. J. Nichol, "Probability Analysis in the Theory of Demand, Net Revenue, and Price," *Journal of Political Economy* (October, 1941); Gerhard Tintner, "A Contribution to the Nonstatic Theory of Production," in *Studies in Mathematical Economics and Econometrics: In Memory of Henry Schultz* (Chicago, 1942), and *idem*, "The Theory of Production under Nonstatic Conditions," *Journal of Political Economy* (October, 1942); James W. Angell, *Investment and Business Cycles*, (New York and London, 1941); W. Fellner, "Monetary Policies and Hoarding in Periods of Stagnation," *Journal of Political Economy* (June, 1943); D. Domar and Richard A. Musgrave, "Proportional Income Taxation and Risk Taking," *Quarterly Journal of Economics*, LVII (May, 1944), 388–422; cf. pp. 394 ff.

[11] G. L. S. Shackle, *Expectations, Investment, and Income* (London, Humphrey Milford, 1938), p. 19.

The concept of the certainty equivalent of uncertain expectations makes explicit a procedure that is implied in most dynamic theories. That the actual expectations cannot be maintained with certainty is recognized in all dynamic theory. Yet, if a theory relates business decisions to definite *ex ante* magnitudes, it clearly proceeds as though definite magnitudes could be substituted for the actual ranges of expected magnitudes. This, however, is not generally permissible, although the procedure may be acceptable in certain specific contexts. Generally speaking, the decisions resulting from a range of expectations are different from those resulting from any single-valued expectation whatsoever. This is another way of saying that there is no such thing as the certainty equivalent of expectations.

The situation of a firm that must make a decision concerning a specific investment project may now be envisaged. The firm must decide whether the investment should be undertaken, and, if so, on what scale it should be carried out. If the case under consideration belonged in a homogeneous universe of cases, to which the probability calculus in the strict sense could be applied, then the firm could feel certain that the average outcome would approximate the mean value of the distribution the more closely, the greater the number of trials. Consequently the firm could, if it wanted to, act as though something approximating the mean value of its expectations was maintained with certainty. In order to do so, it would have to undertake a very great number of trials or it could shift the risk of dispersion to an insurance company.

The actual instances faced by businessmen do not belong in homogeneous universes. The relationship between these instances and a homogeneous universe could at best be rationalized as follows. Entrepreneurs have forecasts concerning the frequency distribution that would be obtained in a hypothetical homogeneous universe consisting of many instances such as the one they face at a particular moment. This forecast is based on "experience" relating to single past instances all of which belong in different universes. In addition, it is based on the assumed ability to appraise the effects on the outcome of those properties of the past instances in which they differed from the instance faced at present. Experience plus the ability to appraise the effects of differences between various universes may lead to a probability forecast relating to an assumed (hypothetical) homogeneous universe consisting of many instances "such as the present one." This probability forecast will not, however, uniquely determine the behavior of entrepreneurs. Their fate depends on a single outcome, or at best on the outcome in a small number of cases because, in reality, there does not exist a universe consisting of many cases "such as the present one." Entrepreneurs are throwing a given set of dice only on a single occasion. The previous throws were with different dice and the subsequent throws will be with still others. The dice are irregular and the entrepreneurs can at best attempt to appraise the effect of the irregularities on the frequency distribution that would be obtained with the "present dice" if they were thrown many times. In these circumstances the frequency distribution estimated for an hypothetical sequence of throws with the present dice is no unique determinant of "intelligent conduct." The actual conduct of the participants may be interpreted as being determined by three types of determinants. (1) The participants' forecast concerning the mode of the frequency distribution that would be obtained in a hypothetical homogeneous universe consisting of many instances such as the present (i.e., consisting of many throws with the present dice, which, however, in reality will be thrown just once). (2) The participants' confidence in the probability forecast under consideration, which in this case is essentially his confidence in his ability to translate past experience (relating to different universes) into terms of the assumed homogeneous universe consisting of many cases such as the present one.[12] (3) The participants' attitude toward the "uncertainty" resulting from the uniqueness of the instance (i.e., of the "throw"), and from the possibility that an improbable outcome might materialize in this single instance.[13]

It would seem that under determinants of type 1, the mode rather than the mean of the assumed frequency distribution expresses its significant property.[14] If it is possible at all to interpret decisions

---

[12] This ability is identical with the ability to "allow" for the differences between the various universes to which his experience relates.

[13] This factor would enter even if the probability forecast would be maintained with certainty for a great number of throws.

[14] For the contrary opinion, cf. Evsey D. Domar and Richard A. Musgrave, "Proportional Income Taxation and Risk-Taking," *Quarterly Journal of Economics* (May, 1944) LVIII, pp. 388–422. Cf. 394 ff.

relating to unique instances as resulting from probability considerations, on the one hand, and from considerations of a different character, on the other (cf. types of determinants 2 and 3 above), then the probability considerations should preferably be interpreted as relating to modal rather than to mean values. It seems more meaningful to postulate that the behavior of a person risking his money at a single throw is determined by the most probable outcome and by his attitude toward the potentiality that a less probable outcome might materialize, than to postulate that the mean enters into the determination of typical behavior in unique instances. Of course, it could be maintained that neither the mode nor the mean is a legitimate concept in the analysis of the problem in question because it could be maintained that the frequency distribution itself is not a legitimate concept. In fact it is true of all concepts of the probability analysis that they can be "rescued" for the purposes under discussion merely by postulating the existence, in the mind of the forecaster, of a hypothetical homogeneous universe consisting of many instances such as the one he is facing, and by postulating that he applies the concept of probability to this hypothetical universe and then takes separately into account the fact that he will not be facing more than a single instance of the universe. Psychologically, this method of "rescuing" probability concepts seems justified because it is a widespread habit to think in terms of probability concepts when unique situations are encountered to which the probability calculus in the strict sense is not applicable. The resulting impure or adulterated concept of probability can be "decomposed," and thereby "explained," by the kind of reasoning contained in the discussion of determinants 1 to 3, above. But although there exists in the human mind an impure concept of the "most probable," which is being constantly applied to unique instances, it is questionable whether the arithmetic mean has ever been conceived of in this manner. A complicated analytical procedure that adapts the concept of the most probable to unique situations has its counterpart somewhere in the human mind. The analogous procedure adapting the concept of the mean to unique situations may well be psychologically unrealistic. The point is of no great significance for the problems to be discussed later; it was raised merely to justify the specific type of "impure" probability concepts which will be used in the next section. It is quite possible that alternative versions would have merits that this specific version does not possess.

THE LINK BETWEEN THE I CURVE AND THE L FUNCTION

The thesis of this section is that substantial downward shifts of the I curve in figure 20 typically are associated with upward shifts of the L function (i.e., with an increase of the distance between the I and the D curve), for reasons dependent on the nature of uncertainty and its relation to the problem of probability. Downward shifts of the I curve result from a lowering of the most probable profit expectations of individual entrepreneurs. And, for the individual entrepreneur, a substantial lowering of the most probable profit expectations is associated with an increased risk of loss and thereby with an increased risk of not being able to rely on the credit market. The link between the I curve and the L function is therefore as follows: The lowering of most probable profit expectations results in a downward shift of the I curves, on the one hand, and in smaller safety margins against losses, on the other. Substantially reduced safety margins against losses result, in turn, in an increased risk of being cut off from the credit market, which is identical with the risk of forced liquidation unless the enterprise can finance itself from contingency reserves. Consequently a substantial downward shift of most probable profit expectations results in increased contingency provisions. To "increase" contingency provisions means to shift to the right along the following two scales: first, long-term securities → short-term securities → cash; second, risky securities → safer securities → cash. Liquidity preference is a matter of shifting along scales such as these. Professor Viner has rightly stressed that it is not simply a matter of hoarding *versus* lending.[15]

A substantial decline in most probable profit expectations therefore typically leads to a shift away from long-term securities toward short-term securities and toward cash, and also to a shift away from risky securities toward safer securities and toward cash, even if the

---

[15] Jacob Viner: "Mr. Keynes on the Causes of Unemployment," *Quarterly Journal of Economics* (November, 1936), 147–167.

risk of rising net rates of interest (i.e., the risk of a fall in the value of "safe" securities) has remained unchanged or has decreased. It is not permissible to interpret a rise in the demand for short-term securities in relation to long-term securities (i.e., a rise in the interest-rate differentials in favor of the long-term rates) as necessarily reflecting the increased expectation of a rise in net rates of interest. Nor is it permissible to interpret a rise in the demand for idle balances in the same manner. The same probability (or even a smaller probability) of rising net rates is quite compatible with an increased demand for more liquid securities at the expense of less liquid securities and with an increased demand for cash at the expense of all securities, provided the likelihood of "contingencies" requiring "own cash" has increased sufficiently.[18]

A substantial downward shift of most probable profit expectations is associated with reduced safety margins against the risk of loss for reasons that are less obvious than they might seem at first sight. The safety margins in question will here be defined so as to measure the difference between the expected most probable outcome and that outcome by which the firm would barely avoid losing. The reasons why a substantial downward shift of expectations diminishes these safety margins will be considered presently in some detail. It may be pointed out in advance, however, that if individual entrepreneurs always invested on such a scale as to maintain given safety margins against losses, the change in most probable profit expectations would merely change the volume of investment, but not the demand for contingency reserves. Entrepreneurs could adopt a policy of constant safety margins. This would imply that if conditions improved they would increase the scale of their operations sufficiently to prevent safety margins from rising. If conditions changed for the worse, they would reduce the scale of their operations sufficiently to prevent the safety margins from shrinking. If no reduction of the scale would maintain the safety margins at an unchanging level, they could refrain from carrying out investments. Such a policy would be quite conceivable. If it were the typical

---

[18] This is not necessarily overlooked, but it is not included in the main line of argument in the otherwise excellent treatment of the problem by F. A. Lutz, "The Structure of Interest Rates," *Quarterly Journal of Economics,* LV (November, 1940), 36–63.

policy of entrepreneurs the views to be expressed in the present section would be invalid.

The view presented here is based on a hypothesis which will be expressed in broad common-sense terms and will later be elaborated upon more technically: In advanced industrial communities the typical entrepreneur attempts to carry out his operations on a scale for which the safety margins against losses are considerable, and therefore the need for contingency provisions is relatively small. If conditions change so that the previously realized safety margins cease to be available irrespective of how the scale of operations is adjusted, the "representative entrepreneur" will operate with reduced safety margins and he will increase his contingency provisions per unit of investment. Obviously, operations will be discontinued altogether if safety margins fall below certain limits. Considering that the safety margins available to different entrepreneurs are different, a general lowering of available safety margins will always induce certain ("marginal") entrepreneurs to discontinue their operations. Yet, the crucial aspect of the hypotheses relates to those firms which stay in business in spite of the reduction of the individual safety margins. The existing firms may be arrayed according to the safety margins that are available to them. It may then be argued that a general lowering of the available safety margins for all firms will not merely push the weak entrepreneurs[17] "below the mark" (i.e., below the margin of investment), but that at the same time the position of those entrepreneurs situated higher in the array will come closer to the position of the marginal entrepreneur than was true before. In periods in which most probable profit expectations are high, so that high safety margins are available to the average entrepreneur for certain scales of operations, the typical scale of individual operations will be such as actually to result in the realization of high safety margins plus a relatively small demand for contingency balances. From this it follows that a decline in most-probable profit expectation which is substantial enough to preclude the maintenance of the previously realized safety margins for any scale of individual operations, is associated with an increased demand for contingency balances per unit of investment on the part

---

[17] That is, the entrepreneurs to whom relatively low safety margins are available.

of the firms not actually going out of business. For reasons indicated above, a rise in the demand for contingency balances per unit of investment is typically coupled with two shifts of a similar character; namely, with a shift of demand from long-term securities to short-term securities (i.e., with the appearance, or the increase, of interest-rate differentials in favor of long-term rates) and also with a shift of demand from securities implying a higher risk of default to safer securities.

The Lack of Symmetry Between Favorable and Unfavorable Surprise

The analysis is not particularly well suited for graphic illustration because the number of "variables" included is high. Nevertheless, it may not be useless to illustrate the situation of the individual firm in face of shifting expectations by the following simple device.

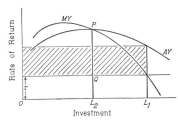

Fig. 21. Individual output in view of uncertainty.

Along the abscissa is measured, in dollars, the amount of gross investment undertaken by the firm during a given period, and along the ordinate the expected most probable rate of return from the investment (including interest in the return even if the capitalist and the entrepreneur are distinct).[18] The expected most probable rate of return is a function of the scale of investment. It is affected by the **U** shape of the cost curves and, except in pure competition, also by the downward slope of the expected demand curve. The most probable rate of return, as a function of the scale of investment, is labeled AY in the figure. "Most probable" is to be interpreted in the "impure" sense discussed in pages 152–156.

If it were realistic to assume that the typical entrepreneur (or the typical hired manager) is concerned exclusively with maximizing "most probable" profits, the actual scale of gross investment would be determined by the intersection of the MY curve[19] with the curve

---

[18] It is implied that the factors of production are combined optimally for each potential output, given, however, the commitments previously entered by the firm.

[19] The MY curve is the marginal curve corresponding to the average curve AY.

that is marginal to the supply curve of credit faced by the firm. For the sake of simplicity it is assumed that the supply curve of credit to the individual firm is a horizontal line in the relevant range. The line is drawn in the figure at the level r, indicating that the firm could borrow a practically unlimited amount at the interest rate r. In this event the scale of most probable profit maximization is determined by the intersection of the MY curve with a horizontal line at the height of r.

In reality the supply curve of credit to individual firms may have different shapes, and, if the shape is not horizontal throughout the relevant range, the point of most probable profit maximization is derived from MY and the marginal curve to the supply curve of credit. It is obvious that allowance can be made for this case. It is not possible, however, to make allowance in a simple scheme for another difficulty. If the enterprise uses its own funds rather than borrowed ones, the "supply curve of credit" clearly should express the opportunity cost arising through not lending. This opportunity cost, however, is a matter of the probable yield of securities just as the outcome of a specific physical investment project is a matter of probabilities. In other words, the same kind of impure probability analysis as the one applied to the rate of return from the planned investment should also be resorted to in connection with the supply of funds. Moreover, a great number of competing alternative opportunities would have to be included on the supply side. What this implies should become obvious once the analysis has been carried out for the rate of return from a single investment project, given the supply function of credit. To make allowance for this circumstance, however, involves "complications" that render the problem unmanageable on the level of simple graphic technique. It will therefore be assumed that the enterprise borrows the funds required for the investment on the credit market at a definite cost, and that, for institutional reasons, the project under consideration is the only one accessible to the enterprise.

The assumption that the enterprise is interested exclusively in "most probable" profit maximization would clearly be unrealistic. If this was a case of true probability considerations relating to homogeneous universes, the firm—or the insurance company from which it could buy a policy—might be concerned exclusively with a limited number of properties of the statistically established frequency distribution. An impure concept of the "most probable" has been postulated for problems, such as the one considered, to which probability concepts in the strict sense are not applicable. But it cannot be maintained that business decisions are based exclusively on what seems to be most probable in this extended sense. They may be interpreted as being based on such an extended concept (or "impure" concept) of the most probable, plus the notion that allowance should be made for the possibility of less probable outcomes.

The kind of allowance that is made for the potentiality of relatively unlikely outcomes depends, of course, partly on the genuinely "psychological" propensities of the persons making business decisions. These psychological propensities enter into the decisions in two distinct ways. The question of what the most probable outcome is cannot be answered on purely objective evidence. The answer to this question is already psychologically colored, to say the least. Employing previous terminology, it may be said that psychology enters here at the point of translating past experience, derived from instances belonging in different universes, into terms of a hypothetical homogeneous universe consisting of many cases such as the (actually unique) case faced "at present." This implies appraising the effect on past outcomes of those properties of the various universes in which they differed from one another and in which they differ from the universe into which the present instance belongs. Psychological propensities enter into this process of appraisal. In addition, it enters into decision making after the appraisal is completed, on an equal footing with the "probability judgment" itself, because the nature of the provisions for relatively unlikely outcomes is also partly psychologically determined. Whether the provisions to be made for possible outcomes other than the most probable are influenced more by the potentiality of such outcomes as are more favorable than the most probable or by the potentiality of less favorable outcomes depends partly on the psychological characteristics of the entrepreneur.

Yet, the nature of the provisions for the possibility of less probable outcomes depends but partly on psychological propensities.

The character of these provisions is partly—it could be said, largely—determined by institutional factors acting in a broadly predictable direction. To summarize this section of the argument in advance: certain institutional characteristics of well-developed industrial communities make it seem very likely that the provisions for possible deviations from the most probable outcome will be influenced more by the potentiality of unfavorable surprise than by that of favorable surprise. This is true because originally moderate losses tend to become cumulative through the reaction of the credit market, whereas originally moderate favorable surprise does not show this tendency in a comparable degree.

If the actual outcome of a business venture is less favorable than the expected ("most probable") outcome, by a margin sufficient to cause losses, then these losses are likely to be significantly increased in consequence of a sudden deterioration of the conditions on which the enterprise is capable of borrowing on the credit market. Originally moderate losses frequently do not stay moderate. They tend to become cumulative because the standing of a firm that suffers losses deteriorates and this gives rise to further losses. Complete blocking of the credit market, or even a significant upward shift of the credit supply curve facing the individual enterprise, forces liquidation in highly unfavorable circumstances, unless the firm is capable of resorting to its own liquid funds. In consequence of the imperfections of the markets for used physical assets and for goodwill, forced liquidation is tantamount to almost complete loss of all values invested in the enterprise. This situation is not symmetrical with respect to deviations from the most probable outcome in the two conceivable directions. It is quite possible to argue that consistently favorable business results improve the credit standing of an enterprise and that this tends to increase further the profitability of its ventures; but the losses arising in the event of forced liquidation have no *equivalent* counterpart on the favorable side. The factor by which originally moderate losses are multiplied if credit facilities are withdrawn from an enterprise is entirely out of line with the proportion in which originally moderate gains may increase in consequence of the improved standing of the firm.

The asymmetry just considered has "objective" (institutional) roots. It will result in emphasizing the potentiality of unfavorable surprise more than that of favorable surprise unless at least one of two specific conditions is satisfied. These two conditions, which may have been satisfied in the typical "frontier" environment, but which are not typically satisfied in advanced industrial communities, are these: Either the likelihood of favorable deviations from the most probable outcome must be considerably higher in some range than those of unfavorable deviations (aside from the cumulative tendency considered above), or the genuinely psychological elements entering into decision making must be such as to emphasize primarily the potentiality of favorable surprise. An entrepreneur to whom favorable surprise seems as likely as unfavorable surprise (aside from the cumulative tendency of losses), and to whom the disutility of losses amounting to x dollars is psychologically equivalent to the utility of gains amounting to x dollars, *should* be more influenced by the potentiality of outcomes falling short of the most probable than by outcomes exceeding it, because the former become cumulative with a higher intensity than the latter. If, in addition, he attaches a higher psychological weight to unfavorable than to favorable surprise, the "objective" consideration is reinforced by the "psychological" element. Only if, aside from the cumulative tendency, favorable surprise seems more likely than unfavorable surprise or if a considerably higher psychological weight is attached to the potentiality of high gains than to that of the complete loss of assets, could the final decision be more influenced by the potentiality of outcomes exceeding the most probable than by the potentiality of outcomes falling short of it. The kind of environment associated in the United States with the frontier was characterized by a relatively high likelihood of the realization of gains, within short periods, that exceed in amount the value of all assets risked. The frontier environment may also have been characterized by the existence of "investors" who attached a higher psychological weight to gains than to losses. In advanced industrial communities the likelihood of profits amounting to a high multiple of the most probable is typically slight, and the psychological weight attached to the unfavorable potentiality of bankruptcy or receivership is high. It may be concluded therefore, that the asymmetry in the intensity with which losses, on the one hand, and gains, on the other, become cumulative, will be reflected in the final decisions themselves. This asymmetry is typically even reinforced by an asymmetrical psychology that weights unfavorable surprise more heavily than favorable surprise. It is not typically weakened or offset by objective or psychological elements of an opposite character.

The asymmetry expresses itself in two distinct ways. It leads to a scale of operations that deviates in the direction of greater safety from the intersection of the MY curve with the r line in figure 21, thereby reducing the risk of loss. It also leads to contingency provisions, that is, to the maintenance of liquid reserves, which are intended to prevent potential losses from becoming cumulative through repercussions in the credit market.

The scale of operations determined by the intersection of the MY curve with the r line in figure 21, would be the scale of the highest safety margin only if all potential losses were lump-sum losses, independent of the scale of operations. The scale, by definition, is that of most probable profit maximization. Consequently it is also the scale minimizing losses if the outcome is less favorable by a lump sum than that deemed to be "most probable." The scale, however, is not that which would maximize profits or minimize losses if the rate of return on the investment were to be x per cent less favorable than appears to be most probable. This can be expressed by saying that the safety margin against losses in the nature of fixed costs is the highest for the scale of most probable profit maximization and that the margin in question is measured for that scale, in 100 dollar units, by the shaded area in figure 21. On the other hand, the safety margin against losses in the nature of proportionate costs[20] is the highest for the scale for which the vertical distance between the AY curve and r is the greatest and this safety margin is measured in rate-of-return units by the vertical distance in question, (i.e., by the distance PQ). Conceptually, the safety margin is in both cases a margin by which the outcome may fall short of the most probable without causing losses.

Although some of the potential losses may be in the nature of fixed costs, others are clearly like variable costs, although not neces-

---

[20] That is, of costs proportionate to the scale of investment.

sarily like proportionate costs in the strict sense. Even if nothing were known about the appropriate weighting of these two types of potential losses, it would have to be assumed that the actual scale of operations was not that corresponding to the intersection of the MY curve with the r line. If the scale of operations is influenced more by the potential unfavorable surprise than by the potential of favorable surprise, the actual scale of operations will be smaller than that corresponding to the intersection, considering that some of the potential losses would have to be classed as "variable cost losses" in any event. In reality there exists a strong presumption that most potential losses should be classed as variable cost losses, although not necessarily as losses precisely proportionate to the scale. Lower selling prices than those judged to be most probable belong in the variable category, and so do higher input prices than those regarded as most probable. Consequently, safety margin considerations of themselves would undoubtedly justify a scale lying well to the left of the intersection of MY with r (i.e., well to the left of L_1 and near L_2). The actual scale of operations influenced by the objective of most probable profit maximization, on the one hand, and by safety margin considerations, on the other, might frequently be distinctly smaller than that which would be determined by the objective of most probable profit maximization alone.

The lack of symmetry between the consequences of favorable and those of unfavorable surprise results not merely in a scale of operations different from that of most probable profit maximization, but also in liquidity provisions for contingencies. These aim at making self-financing possible if the credit market should be blocked to the individual firm or if the conditions in which credit is available to the firm should deteriorate significantly.

It can be seen from figure 21, that a substantial downward shift of the AY and MY curves must be expected to reduce the available safety margins for all potential scales below those actually realized in favorable conditions, assuming that in favorable conditions the typical entrepreneur operates on a scale leaving him considerable safety margins. This is true because a sufficiently far-reaching downward shift of the functions of expected return will result in small safety margins for all potential scales of operation, regardless of how far the costs of borrowing decline. Even if rates on money loans approximated the zero level, it still would be true that the available safety margins would in "bad times" be smaller for all potential scales than are the actually realized safety margins in "good times." This is another way of saying that the degree of downward shift of the curve of expected return from "good" to "bad" times is much greater than what could be offset by a reduction of rates on money loans, and the upward shift from bad to good times is partly used to increase the safety margins actually realized. A reduction of the safety margins below the levels previously attained will induce marginal or near-marginal entrepreneurs (i.e., entrepreneurs to whom small safety margins were available) to discontinue their operations. The entrepreneurs to whom high safety margins were available will usually stay in business, but in consequence of the reduced safety margins they will tend to develop an increased demand for "liquidity" per unit of investment.[21]

The increased demand for liquidity was discussed here with reference to firms. But it is obvious that in periods in which business contingencies require higher business liquidity, individuals will also be "justified" in increasing their contingency provisions.

THE SHORT-RUN CHARACTER OF THE ANALYSIS

A downward shift of expectations and of the I curve may frequently be a short-run phenomenon, but it is also possible that these shifts mark a long-run change. If there are long-run shifts, certain influences will gradually become effective which tend to reduce the aggregate demand for idle balances. Even if the expectations are limited to single firms (or to the "representative firm") it should not be overlooked that as real assets of the firm become gradually liquidated, the aggregate demand of the firm for contingency balances is likely to be reduced. Moreover, the aggregate demand of business as a whole is likely to be reduced for the further reason that, in the event of a long-run downward shift, the number of firms is gradually reduced. The argument of the preceding sections merely

---

[21] Throughout the array of firms, ordered according to the safety margins available to them, each firm will be pressed downward. Hence the "average entrepreneur" or the "representative entrepreneur" will come closer to the weakest entrepreneur still remaining in business (i.e., to the marginal entrepreneur) than was the case before.

establishes a presumption that the demand for liquidity per unit of real investment (or per unit of commitments) rises when the probable outcome of business ventures changes to the worse. This results in a shift to the right of the L function, and therefore in an increase of the distance between the I and the D curve in figure 20, only if investments are not liquidated (i.e., commitments are not reduced) in a measure sufficient to reduce the aggregate demand for liquidity in the economy as a whole to the previous level or to even lower levels. In the long run such an offsetting effect may tend to develop. This possesses significance for interest theory because it means that the long-run shift of the L function may be quite different from its short-run shifts. In the event of a long-run downward shift of the I curve, the temporarily inflated demand for liquidity may gradually be reduced. However, from the specific point of view of this discussion these further considerations are of no immediate importance. The primary interest here is in the question of why interest rates do not adjust in such a manner as to maintain output. The long-run changes in question are such changes in interest rates as occur only after investment has changed significantly. These long-run forces do not provide a mechanism by which significant oscillations in investment and output would be avoided.

The Elasticity of Hoarding with Respect to Interest Rates

The preceding analysis leads to the conclusion that the demand for idle balances is likely to prove sensitive to the available safety margins, that is, to the margins by which the outcome of business ventures may fall short of the most probable without leading to losses. This, in turn, may be expressed by saying that the demand for idle balances is sensitive to the position of the I curve in figure 20, because higher safety margins will be realized on the average if the individual AY curves in figure 21 (and thereby the I curve in figure 20) are high than if these curves are low. If the AY curves shift to the left to such a degree that the available safety margins are reduced, regardless of how far the rates on money loans decline, the L function must be expected to shift to the right; that is, the distance between and I and the D curves must be expected to rise. These shifts are of great importance.

Most monetary theorists have assumed that the elasticity of contingency hoarding to interest rates is small. This opinion seems plausible. Moreover, it should be repeated that in certain cases even the algebraic sign of the elasticity of the L function may be different from what it is assumed to be in the theory of speculative hoarding. Changes in rates on money loans affect not merely the cost of liquidity. They also affect the safety margins themselves because if the costs of borrowing increase, safety margins decline and vice versa. This effect of the change in interest rates tends to offset the other effect, namely, the effect of the change on the cost of liquidity. The L function slopes upward if the circumstance that entrepreneurial safety margins are decreased, though a rise in interest rates has a greater influence on the demand for liquidity than does the circumstance that a rise in interest rates increases the cost of liquidity. An upward sloping L function would be expressed in figure 20 by letting the distance between the I and the D curve increase (instead of decrease) as the interest rate rises.

On a priori grounds more definite statements about the slope of the L function cannot be made than those applying to the slope of the Sg curve. In both cases influences might be pointed to which make for a negative slope and also to influences which make for a positive slope. In both cases it is also possible to argue that an important portion of the determining influences presumably is unaffected by changes in money rates within the usual range of these changes. The same is true of the M function.[22]

The model most appropriate to these considerations would possess the following main characteristics. The I curve would have to be represented as distinctly downward sloping, and as intersecting with the abscissa at a finite distance from the point of origin. The intersection of the I curve with the abscissa is at a finite distance from the origin because even a zero rate on money loans would leave all potential entrepreneurs with finite safety margins, and even a zero rate would leave some potential entrepreneurs (those whose expectations are unfavorable) with safety margins that are insufficient to induce them to invest. This does not contradict Professor Knight's view, according to which the demand for loans would be

---

[22] That is, of the distance between the Sg and the S curves.

unlimited if everybody could obtain and renew loans without interest charge in any amount desired.[23] Credit that is extended in any amount desired, and the continuous renewal of which is guaranteed in advance, is indistinguishable from unconditional subsidies, the demand for which, of course, is unlimited. This, however, is true even if the unlimited loan facilities are extended at positive rates. In the present analysis it is assumed that the possibility of obtaining a loan, (i.e., of "entering the credit market" on the demand side) depends on the status of the would-be borrower and that therefore no borrower can feel assured that he will be able to renew his loan, instead of repaying it, should he suffer losses in the meantime. In these circumstances, the zero rate on money loans does not produce an infinite demand for credit, and the negatively inclined I function intersects with the abscissa at a finite distance from the origin.

The model appropriate to the foregoing analysis should contain, in addition to the negatively inclined I curve, an L function that usually (but not necessarily always) possesses small elasticity. In other words, the distance between the I and the D curves might not depend very markedly on the interest rate. It is impossible to indicate with general validity the algebraic sign of the comparatively small elasticity of the L function, yet the position of the L function depends in a high degree on the position of the I curve. In the short run, if the I curve shifts to the right, the L curve shifts to the left with the result that the I + L curve (i.e., the D curve) possesses a considerably greater degree of cyclical stability than either of its two constituents. It is impossible to state with general validity whether, on balance, the D curve moves to the right or to the left when the I curve shifts in one direction and the L function shifts in the other. The shift of the L function attending a given shift of the I curve depends on so many factors of a purely psychological character that it is impossible to make statements of general validity concerning the relative magnitude of the two shifts respectively. It can be safely maintained, however, that the cyclical stability of the D curve is much greater than that of the I curve or that of the L function.

Clearly, the cyclical stability of the D curve is even greater if the

---

[23] This is Professor Knight's interpretation of the zero rate. Cf. F. H. Knight, "Diminishing Returns from Investment," *Journal of Political Economy*, LII (March, 1944), 26–47, Cf. p. 26.

analysis is applied to long-term rates than if it is applied to short-term rates, because the average of short-term rates over some longer future period is not expected to change to the full extent of sudden changes in the short-term rate.

Yet, if the shift of the I curve is a long-run shift, the L function need not stay shifted in the opposite direction. In the event of a downward shift of the I curve, the aggregate demand for liquidity

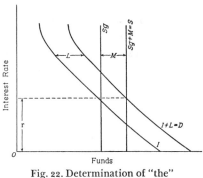

Fig. 22. Determination of "the" interest rate.

might decline in the long run, in spite of the continued high demand for liquidity per unit of "illiquid" (real) assets, because in the long run, "illiquid" assets might become liquidated in a value sufficient to outweigh the effect of the "per unit" rise in total demand. For an ·analogous reason, in the event of an upward shift of the I curve, the aggregate demand for liquidity might increase in the long run in spite of the continued low demand for liquidity per unit of "illiquid" (real) assets.

On the supply side, the Sg curve as well as the M function[24] might be conceived as usually (but not necessarily always) possessing small elasticity. Both these curves may slope upward or downward. The position of the Sg curve depends mainly on the level of the income "out of which" saving takes place; that is, its position depends mainly on the level of disposable income if the Robertsonian model of causation is valid and mainly on the level of expected income if the Swedish model is accepted. The position of the M function—the distance between the Sg and the S curves—depends mainly on the policies adopted by the monetary authority.

All this does not lend itself well to graphic representation in a single figure. In a first and very crude approximation it may be legitimate to draw the Sg and Sg + M curves vertically, and to draw the D curve parallel to the I curve, especially if there is a limitation to the "usual range of changes in rates on money loans." This is

---

[24] Expressed by the distance between the Sg and the S curve.

done in figure 22 in order to emphasize the fact that as a rule the I curve presumably possesses a considerably greater elasticity than any of the other functions. On a simplifying assumption such as this, it is possible to draw a graph which, obviously, cannot be drawn if it has not been determined whether the L, Sg, and M functions should be represented as possessing usually a slight positive or a slight negative elasticity. Yet the figure in question will, in any event, fail to express the main elements of the interest rate determining mechanism, or will express these at best in a very superficial sense. The main elements of the mechanism lie behind the figure. The basic problems of interest theory relate to the questions: in what way does the position of the Sg curve depend on the level of income, on institutional circumstances, habits, and so on? In what way does the position of the M curve depend on policies of the monetary authority? In what way does the position and the elasticity of the I curve depend on profit expectations? In what way are the I curve and the L function interrelated with each other?

SUMMARY

The chapter began with a question which, after some detour, may now be briefly answered. The question relates (*a*) to the causes of the "rigidity" of interest rates; and (*b*) to the consequences which might be expected from an attempt on the part of monetary policy to overcome the downward rigidity of interest rates.

The rigidity of interest rates expresses itself in the fact that the decline in interest rates is insufficient to maintain the level of output in the face of downward shifted expectations. This is partly explained by the inverse shifts of the I function and of the L function in the "short run," that is, during the period in which the stock of investment is not yet adjusted to the change in expectations. It is irrelevant from this point of view that for a smaller aggregate stock of investment the aggregate demand for liquidity may again become smaller and that for a greater aggregate stock it might again increase. This already implies a reduced volume of investment and of output for downward shifts and an increased volume of investment for upward shifts.

It must, however, be realized that hoarding is but partly responsible for the failure of investment and output to be maintained in the face of downward shifting expectations. Unless the demand for idle balances should become perfectly elastic (which is very unlikely if hoarding is mainly of the precautionary variety) it is always possible to overcome the effects of hoarding by changing the supply of money; that is, by shifting the M function and along with it the S curve, to the right. This policy, however, is subject to important limitations because rates on money may be too high for the maintenance of a substantial rate of investment even if they are lowered to the neighborhood of the zero level. A theory taking into account the uncertainty of loan-renewal facilities and their dependence on current business results[25] cannot assume that zero rates on money loans would produce an infinite rate of investment. Even zero rates would leave but a finite number of potential entrepreneurs with finite safety margins. If the rigidity of rates on money loans means the insufficiency of their adjustment for the maintenance of investment and output, they might in many cases be "rigid" downward even if additions to the supply of money lowered them to the zero level. Even a decline to the zero level would fail to induce strongly pessimistic entrepreneurs to carry out large-scale investment projects. In other words, in the event of a significant change to the worse of expectations, interest rates would have to become negative in order not to be "rigid"—assuming that rigidity means failure to adjust in such a manner as to "clear the market." This means that money would have to be supplied at negative rates—that is, that the monetary authority would have to produce an S curve that continues below the abscissa—in order to enforce a sufficiently flexible behavior of the interest-rate structure.

Certain fundamental obstacles stand in the way of such a policy of outright subsidization on a large scale. The conditions on which the subsidy is granted would have to cover the output which the firm is expected to produce, the employment which it is expected to supply, and probably a number of other significant variables. This precludes the adoption of such a policy on the level of generality with which loan policies are pursued. The actual behavior of rates

---

[25] Or, generally speaking, a theory taking into account the fact that credit always is rational in the sense that not everybody can obtain it.

on money loans in the face of downward shifting expectations must be explained largely with reference to the behavior of the L function. It must be added, however, that deliberate policies of the central bank could always overcome the downward rigidity of rates were it not for the fact that overcoming this rigidity might imply establishing negative rates.

Upward rigidity of rates, that is, their failure to adjust so as to prevent investment from rising when expectations improve, is also a consequence of the behavior of the L function. Upward rigidity could, however, frequently be overcome by shifting the S function to the left.[20] Aside from inflationary situations, it, of course, is undesirable to interfere with the upward rigidity of money rates. On the contrary, it frequently is desirable not to counteract the willingness of the commercial banks to increase the supply of money when hoarding decreases under the impact of improving expectations. This, of course, increases the upward rigidity of interest rates and the upward flexibility of investment.

Finally, it should be repeated that changes in entrepreneurial expectations leading to an increase (or, alternatively, to a decrease) in the demand for contingency balances, by the same token widen (or, alternatively, diminish) the interest-rate differentials existing in favor of the long-term rates, and also the differentials existing in favor of the rates on risky securities. The expectations of rising net rates may produce a significant demand for idle balances and it may also produce interest-rates differentials in favor of long-term rates. Yet the expectation of rising net rates is not a necessary condition of hoarding or of the interest-rate differentials in question. As long as the possibility of rising net rates (i.e., of a fall in all security prices) is not completely excluded, a decline in the available entrepreneurial safety margins must be assumed to produce preferences for short-term as against long-term securities. It must also be assumed to produce preferences for safe as against risky securities, and for cash as against securities in general. The differentials in favor of risky rates rise also for the additional reason that the "risky security" is more risky than it used to be.

---

[20] For qualifications, cf., pp. 183–185.

CHAPTER VI

Alternative Monetary Policies

Expansionary Monetary Policies and the Elasticity of Hoarding

THE EFFECTIVENESS of certain types of monetary policy in maintaining the level of employment in the face of downward shifted expectation depends greatly on the elasticity of liquidity provisions and on that of private investment with respect to rates on money loans. The present section summarizes the relationship between expansionary monetary policies, on the one hand, and elasticity considerations, on the other.

1) *The sale of government securities to the public and the use of the proceeds of the borrowing operations for public expenditures* can become reasonably successful only if the L functions expressed in figures 20 and 22 are downward sloping and if they possess considerable (negative) elasticity. The sale of government securities to the public tends to raise interest rates beyond the level at which they otherwise would be. If the L function is upward sloping—which, as was pointed out in the preceding chapter, is a possibility[1]—the public increases its idle balances. Consequently, the policy under consideration has contractionary effects whenever the movement occurs along a reasonably stable, upward sloping L function. Effectiveness of the policy requires that idle balances rather than active money be borrowed and spent by the government and this condition is identical with that of downward sloping and considerably elastic L functions. In the limiting case of perfectly elastic L functions it could be maintained that only hoards are borrowed and spent by the government. In this limiting case interest rates do not rise at all, so that private investment and the amount of working balances do not decline. The entire government expenditure constitutes a

---

[1] Cf. above, chap. v, p. 168.

net addition to the expenditures of the community. Whenever the L function is downward sloping and possesses finite elasticity, it is true that partly idle money and partly active, or "working" money is being borrowed and spent by the government. Other things remaining equal, interest rates do rise in this case beyond the level at which they otherwise would be, and the rise in rates has the double effect of reducing idle balances (favorable effect) and of reducing the rate of private investment (unfavorable effect). The greater the negative elasticity of the L function, (i.e., the greater its elasticity, assuming that it slopes downward), the more idle balances are being borrowed per unit rise of money rates; and the smaller the interest elasticity of private investment, the less private investment is being suppressed per unit rise of rates. In the limiting case of a perfectly inelastic L function all government borrowing is at the expense of private investment and the government spending creates no net addition to total expenditures.

To clarify the terminology used, it might be well to call to the reader's attention that the interest elasticity of hoarding does not uniquely determine the interest elasticity of private investment, or vice versa. If, for example, hoarding declines slightly per unit rise of interest rates, private investment need not decline substantially. It may also decline slightly *per unit rise of interest rates*. This should not be confused with the decline of hoarding and private investment, respectively, *per unit of government borrowing*. Assuming that the M function is inelastic and that it does not shift, it is true that the borrowing reduces either hoarding or private investment and that it reduces the one to the extent to which it fails to reduce the other.

According to the foregoing presentation the expansionary monetary policy here under consideration presupposes that the interest elasticity of hoarding should be negative and that it should be high in comparison with the (always negative) interest elasticity of private investment. Statement of the case in terms of elasticities implies, however, stable L and I functions. It must therefore be added that effectiveness of the policy also requires that the indirect repercussions of the deficit-financing operations should not shift the I function to the left, or the L function to the right, to a degree sufficient to outweigh the direct stimulus. This might be expressed by saying that the direct expansionary effects of the policy must not be offset by negative pump-priming effects. Shifts of the relevant functions (as distinct from movements along the functions) may be termed pump-priming effects, because pump-priming programs are based on the notion that the economic system maintains itself automatically on a changed level if a change in the level of activity is brought about temporarily by monetary policies. This, of course, means that the policies shift the I and the L functions.

Assuming that the elasticities considered above are such as to result in a primary expansionary effect and that this is not offset by a negative pump-priming effect, the total increase in MV depends, in addition to the circumstances so far mentioned, on the secondary rise in consumption and in investment (Angell's multiplier effect) generated by the original increase in money income. It is true of the policy now under consideration, and of all policies to be considered subsequently, that the secondary rise in consumption and in investment depends on the marginal propensity to spend[2]—provided the primary increase[3] is assumed as given. It also is generally true that the marginal propensity to spend is the greater, the greater the marginal propensity to consume, the smaller the interest elasticity of hoarding and the greater the interest elasticity of private investment. These interest elasticities enter into the determination of the secondary rise, and they enter in the same way for all policies to be considered, because they determine (*a*) the extent to which interest rates decline in consequence of the saving out of additional income; and (*b*) the additional investment produced by this decline in interest rates.

2) *The sale of government securities to commercial banks, and the use of the proceeds of the borrowing operations for government expenditures* is effective if conditions are satisfied that are closely analogous to those discussed in the preceding paragraphs. The only difference is that the policy requires high elasticity of bank reserve ratios (rather than of "hoarding") to interest rates. The banks must

---

[2] As defined by Professor Angell in *Investment and Business Cycles,* p. 196.

[3] The primary operation here is interpreted as consisting of the sale of government securities to the public and of the use of the proceeds of the borrowing operations for public expenditures. The "respending" on the part of the public is "secondary."

be willing to create new money in consequence of the rise in money rates attending the borrowing operations. They must be willing to buy the government securities "with new money." This implies that the reserve ratios actually maintained must decline in consequence of a rise in interest rates. At the same time it is again true here that the accompanying decline in private investment is the smaller per unit rise of interest rates, the smaller the interest elasticity of private investment is. Effectiveness of this policy presupposes, just as that of policy 1, that the pump-priming effect, reflecting itself in shifts of the relevant function should not be negative; or, if it is negative, that it should not outweigh the positive direct effects. The secondary consumption and investment to which the original increase in income gives rise enters here too into the determination of the aggregate increase in MV, and it enters in the same way (cf. the last paragraph under policy 1).

3a) Open-market purchases of securities from the public or from the commercial banks are the more effective, the less the conditions discussed in connection with policies 1 and 2 are satisfied. The policy now under consideration is based on the assumption that private investment is elastic to interest rates, and that hoarding and bank reserve ratios are not. If hoarding is elastic (or if bank reserve ratios are), interest rates will not decline much under the impact of the policy. If private investment is not elastic, the decline in interest rates will not bring forth much additional investment. The difference between the conditions of effectiveness for this policy, on the one hand, and the policies previously considered, on the other, relates merely to the "primary effect." This is interpreted as including the investments brought about by the decline of interest rates directly attributable to the open-market purchases, but not the respending governed by the marginal propensity to spend. The magnitude of the respending effect per unit of primary increase depends for all policies on the identical circumstances (cf. the last paragraph under policy 1).

It should be added that the raising of required reserve ratios, if carried far enough, possesses the same type of contractionary effect as that possessed by open-market sales. The lowering of required reserve ratios, if effective at all, possesses the same type of expansionary effect as that possessed by open-market purchases. Yet the lowering of required reserve ratios presumably is ineffective as long as all banks possess legal excess reserves.

3b) *The purchase of monetary metals by the central bank from the public* has effects very similar to those of the open-market purchase of securities. The policy in question increases the reserve ratios of the commercial banks in spite of the fact that there exists no indication of an increased demand for liquidity on the part of the banks.[4] There does exist an indication of an increased demand for money on the part of the public that sells the gold, and if banks are the sellers of gold there also exists an indication of an increased demand for liquidity on their part. Yet, if the public sells the gold, the banks simply find themselves with increased reserve ratios which they have not sought. Consequently, the banks must be expected to increase their liabilities. The expansionary effectiveness of this depends on the interest elasticity of private investment and on that of hoarding in the same manner as that in which the effectiveness of open-market purchases (policy 3a) depends on these factors. In both cases it is necessary to take into account the algebraic sign and the magnitude of the pump-priming effect (i.e., of the shifts of the relevant functions), for a final appraisal of the consequences of the policy. It is also necessary to include the secondary rise in consumption and in investment generated by the original increase in income (multiplier effect).

4) *Government expenditures financed by a government bank, or by a central bank supporting the government policy,*[5] are effective regardless of the elasticities so far considered. This policy amounts to the creation of new money by the monetary authority for the purpose of public expenditures. It must result in a net increase of expenditures (regardless of elasticity considerations) unless the pump-priming effect is negative and substantial. The aggregate net

---

[4] This, generally speaking, is true of all instances in which the central bank instructs a commercial bank to credit the account of a private person or institution with an amount. In all these cases, the commercial bank acquires a 100 per cent reserve for that specific deposit and this implies an increase in the average reserve ratio maintained by the bank.

[5] The assumption here is that the central bank is capable of decreasing its reserve ratio.

increase depends on the pump-priming effect and also on the secondary consumption and investment spending generated by the original increase in income. The magnitude of the secondary effect per unit of primary increase depends on the marginal propensity to consume and on elasticity considerations, in the manner indicated in the last paragraph under policy 1 (and applying to all policies considered).

5) *Combinations of policy 1 or of policy 2 with policy 3* amount to the application of policy 4 in a roundabout way. If the government, or if the central bank, buys securities from the public or from the commercial banks, and if this policy is supplemented by government borrowing from the public or from the banks, then the monetary authority provides additional liquidity to groups from which the government borrows the amounts thus provided. The same is true if the government buys gold from the public and if simultaneously it borrows from the banks. In this case, too, a group of potential lenders, namely the commercial banking system, finds itself with additional liquidity which is tapped by the Treasury. The difference between direct government borrowing from the central banks and the indirect method in question is immaterial so far as expansionary effects are concerned, unless the psychological effect on investors (i.e., the pump-priming effect) should be different. The pump-priming effect might in certain cases be different, but this question will be considered later. What matters here is that the elasticity of the L function and of the I function cease to be determinants of the primary[6] consequences of the expansionary policy if the policy resorts to direct borrowing from the central bank, or alternatively, if it resorts to such a combination of policies 1 or 2 with policy 3 as results in indirect borrowing from the central bank. This is emphasized here because it will be maintained presently that such a combination of policies actually was characteristic of monetary developments during the 1930's.

In case the public, including the banking system, is thoroughly convinced that government securities are free from any risk of de-

---

[6] The qualifying adjective "primary" expresses here the fact that elasticity considerations do enter into the determination of the responding effect (multiplier effect in Angell's sense).

fault whatsoever, the sale of securities with a guaranteed constant capital value also should be regarded as a case of deficit financing through the government itself. Assuming zero default risk and a constant capital value, the securities come very close to being perfect substitutes for money because it is almost correct to say that any amount of such securities is salable for money at a discount that merely expresses the costs and the inconvenience of handling security portfolios as compared with the costs and the inconvenience of handling check deposits. The only qualification is that the costs and the inconvenience might be evaluated somewhat differently by different groups of persons. This qualification is quite unimportant, and, consequently, the government may in this case be interpreted as issuing (perfect substitutes for) money in order to finance its own expenditures. The policy belongs in the same category as that of deficit financing through a government bank or through the central bank.

Expansionary monetary policies are adopted on the assumption that otherwise saving would exceed investment at high levels of employment, with the result that hoarding would occur until income and employment have declined to lower levels. Of the policies surveyed in the preceding pages, 2, 4, and 5 aim at offsetting the decline in velocity (hoarding) at high levels of employment, by increasing the stock of money. Policy 1 aims at preventing the decline in MV at high levels of employment, by absorbing the idle balances, which tend to accumulate, and by transforming them into active balances. Policies 3*a* and 3*b* aim at creating a situation in which there ceases to exist a tendency to hoard at high levels of employment.

The Problem of the Impasse: Expansionary and Counterinflationary Policies

The reasoning leads to the realization of the possibility of an impasse that is different in character from the so-called Keynesian impasse. The Keynsian impasse rests on the notion that open-market policies are incapable of lowering interest rates below a certain level because the L function supposedly becomes very elastic as rates decline. Consequently, open-market purchases result in a substantial increase of idle balances (or, if the securities are bought from commercial banks, in a substantial increase of excess reserves). In the limiting case of a perfectly elastic L function, they result exclusively in increased liquidity provisions at unchanging interest rates, rather than in increased private investment at declining interest rates. In this event, deficit financing by borrowing from the public or from the commercial banks should be highly effective, as was pointed out under policies 1 and 2. This is because the borrowing operations of the Treasury result in a substantial decrease of idle balances (or, if the securities are sold to commercial banks, in a substantial decrease in the reserve ratios actually maintained). In the limiting case of a perfectly elastic L function, they result exclusively in reduced liquidity provisions at unchanging interest rates rather than in reduced private investment at rising rates. In spite of the effectiveness of this policy the Keynesian assumptions establish an impasse, so far as private investment is concerned, because on these assumptions aggregate investment can be increased to a level corresponding to full employment only by means of investments undertaken by the government.

The specific difficulty to which the Keynesian reasoning points is unlikely to exist if the hoarding of the public and the liquidity provisions of the banks are mainly of the precautionary variety (contingency hoarding). Assuming that liquidity provisions are predominantly of this variety, and that these provisions possess little sensitiveness to interest, it may be concluded that open-market policies are effective means of lowering interest rates. The open-market purchases result in increased private investment at declining interest rates rather than in substantially increased liquidity provisions. On the other hand, on these assumptions, borrowing from the public or from the commercial banks does not result in any significant decline in hoarding or in the creation of new money at any significant rate. In the event of borrowing from the public or from the banks, the rise of interest rates attending the sale of additional government securities is the only change from which a reduction of liquidity provisions could be expected. Yet the rise of interest rates will not produce a reduction of liquidity provisions if these provisions are insensitive to interest rates. Instead of producing a reduction of liquidity provisions, it will produce a reduction of private investment. Consequently, borrowing from the public or from the commercial banks for government expenditures results mainly in the substitution of government spending for private spending, whereas open-market purchases do have the beneficial effect of lowering interest rates and of thereby raising the level of private investment.

However, the decline in interest rates brought about by open-market purchases may be insufficient to raise private investment to a rate corresponding to a high level of employment. The intersection of the I curve with the abscissa in figure 22, may occur at a point expressing a rate of investment which, given the consumption function, is too small to create a high level of employment. This may be expressed by saying that chronic depressions may well be characterized by the simultaneous occurrence of the following two facts: (1) the elasticity of the L function is too small to render reasonably successful such deficit-financing operations as are carried out by borrowing from the public or from the commercial banks; (2) the elasticity of private investment with respect to interest rates is too small to render open-market purchases reasonably successful. In a situation characterized by both these facts open-market operations are effective in lowering interest rates and this does result in some increase of private investment. The increase in private investment, however, is insufficient to reduce unemployment to a moderate level, provided it is impossible to establish negative rates on money loans. If the liquidity provisions of the public and of the commercial banks are mainly of the contingency variety, the elasticity of the L function is not likely to be high. Furthermore, if it is correct to assume that long-period stagnation of investment should not typically be attributed to high interest cost, the intersection of the I curve with the abscissa does not in these periods mark a high level of investment. In these circumstances an impasse arises which, in contrast to the Keynesian impasse, is not a consequence of the flattening out of the hoarding function. The impasse in question is a consequence of the simultaneous insufficiency of two elasticities, namely, of the elasticity of liquidity provisions with respect to interest rates and of the elasticity of private investment with respect to the same variable.

This impasse differs from that considered by Keynes not merely as concerns the analytical explanation. A difference consists also in that the simultaneous insufficiency of both elasticities renders unsuccessful such deficit-financing operations as are carried out through borrowing from the public or from the commercial banks. These operations should be successful if the difficulties faced by monetary policy in periods of stagnation were caused by the high elasticity of liquidity provisions to interest. The difficulties caused by highly elastic L functions reduce the effectiveness of open-market purchases but they do not apply to borrowing from the public or from commercial banks. The difficulties arising from inelastic liquidity provisions and from insufficiently elastic private investment apply to both these policies.

Even this impasse does not extend to deficit financing by borrowing from central banks, or from government banks (policy 4). Nor does it extend to deficit financing by the outright issuance of banknotes (or of government securities with guaranteed constant capital value, assuming that the default risk attached to these is commonly considered zero). Finally, the impasse also does not extend to combinations of policies possessing the net effect of borrowing from central banks for government expenditures (policy 5). In these cases the central bank provides the excess liquidity which the government taps. The government borrows indirectly from the central bank and a rise in MV by the full amount of the deficit-financing operation must ensue, unless the indirect repercussions of the process result in an adverse effect on private investment (in a negative pump-priming effect). Moreover, unless the original stimulus is completely offset by a negative pump-priming effect, the consumption generated by the original government investment gives rise to further ("secondary") additions to income. Yet the "impasse" considered here is more comprehensive than the Keynesian impasse because it extends to such varieties of deficit financing as are unaffected by the Keynesian impasse.

Does a similar impasse apply to policies aimed at counteracting inflation? As long as inflationary developments require the creation of new money it is always possible, although it is not always politically feasible, to counteract them by methods of credit policy. Raising interest rates to high levels may not always of itself prevent inflationary borrowing because the expectation of a further rise of interest rates may be created and, in the short run, such expectations increase the inducement to borrow. But, "in principle," it is always possible to manipulate reserve requirements so as to force the banks to ration credit and thereby to abstain from the creation of new money. This presupposes the existence of legal reserve requirements and the unlimited power of the central bank to change them—a highly desirable reform, so far as the United States is concerned. The main reason why preventing the creation of new money may sometimes not be politically feasible is that it leads to a sharp decline in bond prices, and important segments of the economy are interested in the maintenance of the bond market. It is true that, when bond prices in general decline, the bond holdings of the credit institutions could be exchanged for special types of securities with unchanging and guaranteed capital values. The inflationary consequences of the guarantees could be precluded either by adjusting reserve requirements or by requiring the maintenance of bond reserves. But in substance this would amount to freezing the bond holdings of the credit institutions and to bringing about a decline in other bond values, whereas the Treasury, if it wants to keep the door open toward a later resumption of deficit-financing operations, may be interested in keeping bond holdings liquid. (This obstacle would, of course, be eliminated if borrowing from the central bank were envisaged for the future.) In war periods, and generally speaking in emergencies during which the Treasury is forced into spending more than what a politically feasible tax structure will yield, there of course exist even stronger reasons why counterinflationary credit policies are not adopted in the appropriate measure. It still remains true, however, that it is possible to describe methods of credit policy by which inflation could be prevented, assuming that inflationary developments require the creation of new money. In principle, the banks can always be forced into rationing credit.

Yet if a significant amount of idle balances exists and the public tends to dishoard these suddenly—as may happen if policies 2, 4, or 5 have previously been adopted on a large scale, either to maintain employment or to finance a war—inflation might develop without the creation of new money. In this event it may be impossible even "in principle" to describe a monetary policy that would preclude a sudden and significant rise in the price level.[7] The dishoarded balances could be sterilized only if they could be absorbed by the sale of new government bonds. The government would then be in a position to hoard the balances which the public dishoarded. But it cannot be taken for granted that the public can always be induced to dishoard into bonds rather than into goods. An attempt to induce the public to buy bonds rather than goods for the money it dishoards, implies that bond prices are reduced sharply and suddenly. If commodity prices are expected to rise sharply and at the same time a significant decline in bond prices is expected, it may be impossible to absorb the funds dishoarded by selling bonds at reduced prices. It is likely that, within a wide range of possible bond prices, reductions of the price would produce the expectation of further reductions. Therefore, the funds dishoarded by the public may flow into the commodity markets, regardless of how far bond prices are reduced. It seems unlikely that government bonds could be made attractive to the public "in the short run" by having the owners of old bonds suffer significant capital losses.

It has been maintained that the appropriate credit policies could always prevent inflationary developments, although they could not always put an end to a depression. As has been shown, such a statement should be qualified because if the public tends to dishoard significant idle balances, credit restrictions and rising interest rates may be ineffective means of precluding inflation. For this reason an impasse may develop not merely for expansionary credit policies, but also for credit policies aimed at precluding an inflationary spiral.

The question of how the "inflationary" and "deflationary" developments that are to be counteracted should be defined, cannot be answered with general validity. The answer depends on whether more stability (in output and employment) can be expected from the one or the other set of circumstances at which it is possible to aim. Preventing significant changes in the general price level means something different from preventing significant changes in money

---

[7] Except, of course, by freezing money stocks.

earnings per unit of real input, unless productivity remains unchanged. Given the secular rise in productivity, the pressure for
wage increases, and the resistance to price reductions, it would seem
that, normally, a policy directed at a stable general price level has a
better chance to secure "economic stability" in the relevant sense
than does a policy directed at stable money income rates. Such a
policy would aim at having money income rates, including wage
rates, rise secularly with the increase in over-all productivity. However, constancy of the general price level must not be considered an
axiom, and rigid devices of accomplishing a constant price level
could scarcely be justified.

CREDIT POLICIES AND SUBSIDY PROGRAMS

In earlier sections of this volume it was suggested that credit policies
at positive rates should be regarded as being qualitatively different
from "credit policies at negative rates" which in reality are subsidization policies. Only, if this distinction is made, can it be maintained—as it is—that easy credit may be insufficient to overcome
deflationary influences.

The difference between the character of credit policies and subsidy policies—that is, between credit policies at positive and at
negative money rates—is especially marked if the credit policies in
the usual sense which are compared with subsidization plans, are
limited to transactions in government securities. The subsidization
policies differ in this case qualitatively from the credit policies at
positive rates not merely because of the basic difference between
credit conditions and the conditions on which subsidies could be
granted. In addition, there exists the difference that the monetary
authority must grant the subsidies to *private business* in order to
establish negative rates, whereas in the case considered here the
credits in the usual sense (i.e., the credits at positive rates) are
granted by means of purchasing *government securities*. The monetary authority is in no position to establish negative rates to business
by giving credits to the government at negative rates, that is, by
subsidizing the government. To have the central bank grant credits
to the government at negative rates would serve no useful purpose.
Such a policy would not induce private lenders to subsidize private

borrowers as long as it is certain that money stocks retain their nominal value. The establishment of "negative rates" implies the direct subsidization of private investors (or possibly of their creditors) by the monetary authority itself. Reducing or raising interest rates to private business, within the positive range, does not, however, necessarily imply buying or selling private securities. By dealing in government securities the monetary authority exerts a pressure on the entire interest structure in the one direction or the other. If the yields from government securities rise, yields from other securities also tend to increase (or, at least, to decline by less than would otherwise be the case) and the analogous statement is true of a decline in yields from government securities. This, however, is subject to the qualification that rates on business loans will not tend to decline below a positive level expressing the bare risk premium, even if the yields from government securities are lowered successfully to the zero level or below it, assuming that hoarded money retains its nominal value.[8]

Yet, the effect of dealings in government securities on business credit is obviously indirect. After a change in the yields from government securities, the automatic restoration of the previous differentials within the structure of interest rates may take time (although there is no reason to assume that the process should induce a permanent change in the relative appraisal of different types of securities). The time lag in question could be avoided only if the monetary authority extended its open-market transactions to long-

---

[8] Legal arrangements resulting in a continuous decrease over time of the nominal value of any given banknote, coin, and deposit (i.e., stamped money schemes extended to deposits) would automatically establish negative rates. Yet it is very questionable whether business activity would be stimulated by such arrangements. Hoarding would doubtless be discouraged. But borrowing from banks for investment might also be strongly discouraged because the legal arrangement under consideration would tax profits heavily in case the profits are hoarded. Profits that lose their value if hoarded seem to be worth less *ex ante* than profits that retain their value even if not reinvested (i.e., even if hoarded). Consequently M might decrease in a higher proportion than that in which V increases. (Cf. G. L. S. Shackle's review of A. Dahlberg: "When Capital Goes on Strike," *Economic Journal*, September, 1938). Moreover, if a stimulus is produced, it would have to come through continuously rising prices, that is by an inflationary process. The mere fact that money loses its nominal value gradually, makes the holding of goods more profitable in relation to the holding of money, but it does not make the production of goods more profitable in relation to the holding of goods. Production will be stimulated only if prices start rising owing to the increased demand for goods by hoarders.

term business securities. This, at the same time, is the only method by which the rates on business loans could be lowered below the positive level expressing the risk premium.

In reality, the credit policies of the monetary authority are usually limited to dealings in governments so far as long-term securities are concerned. As concerns short-term paper, they are usually limited to dealings in government securities and in some practically riskless private securities. Consequently, the effect of these policies on the most important varieties of business credit is indirect.

Extending the scope of open-market operations to a broad range of private securities would, however, create difficulties which are partly similar to those arising in connection with subsidy programs. There still would remain a substantial difference between these extended credit policies at positive rates on the one hand, and credit policies at negative rates (subsidies) on the other. This difference would still warrant regarding these two types of policy as qualitatively distinct. Extension of the open-market policies to risky securities (i.e., to business credit in a general sense) would not require the "additional output" clauses or "additional employment" clauses that would have to enter into subsidy contracts. But such an extension of the scope of credit policies would necessitate a considerable degree of discrimination between potential private borrowers. The "principles" on which central bank credit is granted are simple and they do not tend to become objects of pressure politics so long as long-term dealings are limited to governments, and short-term dealings are limited to governments and to bankers' acceptances. It would be exceedingly difficult to describe the so-called principles on which the monetary authority might elect risky private securities, and might grant business credit to certain firms, except if these dealings were limited to a comparatively small volume of issues highly placed on the scale of political preferences. The procedure of the monetary authority would have to be very arbitrary and it would lend itself readily as an object of pressure politics. The "extended" credit policies at positive rates would share this feature with subsidy plans (or with "credit policies" at negative rates). Therefore, credit policies extended to risky loans would differ less substantially from subsidy policies than do the actual credit policies of central banks, although there would still exist a considerable difference. It would still remain true that subsidies could be granted only on quite specific conditions concerning the additional output to be produced by private firms and that these conditions could not be based on theoretically valid calculations. Credit, however, could always be given against "security" on condition that it be repaid.

Experience with easy-money policies does not of itself prove the thesis that it takes more than lowering interest rates to keep employment permanently high. Yields from long-term governments have never been lowered in the neighborhood of the zero level and monetary authorities have not included private long-term securities in the scope of their operations on any substantial scale. Yet most experienced persons would probably not subscribe to the opinion that further reductions of interest rates in stagnant periods would have increased the aggregate rate of investment by a significant margin. At the same time it would be very difficult to establish a statistical relationship between investment and interest rates *ceteris paribus.* In consequence of the high degree of intercorrelation between the relevant variables, the statistical series typically show a tendency of both investment and interest rates to rise under improved expectations and to decline in periods of contraction.

INTEREST RATES AND THE BUSINESS CYCLE

For a period of considerable length preceding the First World War, Frederick R. Macaulay has found that short-term rates tended to lag behind the physical volume of production, and that long-term rates tended to lag behind short-term rates in the cyclical process.[9] For a decade preceding the first war, a lag of interest rate turning points behind pig-iron production turning points can also be read from diagrams published in Warren S. Person's study concerning the construction of the Harvard Index of Business Conditions.[10] Inspec-

---

[9] Frederick R. Macaulay, *The Movements of Interest Rates, Bond Yields and Stock Prices in the United States Since 1856* (New York, National Bureau of Economic Research, 1938), cf. chap. vii in general, and p. 221 in particular.

[10] However, the bond yields included in Person's study (railroad bonds) do not lag behind short-term rates. Cf. Warren M. Person's, "Indices of Business Conditions," *Review of Economic Statistics,* I (1919), 88–89. And *idem,* "A Non-Technical Explanation of the Index of General Business Conditions," *Review of Economic Statistics,* II (1920) 42–43.

tion of these diagrams shows that establishment of the lag of interest rates behind pig-iron production does not require any trend-elimination techniques of doubtful logical validity. The trend for the decade in question was not powerful enough to wipe out the turning points from the unmanipulated series. These are readily discernible even if the trend is not eliminated. The proposition that output and interest rates tend to move in the same direction, with a lag of the latter behind the former, is consistent with the notion that changes in interest rates may have belonged among the factors instrumental in bringing about turning points. The lag implies that interest rates still rose when the downturns occurred and that they still declined when upturns took place. Yet, generally speaking, interest rates and pig-iron production show a tendency to move in the same direction and such a tendency can also be established for interest rates and other important constituents of output. This, of course, means that the character of the observable relationship is different from that of causal relationship from rates to output.

For the period following the "postwar depression," of 1920–1921, even the foregoing lead-lag propositions must be qualified. Throughout the 1920's short-term rates continue to rise in expansion and to decline in contraction, and they tend to lag behind industrial production (although there exists no complete consistency in this respect). The same statement concerning the general tendency toward lagging is true also of long-term rates during the 1920's, for such turning points as are discernible at all in the long-term rate series. Yet, unless highly arbitrary trend-elimination techniques are applied, only the upper turning points of 1923 and 1929, and the lower turning points of 1928 are clearly discernible for bond yields. The lower turning point of 1924 and the upper turning point of 1927 are not discernible because the general downward trend of the series dominates their movement. In the 1930's both the long-term and the short-term series are dominated by the downward drift so that the lower turning point after the depression of 1929–1933 is not discernible. Immediately preceding the cyclical peak of 1937 there occurred a slight contra-trend upward movement of bond yields[11]

---

[11] For the yields on government bonds the upward movement was small enough to be comparable with the minor oscillations that occurred in the preceding years on various occasions.

and also of some short-term rates, but with the downturn of business activity interest rates also declined. On this downturn, rates on Treasury bills, rates on government bonds, and rates on comparatively riskless corporate bonds led industrial production, national income, and investment, whereas rates on more risky bonds lagged behind these magnitudes.

The experience for the period prior to the First World War and for the period lying between the two wars, might therefore be summarized as follows: (1) there existed a tendency for interest rates to move in the same direction as that in which output moved, except for subperiods in which the interest-rate series were entirely dominated by their own secular trends; (2) in the period preceding the First World War interest rates lagged consistently behind pig-iron production both on upturns and on downturns; in the period between the two world wars they tended to lag behind industrial production but this tendency was not quite consistent. Such a situation makes it very difficult to evaluate the quantitative significance of interest-rate movements in producing movements of output. It can at best be said that the leads and lags in the period preceding the First World War, and also some of the leads and lags of the interwar period, were not inconsistent with the assumption that interest-rate movements were contributing factors in producing turning points.

INDIRECT BORROWING FROM THE CENTRAL BANKING SYSTEM IN THE 1930's

It would also be very difficult to lend plausibility to the assumption that the elasticity of hoarding to interest rates is sufficiently dependable to warrant basing monetary policies on this factor. Before turning to this problem it might be advisable to call to the reader's attention that the "monetary experiment" of the 1930's was not in fact based on the interest elasticity of liquidity provisions. It is not possible to interpret monetary developments of the post-depression period as tests of the efficiency of policies 1, 2, or 3 of the classification given on pages 174–180. The policies adopted in the period under consideration are characterized by the fact that the borrowing operations of the government from commercial banks were consistently outweighed by the purchase of gold. This should be understood to mean that gold purchases provided excess bank liquidity which was but partly absorbed by the government through the sale of new securities to banks. The combined operations of the monetary authority and of the Treasury had substantially the same effect as that which would have been produced by direct borrowing from the Federal Reserve banks for public expenditures. The difference of course is that borrowing from the Federal Reserve banks might have been rendered practically free of costs by the issuance of noninterest-bearing securities, or by regulating the profits of the Federal Reserve banks in some appropriate fashion.[12] The gold stock, on the other hand, does not yield any income that could be set against the costs of the borrowing operations of the Treasury. Yet, aside from this, there exists no difference between the policy of borrowing directly from the Federal Reserve and the policy of borrowing from lenders who simultaneously acquire excess liquidity by selling gold to the Federal Reserve. To use the terminology employed in the foregoing analysis, policy 5 is identical with policy 4 in significant respects (cf. above, pp. 178–179). The "primary" effectiveness of these policies does not depend on the interest elasticity of liquidity provisions or on that of private investment (although these elasticities enter into the determination of the magnitude of the "secondary" or "responding" effect).

The borrowing from the commercial banks during the period lying between the depression and the outbreak of the Second World War was undoubtedly outweighed by the gold purchases. In other words, the increase in bank-reserve ratios brought about by the gold purchases was considerably greater than the diminution in reserve ratios brought about by the borrowing operations of the Treasury. Consequently, the deficit financing was in the nature of policy 5 rather than policy 2; and the margin by which the gold purchases "outweighed" the Treasury borrowing left a residual in the nature of policy 3b. This is shown in table 7.

[12] Until 1933 the profits of the Federal Reserve banks in excess of a 6 per cent cumulative dividend on the capital stock plus certain additions to the surplus had to be paid to the Treasury. Along these lines it would be possible to render borrowing operations from the Federal Reserve banks entirely free of cost. At present the profits in excess of a 6 per cent cumulative dividend are added to a surplus account which cannot be distributed to the stockholders. In the event of liquidation, such parts of the surplus as are not required for specified purposes belong to the Treasury.

Column 1 of the table (R/D) contains the ratio of member bank reserve balances plus cash in vault to member bank deposits.[13] Columns 2 and 3 of the table ($\triangle$G and $\triangle$S, respectively) show the increase in the holdings of gold certificates,[14] and the increase in

TABLE 7

EFFECT OF GOLD INFLUX AND GOVERNMENT BORROWING ON MEMBER BANK LIQUIDITY RATIOS*

Year	R/D	$\triangle$G	$\triangle$S	Change in R/D from gold influx alone, *c.p.*†	Change in R/D from gold influx and borrowing, *c.p.*	Actual change in R/D
	1	2	3	4	5	6
1933 I........	12.6	....	....	....	....	....
II.......	14.4	26	367	0.1	−0.1	1.8
1934 I........	17.2	1239	2159	4.6	2.9	2.8
II.......	17.6	335	1482	1.1	0.0	0.4
1935 I........	19.5	1060	535	3.2	2.8	1.9
II.......	21.0	1368	838	3.7	3.1	1.5
1936 I........	19.9	548	1404	1.4	0.4	−1.1
II.......	21.9	746	−127	1.8	1.9	2.0
1937 I........	22.7	−19	−856	−0.1	0.5	0.8
II.......	23.4	283	−317	0.7	0.9	0.7
1938 I........	26.6	1516	−29	3.4	3.4	3.2
II.......	27.4	1153	879	2.5	1.8	0.8
1939 I........	30.0	1726	555	3.5	3.0	2.6
II.......	32.7	1685	551	3.1	2.6	2.7
Entire period....	....	11666	7441	31.2	23.1	20.1

* Data from *Twenty-fourth Annual Report of the Federal Reserve System* (Washington, D.C., 1938), table 52, pp. 112–114, for reserves, deposits, and United States government obligations, 1933–1937; *Federal Reserve Bulletin*, for later figures. U. S. Bureau of Foreign Commerce, *Survey of Current Business, Annual Supplement*, 1936, p. 45; 1938, p. 54; and 1940, p. 49, for gold certificates held by Federal Reserve banks.
† *ceteris paribus.*

government security holdings[15] of member banks respectively. The changes indicated in columns 2 (gold certificates) and 3 (government security holdings of member banks) relate to the period *ending* at the date in the line of which the figures of columns 2 and 3 appear and beginning at the preceding date. The data for gold certificates (column 2) relate to June 30, and December 31, precisely; the data

[13] Demand deposits adjusted plus time deposits plus United States government deposits.
[14] On hand and due from Treasury to Federal Reserve banks.
[15] Member bank holdings of direct and fully guaranteed Federal securities.

of the other columns relate to the call dates nearest the end of the first half and of the second half of each calendar year, the divergences from June 30, and December 31, being small wherever they occur.

Column 4 "isolates" the effect of the gold inflow on the ratio R/D, in the following sense: the column contains that hypothetical increase in the ratio R/D which would have occurred, from the preceding date to the date in question, if merely the stock of gold certificates had changed in the manner in which it actually changed, but all other factors influencing the magnitude of deposits and that of reserves had remained unchanged.[16]

The figures of column 5 are of the same character as those of column 4, with the exception that they isolate the combined effect on the ratio R/D of the gold inflow plus the borrowing from member banks by the Treasury for simultaneous public expenditure. In other words, the figures of column 5 express the hypothetical increase in the ratio R/D which would have occurred if the stock of gold certificates had changed in the manner in which it actually changed, *and* if the member bank holdings of government securities had also changed in the manner in which they actually changed (but if all other deposits and reserve influencing factors had remained unchanged).[17]

Column 6 contains the actual change in the ratio R/D from the preceding date to the date in question.

---

[16] Let R_{n-1} and R stand for the reserves (including cash in vault) at the preceding date and at the "present" date, respectively; let D_{n-1} and D_n stand for total member bank deposits at these two dates, and G_{n-1} and G_n for the stock of gold certificates at the same dates; then the figure appearing in column 4 is defined as:

$$\frac{R_{n-1} + (G_n - G_{n-1})}{D_{n-1} + (G_n - G_{n-1})} - \frac{R_{n-1}}{D_{n-1}}$$

The formula reflects that *ceteris paribus* the gold inflow increases reserves and deposits by the same amount and therefore increases liquidity ratios.

[17] Using the symbols previously employed and, in addition, letting S_{n-1} and S_n stand for the member bank holdings of direct and fully guaranteed government securities at the two dates, the figures appearing in column 5 are defined as:

$$\frac{R_{n-1} + (G_n - G_{n-1})}{D_{n-1} + (G_n - G_{n-1}) + (S_n - S_{n-1})} - \frac{R_{n-1}}{D_{n-1}}$$

The formula expresses that, whereas *ceteris paribus* the gold increases reserves and deposits by the identical amount, the borrowing from banks only increases deposits. This implies that the Treasury spends the money it borrows "simultaneously." Failure to do so is implicitly regarded as one of the "other deposit and reserve influencing factors."

Below the figures relating to the last call dates (i.e., at the bottom of the table) are the figures relating to the change over the total period extending from the first to the last call date indicated in the table. For columns 4 and 5 these figures are not "additive."[18]

The most obvious conclusion from the table is this: the increase in the ratio of reserves to deposits that *ceteris paribus* would have been brought about by the gold influx alone was absorbed only to a small extent by the borrowing operations of the Treasury. During the period as a whole, the ratio of reserves (including vault cash) to total deposits would have increased by 31.2 per cent under the impact of the gold influx alone, as is indicated by the last (lowest) figure in column 4 of table 7. This means that the gold influx alone would have raised the reserve-deposit ratio in question from 12.6 per cent (cf. top figure in column 1) to 43.8 per cent, that is, by the 31.2 per cent mentioned above[19]—provided that all other deposit and reserve influencing factors had remained unchanged during the entire period to which the table relates. The government borrowing from member banks, considered by itself, would have *reduced the increase* of the reserve-deposit ratio in question merely from 31.2 per cent to 23.1 per cent, as is indicated by the last figure in column 5. In other words, if merely the gold influx *and* the borrowing from member banks had taken place *ceteris paribus*,[20] the ratio in question would have increased from 12.6 per cent to 35.7 per cent, that is, by 23.1 per cent. Actually the increase was from 12.6 per cent to 32.7 per cent, that is, by 20.1 per cent (cf. the last figures in column 1 and in column 6, respectively). Starting from the hypothetical condition in which the gold influx would have been the only factor producing a change in the ratio of reserves to deposits,[21] it may therefore be stated that, in consequence of the borrowing from member banks, the ratio of reserves (including vault cash) to total deposits increased by 23.1 per cent instead of by 31.2 per cent and that in

---

[18] That is, they cannot be derived for the period as a whole by adding up the hypothetical changes in reserve ratios during the subperiods because the hypothetical change is calculated each time from the actual reserve ratio of the beginning date *of that subperiod*.

[19] This is *not* 31.2 per cent of the 12.6 per cent, but 31.2 absolute per cent.

[20] That is, if the other deposit and gold influencing factors had remained unchanged.

[21] In which case the ratio of member bank reserves plus vault cash to total number bank deposits would have risen by 31.2 per cent (i.e., from 12.6 per cent to 43.8 per cent).

consequence of further deposit and reserve influencing factors, the actual increase of the ratio in question turned out to be 20.1 per cent. The borrowing from member banks absorbed but a small part of the increased liquidity provided by the gold influx.

It should be remembered that the actual increase of the reserve-deposit ratio considered here does not express a rise of liquidity ratios in any uniquely relevant sense. Nevertheless, it seems preferable to express the change in the cash reserve position of the member banks by the change in some ratio such as that employed above (R/D) than by the change in legal excess reserves. The existence of legal excess reserves does not necessarily indicate excess liquidity in the economically relevant sense. Moreover, changes in excess reserves may be a consequence of changes in reserve requirements as well as of changes in reserve ratios actually maintained. In fact, the rise of the ratio expressed in column 1 of table 7 does not adequately measure the rise in excess reserves during the period. This is true for several reasons. Not only have required reserve ratios been repeatedly changed during the period but, although both demand and time deposits rose, the ratio of demand deposits to time deposits shifted considerably in favor of the former. Consequently, an increase in the ratio of total reserve balances (not including vault cash) to total deposits would have been called for even if required reserve ratios had remained unchanged. Yet the actual rise in the ratio of total reserves to total deposits was of course much greater than would have been required in consequence of this factor. Legal excess reserves therefore accumulated rapidly, except in the subperiod in which required reserve ratios were deliberately raised in order to diminish excess reserves (i.e., during the year preceding the downturn of 1937).

During the period as a whole merely a fraction of the additional liquidity provided by the gold influx was absorbed by borrowing from member banks. The reader will notice that what has been found characteristic of the period as a whole, also characterizes much the greater part of the single half-yearly subperiods distinguished in the table, provided that the subperiods in which borrowing from banks was negative are disregarded. Negative figures for borrowing from banks reflect the circumstance that in the subperiod in question the aggregate of member banks decreased its stock of government securities. This occurred from the second half of 1936 through the first half of 1938 (cf. the negative figures in table 7, column 3). With respect to the four half-yearly intervals of which this span consists, it is of course meaningless to ask the question of the relationship between the excess liquidity provided by the gold influx and the liquidity absorbed by the borrowing: in these subperiods there did not occur any borrowing from member banks (on balance). Of the remaining nine subperiods, it is true, with perhaps two exceptions, that the borrowing from banks absorbed but a small part of the increase in the reserve-deposit ratio which would have been produced by the gold influx alone. In other words, typically the increase expressed in column 5 amounts to a substantial proportion of the increase expressed in column 4. The span during which the banks decreased their holdings of government securities extended but slightly beyond the period in which (1) the inflowing gold was sterilized so that the rise in reserve ratios attributable to the gold was unusually small; and (2) required reserve ratios were being increased so as to enforce contractionary banking policies.

Although it is rarely possible to read "experience" from economic statistics in any conclusive fashion, the "suggestion" of the available figures nevertheless is that the policy of borrowing from banks for public expenditures probably did have expansionary effects. The period covered by table 7 was a period of recovery, interrupted by a depression to which the discontinuation of the borrowing policies may well have contributed. The figures expressing the borrowing operations from member banks (column 3) turn from strongly positive to slightly negative in the second half of 1936 and from slightly negative to strongly negative in the first half of 1937. In the second half of 1938 the cyclical upturn roughly coincides with the reappearance of positive figures for borrowing from banks, and the figure in question is but slightly negative in the preceding half-yearly period. The cycle may be said to follow the development of the borrowing operations with a lag. Certain other relationships may also be historically "suggested," in a similar fashion. The period immediately preceding the downturn of 1937 was not merely one in which contractionary monetary policies were applied but it also was a period of important labor trouble. Yet, a comparison of the figures of table 7 with cyclical developments may be said to "suggest" a relationship between expansionary monetary policies and output.

In fact, a priori analysis leads to the conclusion that the financing of public expenditures by the central bank must possess expansionary effectiveness, provided that the psychological repercussions are either favorable or not sufficiently adverse to offset the primary effect. The data of table 7 indicate that the policies of the period should be interpreted as representing indirect financing through the central bank which, in connection with the gold influx, supplied to member banks the additional liquidity tapped by the Treasury. Yet, the fact that this indirect financing arose must be attributed to something in the nature of a "historical accident." Had the government merely borrowed from the banks and had capital not, at the same time, been transferred from Europe to the United States on an unprecedented scale in the form of gold (rather than commodities), the effectiveness of the borrowing policies would have depended largely on the elasticity of liquidity provisions and of private investment to interest rates. In this event, the borrowing operations from commercial banks for public expenditures would not have had significant expansionary consequences, unless the elasticity of liquidity provisions with respect to interest rates should have proved considerable, and the elasticity of private investment with respect to interest rates should have proved comparatively small. It is not, generally speaking, safe to make these assumptions. The problem of the effectiveness of deficit financing on *ceteris paribus* assumptions is very much different from the problem of deficit financing on the assumption that the Treasury operations are coupled with buying operations of the central bank. Elasticity considerations enter significantly in the first of these two problems, whereas they do not enter in the second. In the 1930's deficit financing was coupled with large-scale gold-buying operations of the Federal Reserve System, but these operations occurred because of the entirely abnormal demand for capital transfers from Europe to America and because of the failure of this transfer to give rise to an import surplus.

It follows that the monetary policies of the 1930's cannot be repeated simply by borrowing from banks for public expenditures.

They can be repeated only if a substitute is found for the gold purchases. The necessity of adopting expansionary fiscal policies would require finding such a substitute. The open-market purchase of securities by the Federal Reserve banks could serve as such a substitute. Moreover, if securities, instead of gold, were purchased "with the right hand" while the "left hand" borrowed, the costs of the borrowing would be partly or wholly offset by the yield of the assets purchased, so that even the internal transfer problem usually arising in connection with the growth of the public debt could be partly or wholly eliminated.[22] At the same time, it might become obvious to the general public that the deficit is being financed indirectly by the central bank. This might pave the way toward direct financing by the Federal Reserve banks because it might help to overcome the prejudice that direct borrowing from the central banks is "inflationary" in any sense other than that in which the government attempts to adopt expansionary (or reflationary) policies, when combatting depression tendencies. Direct borrowing could, of course, easily be rendered free of cost.[23] It could even assume simply the form of the issuance of noninterest-bearing securities. In other words, consistent coupling of open-market purchases with deficit financing might be necessary in periods that really call for deficit financing and it might even gradually lead to a policy of issuing money by direct borrowing whenever monetary expansion is desirable and of "selling securities" to the public or to the banks (and of keeping the proceeds idle) merely when monetary contraction is required.[24] But the problem of techniques is less important than the fact that deficit financing is subject to serious limitations unless the additional funds come directly or indirectly from the central

[22] Provided the additional income of the Federal Reserve banks is conducted back to the Treasury. If the costs of the borrowing are wholly offset by the yield of the assets purchased—that is, if the Federal Reserve buys as many securities as the government sells—the expansionary effect exceeds that of the deficit financing proper because, in addition, excess reserves are created. (This ceases to be true only if 100 per cent reserves are required on marginal deposits.) The additional expansionary effect usually is desirable in periods of deficit financing, except if the deficit financing itself is undesirable (i.e., except if it is merely a consequence of the political impossibility of taxing adequately). In the 1930's the gold influx also gave rise to such an additional expansionary effect.

[23] Cf. above, p. 192, n. 12.

[24] Cf. Henry C. Simons, "On Debt Policy," *Journal of Political Economy* (December, 1944).

bank. In the recovery period of the 1930's they came indirectly, by means of the gold inflow.

The factual analysis has so far been limited to the borrowing operations of the Treasury from member banks. For nonmember banks, and for the (nonbanking) public, qualitatively analogous statements could be made; yet since the analogous quantitative analysis cannot be carried out, these statements must be vague. The gold influx increased primarily the reserve ratios of the member banks, but it must be assumed that the liquidity thus created spread partly over the entire banking system. It is impossible to show, however, what the quantitative effect of this spreading was on the liquidity ratios of nonmember banks and how this effect compares with the opposite effects of the borrowing from nonmember banks. As for the public, the same historical accident as that which resulted in the gold influx undoubtedly also created a market for newly floated securities. The decision to convert overseas assets into American assets may partly have been a decision to maintain idle dollar deposits, but this is not a correct interpretation of the capital movement as a whole. To the extent to which the gold flow reflected the desire of foreign security holders to become American security holders, the gold purchases of the Federal Reserve banks created not merely such liquidity as was tapped by the Treasury at the banks, but also such liquidity as was tapped by the Treasury on the occasion of its borrowing operations from the public. As a consequence, the expansionary effectiveness of the borrowing operations from the public was less dependent on elasticity considerations than it would have been had the borrowing not been coupled with liquidity providing developments.

The Interest Elasticity of Liquidity Provision

So far merely the a priori view has been expressed that the elasticity of liquidity provisions with respect to interest rate is not likely to be high. In periods of large-scale hoarding the bulk of the idle balances is more likely to fall in the category of contingency balances than in that of speculative balances. It seems unconvincing to argue that the hoarding in cyclical depressions and in periods of protracted stagnation occurs because of an expected rise in net rates of interest.

The belief in the return to "normalcy" should produce a return to "normalcy" rather than an abnormal degree of hoarding. To argue that the belief in the return to normalcy is limited to interest rates, and that it is limited to the "appropriate" number of persons so that large-scale hoarding develops but even the interest rates do not return to normalcy—means shuffling the cards in such a manner that a winning hand is bound to be dealt. It is much more plausible to argue that in periods of unfavorable business results and of high unemployment, contingency hoarding is widespread; and it is unlikely that contingency hoarding should be very sensitive to interest rates within the normal range of changes. Whereas, on the one hand, a decline in interest rates reduces the opportunity cost of maintaining contingency balances, it also increases entrepreneurial safety margins and, thereby, reduces the need for contingency hoarding.

All this, however, is a priori reasoning. So far as the factual material is concerned, it can merely be stated that the historical development does not generally exhibit an inverse relationship between movements of interest rates, on the one hand, and liquidity provisions, on the other, but that such a relationship is exhibited for the post-depression period of the 1930's. Figure 23 illustrates the relationship between Treasury bond yields and the ratio of member bank reserve balances plus vault cash to total deposits,[25] for the period lying between the second quarter of 1933 and the fourth quarter of 1939. If functions were fitted to this set of points, there could easily be obtained a curve exhibiting the characteristics of the Keynesian liquidity preference function. Figure 24 derived from yearly data expresses, for the same period, the relationship between Treasury bond yields and the income velocity of the dollar. The positive slope of the scatter reflects the same type of relationship as that reflected by the negative slope of the preceding scatter, considering that velocity figures are the reciprocals of Marshallian K values (which, in turn, are in the nature of liquidity ratios). Instead of Treasury bond yields, rates on other types of securities might have been used, and instead of the ratio of reserve balances plus vault cash to total deposits, other types of liquidity ratios might be chosen. The character of the relationship would still remain un-

---

[25] This is the ratio R/D of table 7.

202 Monetary Policies and Full Employment

changed. All these relationships are dominated by the fact that interest rates declined and liquidity ratios increased in the post-depression period of the 1930's.

Yet the character of the relationship between the variables in

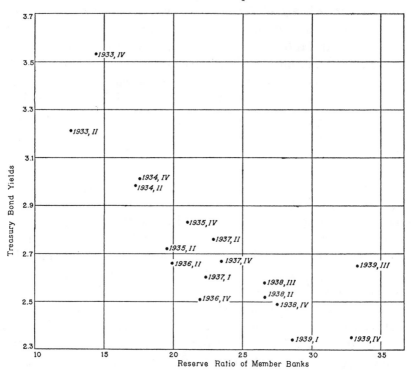

Fig. 23. Reserve ratios of member banks and Treasury bond yields, 1933–1939. Reserves include cash in vault and reserves with Federal Reserve banks at all dates; deposits include demand deposits adjusted, United States government deposits, and time deposits at all dates. Data from *Twenty-fourth Annual Report of the Board of Governors of the Federal Reserve System,* pp. 112–114; *Federal Reserve Bulletins* for reserves and deposits; *Federal Reserve Bulletin* (December, 1938), 1045, and issues following for Treasury bond yields.

question is quite different for the three preceding decades. Velocity, as Professor Angell has shown, exhibited a horizontal trend for the period 1899–1929,[26] whereas the same is not true of interest rates. Long-term rates show an upward trend from the turn of the century until 1920 and a downward trend from there on. Short-term rates

---

[26] Cf. James W. Angell, *Investment and Business Cycles* (New York and London, McGraw-Hill, 1941), cf. chap. ix and Appendix II.

may perhaps be said to show a slight, and not very consistent, downward trend from 1903 to 1920[27] and they doubtless show a marked downward trend thereafter. In the post-depression period of the 1930's the relationship between interest rates and liquidity ratios is determined by the simultaneous downward trend of interest rates

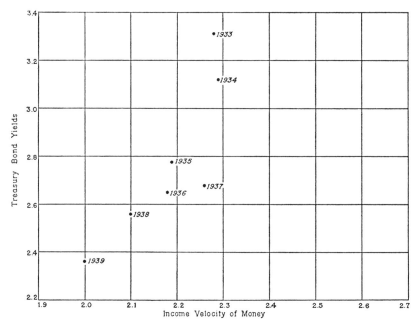

Fig. 24. Income velocity of money and Treasury bond yields, 1933–1939. Data from James W. Angell, *Investment and Business Cycles* (New York, McGraw-Hill, 1949), p. 338, for income velocity; *Federal Reserve Bulletin* (December, 1938), 1045, for Treasury bond yields.

and of velocity. The same relationship is not exhibited by a period in which velocity shows a horizontal trend and interest rates tend either upward or downward.

Figure 25 illustrates the relationship between Treasury bond yields and income velocity for the decade of the 1920's. This relationship is dominated by the fact that, during the decade in question, the trend of income velocity was horizontal whereas that of Treasury bond yields was downward. If, instead of income velocity

[27] Cf. Warren M. Person, "A Non-Technical Explanation of the Index of General Business Conditions," *Review of Economic Statistics*, II (1920), see p. 43.

exchange velocity was used, essentially the same type of relationship would be found (except that in 1928 and 1929—that is, in years of rising interest rates—exchange velocity rose beyond the levels previously attained and consequently a positive slope *is* shown by a very limited section of the scatter). During the depression period 1929–1933 the relationship between interest rates and liquidity

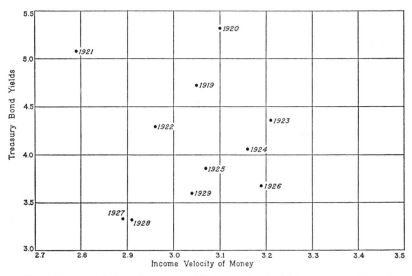

Fig. 25. Income velocity of money and Treasury bond yields, 1919–1929. Data from Angell, *Investment and Business Cycles,* pp. 337, 338, for income velocity; *Federal Reserve Bulletin* (December, 1938), 1045, for Treasury bond yields.

ratios is less consistent. For certain specific pairs of variables, for example, for Treasury bond yields and either income velocity or exchange velocity, the type of relationship that existed during the remainder of the 1930's is obtained, yet for other pairs of equally relevant variables, for example, for Treasury bond yields and bank liquidity ratios, the identical relationship is not obtained.[28] As concerns the first two decades of the century, the relationship between income velocity and interest rates is determined by the circumstance that velocity fluctuated around a horizontal trend line whereas interest rates were subject to the trends previously indicated.

---

[28] Both velocity and Treasury bond yields tended downward in the depression (bond yields with a contra-trend rise in the second half of 1931 and in 1933). Bank liquidity ratios did not, however, increase in this period.

To summarize: Only in the post-depression period of the 1930's do the "historical" liquidity functions in the United States possess the shape which the analytical functions should possess, on the Keynesian assumptions. In asserting this it is taken for granted that any meaningful relationship between interest rates and the demand for idle balances, or the demand for bank reserves, would have to be established for liquidity *ratios*, rather than for aggregate liquidity. This is expressed in the Keynesian theory by making the demand for idle balances depend on income as well as on the interest rate. The liquidity preference of persons or of institutions cannot be said to have changed if only their aggregate liquidity provisions have become different, but they can be said to have changed if their liquidity provisions change in relation to the level of their activities—given the character of these activities. This is the reason the movements of interest rates with those of velocity and with those of the ratio of bank reserves to deposits have been compared.

The mere fact that the historical liquidity functions do not slope downward until the decades of the 'thirties does not prove anything about the shape of the analytical liquidity functions. Downward sloping liquidity functions might have shifted so as to produce a locus curve of an entirely different character. However, if this should have happened, the shifts of the curves must consistently have been such as to wipe out all traces of their "true" shape; and, to say the least, there exists no obvious method of correcting for other variables, by which anything like the "true" shape could be reconstructed.

During the 1930's the historical liquidity functions possess the "Keynesian" shape and this might be regarded as *prima facie* indication of the shape of the true liquidity function in the period. A certain amount of skepticism may, however, be justified concerning the quality of this indication, even on the *prima facie* level. Perfectly reasonable explanations could be given of the decline of interest rates and of the simultaneous rise in liquidity ratios during the post-depression recovery period, without implying a causal relationship between these two phenomena. After the depression, banks and producers were unwilling to expand on the basis of unchanging liquidity provisions. An increase in the level of bankers' and producers' activities was consequently associated with an increase in liquidity ratios as well as of total liquidity. The gold influx resulted, however, in a greater increase in liquidity than was required for satisfying the investment demand at unchanging interest rates and the concomitant rise in liquidity ratios. The excess liquidity provided by the gold influx exerted a downward pressure on interest rates and was absorbed by investment at lower rates. This seems a reasonable interpretation of the increase in liquidity ratios and the simultaneous lowering of interest rates in the period following the depression of 1929–1933. The simultaneous occurrence of a decline in interest rates and of a rise in liquidity ratios during a period of substantial gold influx does not necessarily "suggest" that the rise in liquidity provisions is brought about by the decline in interest rates.

A similar statement could be made with respect to the simultaneous tendency of velocity and of short- and long-term rates to rise in periods of expansion and to decline in contraction. Such a tendency may be said to exist generally—that is to say, not merely in isolated subperiods. Velocities being the reciprocals of liquidity ratios, the coincidence of the two tendencies in question could conceivably be interpreted to mean that *after eliminating the trend* there is found an inverse tendency between interest rates, on the one hand, and certain liquidity ratios, on the other.[29] Yet this of itself does not create a presumption that changes in interest rates produce inverse changes in liquidity ratios. The assumption seems justified that in periods of rising expectations the demand for loans increases with the result that interest rates frequently also rise, and that at the same time entrepreneurial safety margins increase with the result that the demand for liquidity per unit of commitments declines.

SUMMARY

If large-scale dishoarding occurs at a time when bank assets are of such a composition as not to permit a sudden and substantial reduction in the supply of money, it might be impossible to tighten the credit market sufficiently to prevent inflationary developments. An

[29] This is true in a vague sense only. After some experimentation I am doubtful whether the usual trend-elimination techniques lead to any meaningful relationship between interest rates and liquidity ratios.

attempt to conduct the funds dishoarded into the market for government bonds may fail because such an attempt creates the expectation of falling bond prices at a time when commodity prices are expected to rise. Dishoarding therefore cannot always be prevented by means of restrictive credit policy, although the creation of new money can—provided the monetary authority is willing to accept the consequences of a sudden collapse of bond prices and provided the Treasury is not forced to spend more than what a politically feasible tax structure will yield.[30] On the whole, even counterinflationary credit policies are far from being omnipotent (unless the freezing of money stocks is included in the scope of the "policy"). The same is true of counterdeflationary credit policies with the exception of the outright creation of money.

It is not safe to assume that sufficiently low positive interest rates—and a sufficiently "easy" credit—will always start an expansion because the downward interest elasticity of private investment may be insufficient. The reason why it also is not safe to assume that deficit financing by borrowing from the commercial banks and from the public will start an expansion, is that the interest elasticity of liquidity provisions also may be insufficient. The only direct consequence of new government borrowing that might induce banks to create new money, and that might induce individuals to dishoard, is that interest rates are kept on a higher level than would be the case without borrowing. Yet, if the interest elasticity of individual hoarding (i.e., of velocity) is small, and if the elasticity of bank reserve ratios to interest rates is small, then the inducement to create new money and to dishoard also is small. In this event the new government securities are bought with money that would have been used for private investment if the government had not increased its borrowing. It has been argued on a priori grounds that it is not safe to assume that liquidity provisions are considerably elastic to interest rates and it has been argued that the slope of the analytical liquidity functions may in certain circumstances even be positive.

---

[30] This has an obvious bearing on the problem of postwar inflation. If an inflationary outburst should materialize in the immediate future the monetary authority could not do much to stop it. But at least the Federal Reserve Board should be empowered to raise reserve requirements if necessary and to discriminate regionally. Moreover, taxes should not be lowered prematurely, and a rigid policy of constant interest rates should not be adopted.

The historical behavior of the interest-liquidity relationship is, of course, inconclusive from this point of view, but there is nothing in the historical development that would call for interpretation in terms of elastic liquidity functions. At best it could be said that the development during the 1930's could be interpreted with equal ease on the assumption of elastic and on that of inelastic liquidity provisions. If the developments during the three preceding decades were to be explained in terms of elastic liquidity functions, a great many "visible" relationships would have to be interpreted away by assuming shifts of the analytical functions. In general, it is not safe, therefore, to base policies on the assumption of substantially elastic liquidity provisions.

These doubts concerning the effectiveness of certain monetary policies relate to difficulties of a less complex character than does the general objection that monetary policies must not be accepted as "panaceas." It is possible to argue that even those policies which must be regarded as effective from the points of view adopted in this chapter may fail to solve the basic problems of a chronically stagnant economy. Such an argument would have to move on a more complex level, along lines to be examined in the next chapter. So far it merely has been argued that the policy of open-market purchases, and that of deficit financing by borrowing from the public or from the commercial banks, fail in a very "elementary" sense if the downward interest elasticity of private investment and also the interest elasticity of liquidity provisions is small. In this case the two policies in question fail at the outset because the lowering of interest rates, which is brought about by open-market purchases, does not produce a substantial volume of additional private investment; and because the government, if it embarks upon a deficit-financing program, conducts previously active money, instead of dishoarded money or new money, into the channel of public expenditures. This statement does not imply any theory of adverse indirect effects. In the circumstances here envisaged, the two policies fail, regardless of possible "repercussions," simply because the basic functions along which they operate do not possess the shape explicitly or tacitly assumed when these policies are advocated.

On this level the policy of deficit financing through the central bank cannot fail. Nor can policies fail in this elementary sense, if they represent deficit financing through the central bank in disguise—for example, if the central bank creates excess liquidity which is being simultaneously tapped by the Treasury. The direct expansionary effect of these policies does not depend on the elasticity of liquidity provisions or on that of private investment.[31] Assuming, therefore, that expansionary monetary policies are called for, it seems to be "safer," as well as less costly, for the Treasury to stimulate business activity by financing deficits *directly or indirectly* via the central banking system. Whatever the more complex dangers of sustained expansionary policies may be, it is not clear why they should be assumed to increase through central bank financing.

---

[31] However, the magnitude of the "respending" effect (or of the multiplier effect in Angell's sense) does depend on these factors. This secondary effect is the greater, the smaller the interest elasticity of hoarding and the greater the interest elasticity of private investment (and, of course, the greater the marginal propensity to consume).

CHAPTER VII

Underutilization and Full Employment Policy

SOME ADVERSE FACTORS

THE EARLIER PARTS of this volume include observations concerning social and economic factors that may produce stagnant trends. Conclusions relating to these factors will now be briefly reviewed. The analysis concerning full employment policies is summarized in the second section of this chapter.

The distribution of income has considerable bearing on trends in output and employment. If real wages are very high and (average and marginal) profit rates very low, the reward for the bearing of uncertainty is insufficient. Uncertainty declines but it does not tend to zero when real wages, and thereby the average propensity to consume, become very high. Consequently, if real wages are successively increased and profit margins diminished, there must exist a point beyond which profit margins become insufficient. On the other hand, if real wages are successively diminished and (average and marginal) profit rates increased, there also must exist a point beyond which the growing profit margins become insufficient to compensate for the even faster growing uncertainty. Instability and thereby uncertainty would grow beyond all reasonable limits if, in consequence of a decline of the average and of the marginal propensity to consume, investment for further investment became the only significant source of the demand for goods. The adverse effects of such a degree of uncertainty could not be ruled out by the circumstance that a very high fraction of the price would consist of profits if the goods produced should be salable. They would be salable on a large scale only in periods in which the mentality characteristic of stock-exchange booms extends throughout the entire industrial community. Normally, the instability of demand would preclude industrial activities on a scale sufficient to produce a high level of employment.

Although it may be inferred that a "balanced" distribution of income helps to maintain business activity at a high level, definite criteria do not exist on which it could be decided whether in given periods of underutilization the distribution of income should be corrected in the one or in the other direction in order to increase the level of activity. There exists, however, a likelihood that in advanced depressions a reduction of unit labor costs, and in advanced stages of an expansion a rise in unit labor costs, frequently is conducive to the maintenance of a high level of output and of employment. This is true because it seems appropriate to characterize advanced depressions as periods in which the average propensity to consume is high and in which unsatisfactory profit margins are expected with comparatively little uncertainty. Advanced expansions, on the other hand, are periods in which satisfactory profit margins are expected with a relatively high degree of uncertainty. Whenever unsatisfactory profit margins are expected in periods of a high average propensity to consume, it seems likely that output could be increased by raising average and marginal profit rates even at the cost of some increase in uncertainty—that is, even at the cost of some reduction in the average propensity to consume. Whenever large profit margins are expected in periods of low average propensity to consume, it seems promising to raise unit labor costs, that is, to increase the average propensity to consume, even at the cost of reducing the profit margins per unit of output. This makes it seem probable that in the first type of situation a reduction in unit labor costs, and in the second, an increase in unit labor costs, might frequently have favorable effects on the level of output. Rising unit labor costs in depressions and declining unit labor costs in expansion are potential adverse factors. It should be added that there exists a presumption that changes in money wage rates are associated with changes in real wage rates in the same direction (and, of course, also with changes in unit labor costs in the same direction, unless the change in productivity goes in the opposite direction and outweighs the change in real wage rates). This presumption is based on the fact that the total money demand for goods is not likely to rise in the same proportion as that in which money wage rates rise, nor is it likely to decline in the same proportion, because the size of wage income does not bear directly on the investment demand for further investment. Furthermore, it should be borne in mind that secularly money wage rates should be given a rising tendency, provided policy aims at a reasonably stable price level. Otherwise, as a consequence of technological progress, unit labor costs would display a secular downward trend whereas prices would not.

Obviously, if a "balanced" distribution of income has favorable effects and if "unbalanced" distribution gives rise to adverse developments, the degree of progressiveness of the tax structure must be of considerable significance. Increased progressiveness has important effects in common with a rise in real wages at the expense of profit margins, and reduced progressiveness shares important effects with a rise of profit margins at the expense of real wages. On the assumptions previously outlined on the character of periods of advanced expansion and of advanced depression, it follows that increased progressiveness in depression and reduced progressiveness in expansion are potential adverse factors. This position, of course, is quite compatible with the fact that it is possible to put an end to a period of expansion by means of progressive taxation, if this type of taxation is carried beyond certain limits.

Turning from the problem of income distribution to that of the supply of money, it may be inferred that underutilization of resources calls for easy money policies. *Ceteris paribus* the willingness to invest is always greater at low than at high rates on money loans, and it is always greater when credit is easy than when it is tight. This fact apparently is not contested by anyone. Nevertheless, it seems to be true that central banks are not always aware of the bearing of their policies on the general level of business activity. Laughlin Currie, for example, argued convincingly that in the depression of 1929–1933 the Federal Reserve System acted more on the basis of certain ill-defined rules and conventions than on the principle that it is the regulator of the money supply. The supply of money was allowed to shrink abruptly, especially after 1930, although open-market purchases, if they had been undertaken on a sufficiently large scale, could have prevented such a development. Yet, from the downturn in 1929 to March, 1932, the Federal Reserve banks bought no more than 690 million dollars in government securities, and, aside from this they limited themselves to their traditional activities of discounting eligible paper and of buying bankers' acceptances at interest rates which, measured with predepression standards, were considered to be low rates. It is entirely meaningless to maintain that, by so doing, the Federal Reserve System satisfied the "needs of legitimate business" for commercial credit.[1] It is quite correct to maintain that it neglected to counteract a vigorous deflationary tendency, and that instead of increasing the supply of money at a time when velocity declined, it allowed a violent reduction of the stock for no good reason. An attempt to counteract this tendency by open-market purchases would have further lowered the entire interest-rate structure, and it is safe to conclude on purely a priori grounds that this would have resulted in a higher level of activity than that actually attained. It is of course quite uncertain whether such a policy alone would have resulted in a satisfactory level of activity, even if it had been started at an early stage. Yet the fact that an institution cannot accomplish a desired objective by itself does not justify its failure to act.

In what was the most critical period from this point of view, that is during the year 1931, when the economy showed signs of an incipient recovery, the Federal Reserve System was prevented from taking reasonable measures by eligibility requirements based on orthodox and ill-defined theories of central banking.[2] The criticism should therefore not primarily be directed at persons, but at irrational theories and legal arrangements which determined the attitudes of institutions. It is irrational to deny that, in the contemporary setting, the main function of central banks is that of regulating the supply of money, including bank deposits. If in the depression of 1929–1933 this had been clearly realized, it is highly unlikely that any important group would have advocated "regu-

---

[1] Laughlin Currie, *The Supply and Control of Money in the United States* (2d ed.; Cambridge, Harvard University Press, 1935), cf. mainly chaps. iv, ix, xiii, and xiv.

[2] The eligibility requirements assumed increased importance in 1931, owing to the outflow of gold. Cf. W. Randolph Burgess, *The Reserve Banks and the Money Market* (rev. ed., New York and London, Harper and Brothers, 1936), pp. 282 ff.

lating" the supply in such a manner as to have it shrink all the time and especially from 1931 on.

Although irrational monetary management may prolong depressions and may be responsible for longer periods of underutilization, an interpretation of the periods in question in terms of this factor alone seems inadequate. A good case can be made, on a priori grounds, for the assumption that long-run trends toward shifts in the composition of output exert a favorable influence on the aggregate level of output and that the absence of such trends is a potential adverse factor. During expansions, these trends add substantially more to the amount of investment in the fields that are favored than what is deducted from the amount of investment in the fields adversely affected. What is added to the amount of investment in the fields favored is new investment, what is suppressed in the fields adversely affected is replacement. Even over reasonably long periods the resultant of these two component forces is a positive force, tending to raise the level of activity. Moreover, in cyclical depressions the belief in the existence of an upward trend for specific fields may become the initiating force of early recoveries, whereas the belief that all specific trends are dominated by the trend of business as a whole may prolong the vicious circle of deflation. It is possible to lend some plausibility to this proposition by referring to factual material, although the statistical argument itself is inconclusive. Theories of economic development stressing the significance of innovations can be fitted into this reasoning, although it should not be taken for granted that innovations always are the initiating forces of shifts in the composition of output.

The above pages are not intended to convey a generally valid explanation of periods of stagnation. There exists no such explanation. A possible combination of circumstances was outlined that might exert an adverse influence on business activity for periods of time considerably exceeding the "usual" duration of depressions. This combination of circumstances is characterized (*a*) by the absence of significant trends toward shifts in the composition of output; (*b*) by the fact that equalitarian policies become reinforced in periods of depression and that they weaken in periods of high activity so that measures resulting in an increased average propensity to consume at the expense of profit margins are introduced not when the average propensity to consume is low and profit margins are high, but when the average propensity to consume is high and profit margins are low; (c) by a monetary management that is not consistently aware of its being the regulator of the supply of money. Such a combination of circumstances may exert a depressive influence on the level of activity especially if monopolistic tendencies become reinforced at the same time. Temporary saturation in specific fields of investment activity, for example in the important field of residential construction, may seriously aggravate conditions. All "protracted depressions" have fallen in downgrades of the building cycle (although not all downgrades of the building cycle have produced protracted depressions).

Circumstances of an entirely different character may, of course, also lead to protracted or chronic underutilization. All that is required for a stagnationist constellation, is the insufficiency of investment for further investment to absorb the resources not used for the production of consumers' goods and for investment for consumption. It is impossible to prove or to disprove, in any rigorous sense, propositions according to which certain factors are capable of producing an insufficiency of investment. However, doubts may be expressed about the strategic significance of some circumstances emphasized in the Keynes-Hansen argument concerning "stagnation" in mature economies. So far as the significance of extensive growth is concerned, the Keynes-Hansen argument would seem to rest largely on the assumption that an economy with an unchanging territory and with a slight population growth could only move upward along a different (less "favorable") consumption function than an "extensively" growing economy and that the upward movement does not materialize along such a (less "favorable") consumption function. In reality, however, it is not possible to substantiate with facts these assumptions concerning the relationship between extensive growth and the shape of the over-all consumption function. This weakens the argument that further movements along the actually observable consumption function have constituted a more difficult process than upward movements along those consumption functions which would have prevailed if new territories and new population had been added to the existing stock. It may still be true that movements along one and the same over-all consumption function materialize more readily when the population grows rapidly than when it stagnates, because it is easier to forecast the kind of goods that will be demanded when new persons want more of the same things than when the same persons want more things. Yet it should be remembered that even in periods of rapid population growth the rise in aggregate consumption expressed itself to an important degree in increased per capita consumption.

On somewhat different grounds it may, perhaps, be argued that extensive growth is necessary if stagnation is to be avoided, because diminishing returns tend to be counteracted by the acquisition of new resources. But, so far as the United States is concerned, it would be unconvincing to attribute stagnation to diminishing returns. Even when extensive growth had slowed down per capita output continued to grow at a rapid rate, and the rate of growth of output increased in relation to the rate of growth of real capital. Diminishing returns have been consistently outweighed by improvement. The objection that improvement was a better offset in the past because it brought more "deepening of capital" is not valid. The distinction between deepening and merely widening innovations is irrelevant for long-run analysis.[3]

On the other hand, it should not be overlooked that the acquisition of new resources may alleviate the social tension in the expanding community and that this may delay the growth of trends that might interfere with the maintenance of a high average degree of employment. The existing power groups, which produce institutional rigidities, extend their influence automatically over new segments of the economy within a given economic area. Additions to the given economic space are comparatively unorganized in the beginning and consequently they frequently are freer from institutional rigidities. In this somewhat indirect sense the extensive growth argument may contribute importantly to the understanding of stagnant tendencies.

---

[3] Cf. above, pp. 74–82.

Full Employment Policies

There exist only three methods which, if carried far enough, are capable of eliminating "nonfrictional unemployment,"[4] regardless of the initial state of entrepreneur expectations. It is true, however, of many policies that they are likely to diminish unemployment, and these are likely to produce reasonably full utilization, provided the genuine tendency toward underemployment is moderate.

The three methods may be described as (*a*) the subsidizing of private producers; (*b*) the financing of public investment by the government (or by central banks): (*c*) the financing of consumer subsidies by the government (or by central banks).[5] The first method is probably not practicable on any large scale for political and administrative reasons. The second and third methods may be practicable for periods of considerable length, although the third method probably less so than the second. After an attempt to justify the elimination of the first method (*a*), it will be argued that the basic features of our institutional setting could scarcely be "rescued" by the remaining methods (*b* and *c*) if there should be a secular tendency toward mass unemployment *or* if—regardless of the secular trends—these methods should be applied in the framework of a rigid full employment guarantee. This will be argued in the immediately following passages (pp. 218–229). The emphasis will, however, be placed on a positive statement. Consistent application of these policies against cyclical (rather than secular) depression tendencies does not have to produce abrupt changes in the institutional environment provided the timing of the policies is adjusted to price and wage movements in a flexible manner; and if these policies (*b* and *c*), along with others, will be adopted in early stages of recessions, there is a good chance that the economy will *not* be faced with an adverse secular trend. Consequently, the second and third methods men-

[4] Frictional unemployment, brought about by regional or occupational immobility of resources, could, "in principle," be eliminated by the first two methods enumerated in the text, but such an attempt would be quite unreasonable and it would give rise to very serious difficulties. It is even, "in principle," impossible to eliminate frictional unemployment by the third method (cf. above, p. 217 and p. 226).

[5] Allowing the nominal value of any given banknote, coin, or deposit to decrease continuously over time (i.e., "taxing" money stocks or adopting a "stamped money" scheme) is not a dependable method (cf. above, p. 187, n. 8).

tioned, if applied consistently as anticyclical policies, may greatly contribute to create the secular trends under which they can be used without abrupt institutional changes.

As for subsidizing private producers (cf. method *a,* above), the question of whom to subsidize and of what the conditions of the subsidy should be, must necessarily be answered on highly arbitrary grounds. By paying enough money to a sufficient number of producers it would be possible to induce the aggregate of these producers to employ the whole labor force available to them. But there does not exist any general principle on which it would be possible to decide how many jobless persons should be employed by each producer and by each industry, in addition to those employed in the absence of subsidies. The allocation of the additional employment and of the corresponding subsidy payments being arbitrary, the chances are small of finding a generally acceptable, or even a politically feasible, solution. Moreover, even if some arbitrary pattern of distributing the additional employment, and the corresponding subsidy payments were accepted politically, it still would be impossible to find out to what extent the single producers actually satisfied the conditions concerning additional employment. Aside from the administrative difficulties, it must be realized that the concept of additional employment is not a satisfactory basis for policy because nobody knows what the amount of employment would have been in an industry if the subsidy plan had not been adopted. This question also would have to be decided arbitrarily. On the whole, the government would be paying out significant amounts of money to private individuals and to institutions whose share in the sum total of subsidy payments could not be justified except in terms of admittedly arbitrary decisions of the authority. The resulting allocation of resources would, of course, also be quite arbitrary. It seems practically inconceivable that in a political democracy such a system should prove to be workable on a large scale.[6]

---

[6] The difficulties would partly be analogous to those that have arisen in connection with the concept of additional exports in the Central European exchange control systems. But the subsidies granted on additional exports were on a comparatively minor scale, and the form of government of the countries in question was mostly nondemocratic. Cf. Howard S. Ellis, *Exchange Control in Central Europe* (Cambridge, Harvard University Press, 1941), pp. 18–19.

Of course, it cannot be denied that a public investment program (method *b*, distinguished on p. 217) also distributes gains in a highly arbitrary fashion, and that it also results in a composition of output which is arbitrary in terms of the market mechanism. There exists, however, the politically important difference that the arbitrary effects are mainly the indirect ones, whereas the direct effects can usually be justified, in a more or less acceptable fashion, for periods of considerable length. Countries obviously need highways, dams, and so on. Even if the public "investment" does not result in the construction of valuable assets such as these but is in the nature of a quasi dole, it still can be maintained as a general principle that the government must not let the unemployed perish. The choice of the specific public investment projects, of course, determines the indirect effects on the construction goods industries, the consumer goods industries, and so on. The choice being arbitrary, these indirect effects also are brought about and distributed arbitrarily by the authority. But the political difficulties arising in consequence of this are distinctly smaller than those standing in the way of an arbitrary distribution of direct subsidy payments to private producers.

In fact, among the many objections that have been raised against public investment programs, criticisms of the arbitrary distribution of indirect gains in subsidiary fields is not of outstanding importance. What seems to be the most vigorous criticism of these programs has been based on the claim that the effects of a continuous rise of the national debt must sooner or later become detrimental. The popular argument advanced in support of this view rests on an alleged analogy between private and public debt. This version of the argument is a fallacy because it does not take into account the fact that payments on an internally held public debt are transfer payments. Yet so long as the government borrows from private individuals and institutions (including commercial banks), it remains true that adverse consequences may arise from a significant increase in the public debt.[7]

If the government securities are sold to private individuals and

---

[7] Cf. David McCord Wright, *The Creation of Purchasing Power* (Cambridge, Harvard University Press, 1942), pp. 135 ff. Cf. also *idem*, "The Economic Limit and Economic Burden of an Internally Held Public Debt," *Quarterly Journal of Economics* (November, 1940), 116–129.

institutions (i.e., if borrowing from the central bank is excluded), the government must be prepared to collect the interest cost of its borrowing operations by means of taxation. This is true because a policy that must depend in ever-increasing measure on additional borrowing from certain private groups, in order to pay interest to the same groups, would presumably sooner or later create such distrust as to render the government securities unsalable.[8] It is incorrect to maintain that in these circumstances the credit aspects of an internally held public debt cancel out with its debit aspects, merely because the debtor belongs to the same community as the creditors. The adverse effects of the debit aspects on production may possess a different magnitude from the favorable effects of the credit aspects. If the debt grows high, the adverse effects of the debit aspects tend to outweigh the favorable effects of the credit aspects. The debit aspects reflect themselves in the paying of taxes, the necessity of which diminishes the willingness to bear risk. The incentive-destroying effect of taxation would be reduced if present loss deduction provisions were extended along with the appropriate carry-over provisions; yet such provisions would not eliminate the adverse effect of taxation on the willingness to invest because producers could not take it for granted that profits will be available from which the losses may be deducted. Profits may turn out to be negative not merely in a single year but also over longer periods, in the aggregate; and, particularly, new enterprises might have to liquidate under the impact of initial losses before earning adequate profits. In view of these circumstances, the compensation which the tax system promises *ex ante* for potential losses is less than the equivalent of the penalty which it places on potential profits, even if extensive loss deduction with carry-over is allowed. Eliminating

---

[8] What ultimately distinguishes the credit of the federal government from that of other institutions is the ability of the federal government to tax and to create new money without borrowing from outsiders for meeting its obligations. *Aside from these characteristics,* its ability to meet its obligations by borrowing more from its creditors would be no different from the ability of other institutions to do the same; and it is known that this is no sound basis for the credit of an institution. The process of creating new money without borrowing from outsiders has been excluded from the present context: the concern here is with the sale of securities to private individuals and institutions. The outright creation of money (without borrowing from private institutions) will be considered in the subsequent paragraphs. So long as this alternative is excluded, the distinctive features of the government credit is determined by its ability to tax.

the double taxation involved in the present American corporate plus personal income tax structure might also reduce the incentive-destroying effect of taxation, even if personal income taxes were kept on a correspondingly higher level. This seems likely because corporate managements, on the whole, are more concerned with the net profits earned by the corporations than with the "income net of personal taxes" of the individual stockholders. But, obviously, the fact would still remain that, *ceteris paribus*, incentives become the weaker, the higher the rate of taxation. The debit aspects of the public debt, which are reflected in increased taxation, must therefore be assumed to exert an adverse effect on the willingness to bear risk. The credit aspects of the public debt are reflected in the receipt of interest payments by the owners of government securities. The interest received may be spent or hoarded, and, for the reasons just discussed, it will tend to be hoarded rather than invested if taxes are very high. Consequently, the "public debt argument" against deficit-financed government investment, although usually stated incorrectly, is not really without justification, provided the government borrows only from private individuals or institutions.

What frequently is overlooked, however, is that the argument would lose all validity if the government financed its investment program by selling noninterest-bearing securities to the Federal Reserve banks,[9] or by any method of "outright money creation."[10] The objection that financing through central banks is inflationary has no justification because it is the objective of government policy to induce monetary expansion whenever a public investment program is adopted in order to produce fuller utilization of resources. In fact, it was shown in chapter vi that, in these circumstances, financing

---

[9] Or, by selling interest-bearing securities, provided the extra profits of the Federal Reserve banks are taxed away.

[10] This would seem to be one of the main ideas conveyed by Professor Abba P. Lerner's theory of "functional finance," which has been expressed in several of his writings—most recently in chapter xxiv of his *The Economics of Control* (New York, Macmillan, 1944). Yet Lerner's exposition creates the impression that fears from the consequences of a rising public debt rest on mere prejudices even if the government borrows from private lenders. This is not necessarily so, although it should be pointed out that even a continuously rising *privately financed* public debt need not produce a rise in the service charges *in relation to national income*, provided national income rises sufficiently due to rising productivity (cf. Evsey D. Domar, "The 'Burden' of the Debt and the National Income," *American Economic Review*, December, 1944).

through central banks possesses significant advantages over other methods of financing because the expansionary effect of borrowing from other lenders depends on the elasticity of liquidity provisions to interest rates. If the interest elasticity of hoarding, and of the bank reserve ratios actually maintained, are small, then borrowing from individuals and from commercial banks will not result in any significant rise in MV, whereas borrowing from central banks always possesses expansionary effectiveness.[11]

It was also argued that, from this point of view, the combination of certain apparently independent policies may have identical effects with the policy of direct borrowing from central banks. If, for example, central banks buy securities from the public or from commercial banks and the government at the same time sells securities to the public or to the commercial banks, then this combination of policies differs in form rather than in substance from direct borrowing from the central bank. The same is true of the combination of policies actually adopted in the United States during the recovery period of the 1930's. This was a combination of gold purchases by the central bank with government borrowing. The primary expansionary effect of such a combination of policies does not depend on the interest elasticity of liquidity provisions, just as the effectiveness of direct borrowing from central banks does not depend on this factor.[12] However, in the event of a combination of gold purchases with deficit financing, there does exist the difference that the public debt gives rise to an internal transfer problem which would not exist in the event of direct financing by the central bank or in the event of the appropriate combination of security (rather than gold) purchases with deficit financing. The gold yields no interest to the Treasury, whereas the government securities sold to the commercial banks do cost the Treasury interest.

Financing by central banks seems desirable, whenever the public works program is aimed at an expansionary effect. The policy of direct financing is much less "revolutionary" than it might seem to be at first sight, because combinations of policies differing merely

---

[11] However, the control of the Federal Reserve Board over reserve requirements should be increased if such a policy is adopted and even aside from such a policy.

[12] But the secondary effects depend in both cases on the marginal propensity to spend, which, in turn, is partly determined by the elasticities in question.

in form from direct financing have been adopted in the past. The policy of direct financing would clearly invalidate the argument according to which public works programs lead to detrimental consequences via their effect on the financial position of the Treasury. It is true, of course, that a large-scale direct-financing program might run into substantial political difficulties. But there exists a difference between these difficulties and the ones considered earlier in this chapter. Objections to subsidizing private producers cannot be said to rest on mere prejudices. Nor does a person necessarily express mere prejudices if he maintains that a rising public debt may create difficulties, even if the debt is internally held. But it is a mere prejudice to maintain that a public investment program aimed at expansionary effects is sound, or at least acceptable, if financed by security sales to the public or to the commercial banks but that it is unsound if financed by security sales to central banks.[13] This statement is subject only to the qualification that public interest attaches to the ability of the commercial banking system to maintain itself and that the commercial banks may have an interest in being the holders of future increments to the public debt. But, in the first place, it is by no means obvious that keeping the commercial banks sound requires further increasing their holdings of government securities, and second, even if bank earnings should become inadequate in the future, there exist others ways of meeting this problem.[14] Aside from these implications, the sentiment against *direct* financing is a prejudice, provided reserve requirements are under control. Yet it must, of course, be admitted that prejudices,

---

[13] See also in this connection, David McCord Wright, *op. cit.*, pp. 190 ff.

[14] Deficit financing creates deposits the handling of which gives rise to costs which the commercial banks must be capable of recovering in order to perform their functions satisfactorily. Obviously the commercial banks earn more if they hold interest-bearing government securities than if the Federal Reserve banks hold government securities and the commercial banks merely hold such reserve balances as come into existence when the government remits money from its own Federal Reserve account to a customer of a commercial bank. But to maintain that, in consequence of this, deficit financing via noninterest-bearing securities should be outlawed, means insisting on an entirely irrational solution of a (real) difficulty. Why should the amount "the banks must be allowed to earn" equal a definite percentage of a principal determined by the deflationary gap which the government attempts to bridge by expansionary financing? This certainly is a meaningless formula. And why should it be taken for granted that it is preferable to reserve this channel of earnings for the commercial banks rather than to allow them other benefits or possibly have them increase certain service charges in the appropriate measure?

by giving rise to adverse psychological repercussions, may create their own justification. *Indirect* financing by central banks is more "expedient" and certain methods of indirect financing (combinations of open-market purchases with the usual methods of deficit financing) may, perhaps, accomplish the same objectives as direct financing.

However, even if the internal transfer difficulties arising from the growth of the debt could be eliminated by the method of central bank financing, it still would not follow by necessity that a private enterprise economy and the concomitant political institutions could be kept alive indefinitely by supplementing a chronically deficient volume of private investment with a large-scale public works program. The true difficulties, those which are really unavoidable, presumably would not undermine the system unless a substantial deficiency of private investment were "epochal" rather than merely "cyclical" or even "protracted." These difficulties will be discussed and the question will be raised of how they could be avoided by a policy faced with merely "cyclical" depression tendencies.

In the first place, it is likely that if a substantial flow of public investment was to be generated continuously over a long period of time, much of the public works would have to be on the "wasteful" rather than on the "productive" end of the range of potential projects. The number of productive projects is limited through the circumstance that competition with private investment projects must usually be avoided, if a net increment in investment expenditures, and not merely a substitution of government investment for private investment activity, is to be brought about. In certain circumstances government competition with private industries may open up monopolized fields for private outsiders and may thus become a weapon of antitrust policies aimed at increasing private production.[15] But competition with private investment will have to be kept within rather narrow limits if no reduction of private production is to ensue. The box containing government projects which are "worthwhile," according to generally accepted value judgments,

---

[15] See Howard S. Ellis, "Monetary Policy and Investment," *American Economic Review*, Supplement (March, 1940), 27–38; cf. pp. 37–38 (reprinted in *Readings in Business Cycle Theory*, edited by a committee of the American Economic Association under the chairmanship of Gottfried Haberler, Philadelphia, Blakiston, 1944).

and which nevertheless do not reduce private investment opportunities, is not an empty box by any means. But the content of this box is limited at any moment of time and it cannot be increased indefinitely at will. If the volume of private investment should epochally prove to be deficient by a high margin and if the postulate should be accepted that the gap must currently be filled with noncompeting public projects, it would be unavoidable that a large proportion of these projects should be considered wasteful by public opinion and that the incomes derived from these projects should be considered quasi doles. The state of mind of a community in which this view prevails gradually becomes receptive to proposals directed at substituting for the existing order one in which it is not necessary to waste a significant part of the existing resources. It might then rightly be argued that the waste could be eliminated if the government, instead of avoiding competition with private business, "took over" the private segment of the economy. However, it is most unlikely that such a transition would be compatible with democratic political institutions. A democracy in which a significant share of the population lives on quasi doles[16] is socially less objectionable and politically less unstable than one in which unemployment is high and in which the unemployed are on the verge of starvation; yet quasi doles would presumably fail to render the political order of a democracy stable in the long run.

Second, there exists a more narrowly technical reason why the institutions of private enterprise economies would become obsolete if private investment were chronically deficient and if a high level of employment were produced all the time by means of compensatory public works. *In the event of a chronic large-scale deficiency of private investment, the government would presumably be forced to "guarantee" the level of employment de facto, if not de jure.* Inflationary developments would constitute a threat in such a setting, unless the government was willing to forestall them by an elaborate system of direct controls. It would be necessary to resort to direct interference with the price and wage level to prevent monopolistic groups from raising their money earnings against the background of

---

[16] That is, on incomes derived from public "investment," such as is wasteful except for the multiplier effect.

the government "guarantee." Labor unions, for example, would be in a position to raise money wages without creating unemployment because the government would always absorb the slack. Sir William Beveridge seems to feel that an over-all labor union, organized on a national scale, would exert no inflationary pressure, because to the representatives of labor as a whole it would be obvious that they have nothing to gain from such wage increases as are associated with a rise in the cost of living. Yet even a national union would have to take account of the pressures originating in specific constituent groups and the easiest way of doing this would usually be that of accomplishing wage increases for the various specific groups in succession. Moreover, the union might frequently take the position that wage increases should be granted and that these should not lead to price increases, whereas in reality they would. Given a consistent policy of guaranteed full employment by fiscal means, an upward pressure on money earnings would have to be anticipated from labor groups. In many industries of strategic significance, which would benefit from public investment expenditure, the same would be true of monopolistic entrepreneur groups. The normal penalty for raising supply prices beyond certain limits would be eliminated and the economic penalty would have to be replaced by legal penalties (regulations). The setting would be distinctively conducive to an all-round upward pressure on the price level and it is scarcely conceivable that the government would be capable of coping with this pressure by means other than comprehensive direct controls. The controls would presumably have to extend to important segments of the wage and price structure, to the quality of goods produced and services performed, and also to locational problems and to factors affecting labor mobility. These factors would have to be controlled because it would be most unreasonable to adjust the government spending program to the existing regional and occupational maldistribution of resources instead of proceeding the other way around.

The probability of the emergence of a situation calling for far-reaching direct controls seems to be even greater if account is also taken of the monetary characteristics of an economy in which full employment is accomplished by sustained large-scale public spending. In such an economy a significant stock of idle balances as well as of government bond holdings must be expected to accumulate gradually. Only if the full-employment policies of the monetary authority could be based entirely on the interest elasticity of hoarding, would it be possible to finance full-employment policies exclusively by selling bonds to the public and by spending the proceeds of the borrowing operations; on realistic assumptions it must be assumed that the hoards of the public are but partly absorbed in this fashion and that partly they are merely offset by the creation of new money.[17] Consequently, in an economy of the type considered here, the public is left with large idle balances. It must be assumed, however, that sooner or later the public will make an effort to reduce its liquidity substantially because the depression, in view of the potentiality of which the high degree of liquidity is maintained, does not materialize. In such circumstances it would probably be impossible to prevent inflationary outbursts by the ordinary methods of credit control. In principle it would always be possible to prevent the public from exchanging its bonds for money because the appropriate regulation of reserve requirements would force the banks into rationing credit so as to refrain from creating new money. Even this might not be "feasible" for political reasons, because such a policy would bring a sharp decline of bond prices.[18] Yet to prevent the dishoarding of already existing (idle) deposits may be literally impossible, unless rigorous controls are adopted which interfere with the right to spend money. The monetary authority may not succeed in directing the balances in question into the bond market, merely by reducing the prices of bonds. If a further decline in bond prices and a rise in the prices of goods is expected, the usual methods of credit policy will fail. Therefore both the "income approach" and the "quantity theory approach" lead to the conclusion that, in the secular long run, a policy of government-made full employment may prove to be unworkable without an elaborate system of direct controls.

The two circumstances just discussed would presumably result in thoroughgoing institutional changes of an economic and of a po-

[17] Cf. above, chapter vi, pp. 174–180.
[18] Cf. above, pp. 183–185.

litical character, should the volume of private investment prove to be seriously deficient in the secular long run and should public-investment projects systematically be used to make up for the deficiency. To repeat, these circumstances are: (1) the "wastefulness" of much of the public investment that can be undertaken continuously on a significant scale without competing with private investment projects; (2) the economic impunity granted to concerted wage- and price-raising action of monopolistic groups by a policy that would have to guarantee the level of employment in substance if not in form.

The first of these two circumstances—the "wastefulness" of non-competing public investment projects—may be avoided by resorting to consumer subsidies instead of to direct public employment policies (method *c* p. 217). Consumer subsidization, if carried out on a sufficiently large scale, might result, within the limits set by the available real resources, in any desired amount of additional output through the responding effect. At the same time the allocation of resources to "wasteful" public investment projects is avoided. Therefore, given the necessity of a large-scale deficit-financing program, much could be said for limiting public investment to such projects as are valuable per se (i.e., even aside from the multiplier effect) and for accomplishing the remainder of the desired total effect by consumer subsidies.[19] On logical grounds a strong case can be made for this alternative. Yet some of the difficulties attaching to large-scale consumer subsidization are specific of this method (and of producers' subsidies) in the sense of not being shared fully by public works programs. The difficulties arising from the arbitrariness of the distribution of subsidy payments as between consumers might prove to be very serious. These difficulties would presumably be somewhat less severe than those to be expected in connection with a large-scale subsidy program for private investors, because subsidizing the least wealthy consumers comes closer to putting into effect a generally acceptable principle than does any distribution pattern for the subsidization of private entrepreneurs (cf., the gradual acceptance of unemployment insurance as necessary and

---

[19] Cf. J. H. G. Pierson: "The Underwriting of Aggregate Consumer Expenditure as a Pillar of Full-Employment Policy," *American Economic Review* (March, 1944), 21–55. 21–55.

"sound" in the industrially advanced countries). In spite of this, it is doubtful whether, in a political democracy, a working agreement could be anticipated with respect to the distribution of consumer subsidies on a truly large scale. As for inflationary threat, discussed in the foregoing pages, this applies to consumer-subsidy programs, as well as to public investment schemes. In both cases monopolistic groups would tend to raise wages and prices against the background of guaranteed full utilization; and in both cases an automatic velocity deflation would be counteracted by quantity inflation, with the result that it would be necessary to introduce far-reaching direct controls whenever the velocity of money tended back to prestagnation levels or higher.

It is likely that all difficulties so far considered would either disappear or at least tend to become manageable if the government were faced merely with "cyclical" depression tendencies rather than with a large-scale chronic deficiency of private investment. In this event it is not necessary to "waste" any significant share of the available resources because useful and mostly noncompeting public works should always be carried out on a considerable scale and periodically they might even assume very significant dimensions. As for the inflationary danger, an anticyclical spending policy could afford to time its operations so as to take into account price and wage trends and the behavior of monopolistic groups. In the setting now considered it would presumably not be necessary to guarantee the level of employment either in form or substance. Consequently the expansionary fiscal operations could be discontinued in the event of undesirable price trends, and inflation tendencies might well be controllable by methods not requiring abrupt changes in the institutional setting.

The conclusion is pessimistic for a full employment guarantee but it is hopeful with respect to the possibility of preventing periodic business recessions from developing into major depressions with mass unemployment. Ordinarily, the government should be capable of starting vigorous expansionary fiscal policies in early stages of business recessions and it should be capable of preventing dangerous price trends by the proper timing of its policies. Power groups—by producing significant price increases at low levels of activity—might still be in a position to force the government into abandoning its expansionary policies early and thereby they might force the economy into depression. The possibility of suicidal policies on the part of power groups cannot be excluded, but it is to be hoped that the policies of monopolistic groups would be partly determined by their own vital interest in the avoidance of major depressions. This hope need not be utopian in the same sense in which it would be utopian to rely on the reluctance of monopoly groups to produce inflation in the event of a full employment guarantee. For strategically situated power groups there is something to be gained from inflation but, ordinarily, not from a major depression. *In periods of business recession, monetary and fiscal policies should be started early and on a sufficient scale. But it should be made clear that these policies will be discontinued in the event of certain wage and price trends. These trends should be expressed with regard to the ad hoc requirements of the periods in which major expansionary operations are undertaken.* Even if certain controls were needed to supplement such a policy, these would presumably be of a much milder variety than those required by a full employment guarantee.

The qualification that the policy would be unworkable under a seriously adverse secular trend might well be less important than it seems to be at first sight. This is because the policy might greatly contribute to averting an adverse secular trend. The long-run trend and the cycle do not live independent lives. They interact and, therefore, there is a good chance that consistent, successful intervention in early stages of recession would produce or reinforce favorable long-run trends in private investment activity. There exists no compelling reason for anticipating more than cyclical depression tendencies if expansionary devices will be applied consistently, in early stages of recessions. The adjustments occurring during recession periods could take place much faster and much more smoothly if the cumulative decline in aggregate demand was prevented. The policy should not, however, assume exclusively the form of expansionary fiscal operations. This device should always be associated with measures aimed directly at stimulating private investment.

It is sometimes maintained that to bring forth the amount of private investment required for a high level of employment will in the future be an almost impossible task because the amount required to "fill the gap" at high levels of employment has risen greatly.[20] The absolute size of the gap has, of course, risen very greatly because the rise in productivity has led to a significant increase in the full employment level of output. But this has been true for many decades (probably for centuries) without having resulted in secular stagnation. The relative size of the gap, that is the amount of investment required per unit of consumption, has not so far risen, because the average propensity to consume has not changed much. If there is a continuation along the same historical consumption function, the amount of investment per unit of consumption would not have to rise for the maintenance of a high level of employment. Investment would have to rise merely in proportion to consumption.

Among the policies directly stimulating the rate of private investment, those raising the supply of credit are the least controversial. It is generally accepted that the amount of private investment is increased by the lowering of interest rates, and such a policy is generally believed to be desirable in periods of underemployment. Open-market policies have not been carried far enough in the past and a clearer realization on the part of central banks of their true functions in a modern economy has rightly been urged. Interest-rate policies, however, are subject to limitations in consequence of two distinct circumstances, regardless of how far they are carried. In the first place, important political difficulties stand in the way of substantial lending operations by the monetary authority to private business because the selection of the borrowers would have to be undertaken arbitrarily. Just as in the case of subsidies, the authority could overcome public opposition at best in cases in which the borrowers seem to have a claim for exceptional treatment (war veterans, "small business," and so on) and a program of significant dimensions cannot be carried on along these lines alone. If the lending operations of the authority are not extended to private securities, a floor is set to rates on business loans by the height of the risk premia, irrespective of how far the rates on government securities are lowered.

---

[20] That is, the gap between the output required for full employment and the consumption forthcoming at this output level.

Aside from this, it is not clear in what measure private investment would increase if, in periods of underutilization, rates on business loans could be brought near the zero level. It should be repeated at this point that the zero rate on business loans must not be interpreted to imply that any businessman, regardless of his record, is granted loans at a zero rate. Consequently the zero rate does not imply guaranteed renewal at the same rate, or, for that matter, guaranteed renewal at any interest rate. Clearly, if business loans were granted in indefinite amounts at the zero rate and indefinite renewal were guaranteed, the flow of private investment would become infinite. The same is true, however, of the granting of business loans in indefinite amounts, with guaranteed renewal, at any level of interest rates. Guaranteed indefinite renewal changes a loan into a subsidy, and subsidies, if carried far enough, produce full employment. However, once it is recognized that large-scale subsidy programs imply the arbitrary distribution of gifts and that therefore they are scarcely feasible under "free institutions," this proposition loses significance for policy considerations. The concept of "credit policies" should be limited to the granting of credits in definite amounts without guaranteed renewal, and at positive rates (with the zero rate as the limit). If such a distinction is drawn it ceases to be true that a sufficiently "easy" credit policy could always produce full or even high employment. Profit expectations would undoubtedly improve if, in periods of underutilization, loans could be obtained at lower rates. But even the most consistent easy money policy would leave a finite number of producers with finite safety margins against losses, and in periods with adverse expectations these safety margins may be insufficient to bring about a high rate of private investment.

Increasing the supply of loan by open-market operations and otherwise, is not the only measure the authority can undertake to raise the level of private investment directly.[21] The other policies, however, are more controversial. In the first place, attention should be given to the possibility of using public expenditure programs as the means by which institutional rigidities may be loosened. If fiscal

---

[21] By "directly" is meant: not via the consumer demand generated by public expenditure.

programs were used in such a manner, the average amount of public expenditure necessary to create high utilization would be reduced. There exist at least three ways in which the authority could use the power it possesses as an investing agency, to reduce harmful imperfections of competition. (1) Public investment always is associated with the purchase, by the government, of materials and of equipment, and the government might insist that the producers with whom it places orders should adopt certain price policies. It might be possible to exert in this fashion a favorable influence on the relative price structure. The simultaneous reduction of the prices of complementary producers' goods (for example, of a variety of building materials), which could thus be "enforced" by the buying agencies of the government, might in many cases increase the private demand for these goods in a high proportion, even though no single price reduction would have had this effect. Hence, although no single producer believed it to be profitable to reduce his price, the simultaneous price reduction may prove profitable to all. (2) For the same reason, the buying policies of the government might be coördinated with its antitrust policies. (3) Public investment could in certain cases be used to create additional plants in monopolized fields and to increase the output of the industries in question.

All these policies presuppose an appreciable rate of government investment. But if applied appropriately, they might considerably reduce the amount required for high utilization of resources.

As for measures directed at the distributive shares, it was emphasized in earlier sections of the discussion that changes in the relation of the general level of money wage rates to product prices will usually affect the rate of private investment. The half truth that rising wages mean rising purchasing power and therefore rising output, is especially wrong in cyclical phases with a high average propensity to consume and with low average and marginal profit rates. The half truth that low wages mean high profits and therefore high output, is especially wrong in cyclical phases with a low average propensity to consume and with high profit margins. Awareness of this might at least prevent the democratic authority from reinforcing such tendencies as are adverse to the maintenance of a high level of private employment. The authority should, of course, be aware of the fact that, considering the secular trend in productivity, a policy aiming at reasonably stable prices must result in a *secular* rise in money and real wage rates.

For the reason just considered, collecting a given tax revenue with high progressivity is likely to be more appropriate to the maintenance of reasonably full employment in periods of high activity than in depressed periods. By making the tax structure more progressive, the average propensity to consume is increased but, at the same time, average and marginal profit rates decreased. The opposite is true of diminished progressiveness. Increasing the propensity to consume at the expense of net profit margins is more likely to possess favorable effects when the propensity to consume is low (i.e., when uncertainty is high) and when profit margins are substantial, than in the opposite circumstances. However, in interpreting this statement two pitfalls must be avoided. First, it must not be overlooked that the statement relates to a given tax revenue. Adding further progressive taxes to a given tax structure, or canceling part of the taxes without increasing other elements of the structure, is an entirely different proposition. Whether it is desirable to run a deficit or to collect a surplus depends on whether the volume of private investment should be supplemented by deficit spending or should be partly offset by deflationary measures. Generally speaking, given the rate of government spending, taxation is always a deflationary factor. It is merely maintained here that, for a given aggregate tax revenue, the effects of high progressiveness are more likely to be favorable in periods when the average propensity to consume is low and in which profit margins are high than in the opposite circumstance. Second, it must be remembered that, owing to its disproportionate effect on marginal (incremental) income, progressiveness beyond certain limits cannot fail to have deflationary effects even in periods of high activity.

It follows that it would be desirable to adopt more flexible tax policies than those which are customary. Whether very much more flexible taxes would be "politically feasible" is open to doubt, of course. But it should be possible to make some progress toward greater flexibility, if by no other means than at least by adopting speedier procedures of tax revision. Increased flexibility is of course not the only desirable change in the field of taxation. It was pointed out earlier that the failure to allow adequate loss deduction and the attempt to collect a large share of the tax revenue from "business" (and correspondingly less from personal income recipients) are likely to have distinctly harmful effects.[22] However, if business taxes were significantly reduced in relation to progressive personal income taxes, it would be desirable to adopt an undistributed profits tax, especially in periods of recession. Otherwise the change envisaged here would increase the incentive to retain profits.

In conclusion it may be repeated that secular trend lines do not show the equilibrium path along which the economy would be moving in the absence of "cyclical disturbances." If business recessions can be prevented from developing into major depressions and into periods of mass unemployment the "secular trend" of private investment can thereby be greatly influenced also. The necessary adjustments occurring in periods of recession tend to give rise to a cumulative shrinkage of aggregate demand which delays the adjustments themselves and produces disastrous aftereffects on the "trend." Lasting unemployment of considerable sections of the population has rightly come to be considered an intolerable condition. Yet there is no reason to anticipate a "chronic" tendency toward such a condition if "cyclical" tendencies toward cumulative deflation will be counteracted effectively; and, in the absence of a chronic adverse trend, it should be possible to counteract these cyclical tendencies without producing abrupt institutional changes. Periodic tendencies toward cumulative deflation should prove to be manageable by a combination of vigorous expansionary fiscal policies and the other devices considered, provided they are applied in early stages of contraction. It should be possible to adjust these policies to price and wage trends rather than to regulate prices, wages, and other economic variables by comprehensive controls (as would surely be necessary in the event of a full employment guarantee). If the policy should fail it will be either because monetary and fiscal policy is too timid or because economic power groups choose to adopt a suicidal course and are not prevented from adopting it. In these circumstances our institutions would not deserve to survive, and they would not.

---

[22] For an illuminating analysis of this problem, see Harold M. Groves, *Production, Jobs and Taxes* (New York and London, McGraw-Hill, 1944).

APPENDIXES

APPENDIX I

Empirical Consumption Functions

I. United States Data

PERIOD	EQUATION

(The standard error of estimate is indicated in each equation)

1919–1938 $C = 16.4 + 0.681\,Y \pm 2.329$, in billions of current dollars where Y is national income

1920–1938 $C = 17.1 + 0.676\,Y \pm 1.913$, in billions of current dollars where Y is national income

1919–1929 $C = 3.55 + 0.842\,Y \pm 1.846$, in billions of current dollars where Y is national income

1920–1929 $C = 7.95 + 0.789\,Y \pm 1.585$, in billions of current dollars where Y is national income

1930–1938 $C = 16.1 + 0.706\,Y \pm 1.589$, in billions of current dollars where Y is national income

1919–1929 $C = 0.0364 + 0.898\,Y \pm 1.635$, in billions of 1929 dollars where Y is national income

1920–1929 $C = 4.76 + 0.835\,Y \pm 1.405$, in billions of 1929 dollars where Y is national income

1930–1938 $C = 29.9 + 0.559\,Y \pm 1.228$, in billions of 1929 dollars where Y is national income

1919–1938 $C = 4.42 + 0.864\,Y \pm 2.153$, in billions of current dollars where Y is aggregate income payments

1920–1938 $C = 5.20 + 0.857\,Y \pm 1.655$, in billions of current dollars where Y is aggregate income payments

1919–1929 $C = -0.88 + 0.935\,Y \pm 2.184$, in billions of current dollars where Y is aggregate income payments

1920–1929 $C = 4.34 + 0.870\,Y \pm 1.278$, in billions of current dollars where Y is aggregate income payments

1930–1938 $C = 16.1 + 0.706\,Y \pm 1.589$, in billions of current dollars where Y is aggregate income payments

1919–1938 $C = 2.32 + 0.905\,Y \pm 2.032$, in billions of 1929 dollars where Y is aggregate income payments

PERIOD	EQUATION
1920–1938	$C = 6.27 + 0.853\ Y \pm 1.636$, in billions of 1929 dollars where Y is aggregate income payments
1919–1929	$C = -1.63 + 0.952\ Y \pm 1.724$, in billions of 1929 dollars where Y is aggregate income payments
1920–1929	$C = 2.65 + 0.896\ Y \pm 1.137$, in billions of 1929 dollars where Y is aggregate income payments
1930–1938	$C = 15.9 + 0.728\ Y \pm 1.554$, in billions of 1929 dollars where Y is aggregate income payments
1879–1888 to 1919–1928	$C = -0.04 + 0.889\ Y \pm 0.127$, in billions of current dollars where Y is national income
1879–1888 to 1919–1928	$C = -0.890 + 0.904\ Y \pm 0.370$, in billions of 1929 dollars where Y is national income
1879–1888 to 1919–1928	$C = -42.2 + 0.945\ Y \pm 2.535$, in hundreds of 1929 dollars per consuming unit, where Y is income per consuming unit.

II. British Data

$C = -99.1 + 0.972\ Y \pm 112$, in millions of current pounds where Y is national income. Line of regression fitted to data for 1860–1869 (average for period), 1907, 1924, 1929, 1930, 1931, 1932, 1933, 1934, 1935, 1937.

$C = 691.8 + 0.791\ Y \pm 88.5$, in millions of current pounds where Y is national income. Line of regression fitted to data for 1924, 1929, 1930, 1931, 1932, 1933, 1934, 1935, 1937.

$C = 833.1 + 0.766\ Y \pm 56.2$, in millions of current pounds where Y is national income. Line of regression fitted to data for 1930, 1931, 1932, 1933, 1934, 1935, 1937.

APPENDIX II

*Classification of Industries for Successive Subperiods
1899-1909, 1909-1923, 1923-1929*

TABLE 8

Classification of Industries for Successive Subperiods: 1899–1909, 1909–1923, 1923–1929

Industry	Declining by* More than 66⅔ per cent	Declining by* Not more than 66⅔ per cent	Declining by* Not more than 50 per cent	Declining by* Not more than 33⅓ per cent	Growing: Less than 10 per cent of average	Growing: 10–20 per cent of average	Growing: 20–25 per cent of average	Growing: 25–33⅓ per cent of average	Growing: 33⅓–50 per cent of average	Growing: 50–66⅔ per cent of average	Growing: 66⅔–100 per cent of average	Growing: 100–150 per cent of average	Growing: 150–200 per cent of average	Growing: 200–300 per cent of average	Growing: 300–400 per cent of average	Growing: 400–500 per cent of average	Growing: 500–1,000 per cent of average	Growing: More than 1,000 per cent of average
Asphalted-felt base floor coverings															○			
Butter and cheese										○	△							
Butter, cheese, and condensed milk				○							△							
Buttons																	○	
Canning and preserving: fish, crabs, shrimp, oysters, and clams					○							△						
Canning and preserving: fruits and vegetables, pickles, preserves, and sauces										□ △		○ ○		○				
Carpets and rugs, other than rag																		
Carriages, wagons, sleighs, and sleds																		
Cast-iron pipe									○									
Cement								○			□							
Chocolate and cocoa			○					○				○						
Clay products, other than pottery and non-clay refractories					○							○	□ △					
Coke, not including gas house coke						△ □							○					
Condensed and evaporated milk																		
Cordage and twine									△	□		○						
Corn syrup, corn oil, and starch									□	○ △	□							
Cotton goods					□													
Explosives																		
Fertilizers						△						○		○				
Firearms				○									○ △					
Flour and other grain mill products				○		△						○		○				
Gas, manufactured, illuminating, and heating												○	○					
Gloves and mittens, leather								△										
Hats, fur felt											△		□	△				
Hats, wool felt				□ △														
Hosiery and knit goods							○ ○					○ △			△			
Ice, manufactured												△ ○		□				

Industry	1	2	3	4	5	6	7	8	9	10	11	12	13	14	15	16	17	18
Iron and steel, blast furnaces................	..	..	..	..	..	..	..	..	○	..	□	△	..	..	..	..	..	..
Iron and steel, steel works and rolling mills......	..	..	..	..	..	..	..	..	..	..	..	△□○	..	..	..	..	..	..
Jute and linen goods.........................	..	..	..	□○	..	..	..	..	..	..	△	..	..	..	..	..	..	..
Knit goods..................................	..	..	..	○	..	..	..	..	..	..	..	..	..	..	..	..	..	..
Lime.......................................	..	..	..	..	○	..	..	..	..	..	..	..	..	..	..	..	..	..
Linoleum...................................	..	..	..	..	○	..	..	..	..	..	..	..	..	..	..	..	..	..
Lumber and timber products..................	..	..	..	△□	○	..	..	..	..	..	..	..	..	..	..	..	..	..
Motorcycles, bicycles, and parts..............	..	△	..	○	..	..	..	..	..	..	..	..	□	..	..	..	..	..
Motor vehicles, including bodies and parts.......	..	..	..	..	..	..	..	..	..	..	..	○	..	..	..	..	..	△□
Musical instruments, organs..................	..	..	..	△□○	..	..	..	..	..	..	..	..	..	..	..	..	..	..
Musical instruments, pianos..................	..	○	..	..	..	..	..	..	□	..	..	△	..	..	..	..	..	..
Oil, cake and meal, cottonseed................	..	..	..	..	..	..	..	..	..	..	..	..	..	○	..	..	..	..
Oil, cake and meal, linseed...................	..	..	..	..	..	..	..	..	..	..	..	○	..	..	..	..	..	..
Oilcloth....................................	..	..	..	..	..	..	..	..	..	..	..	..	..	○	..	..	..	..
Paint and varnish...........................	..	..	..	..	..	..	..	..	..	..	△□	..	○	..	..	..	..	..
Paper and pulp..............................	..	..	..	..	..	..	..	..	..	..	△□	..	○	..	..	..	..	..
Petroleum refining...........................	..	..	..	..	..	..	..	..	..	..	△	..	..	..	○	□	..	..
Rice, cleaning and polishing..................	..	..	..	..	..	..	○	..	..	..	□	..	△	..	..	..	..	..
Rubber products.............................	..	..	..	..	..	..	..	..	..	..	..	..	○	..	..	..	..	..
Salt..	..	..	..	..	..	..	..	..	..	..	□○	△	..	..	..	..	..	..
Sand-lime brick..............................	..	..	..	..	..	..	..	..	..	..	..	..	○	..	..	..	..	..
Silk manufactures...........................	..	..	..	..	..	..	..	..	..	..	△□	..	○	..	..	..	..	..
Slaughtering and meat packing................	..	..	..	..	○	..	..	..	△	□	..	..	..	..	..	..	..	..
Soap.......................................	..	..	..	..	..	..	..	..	..	..	○	..	..	..	..	..	..	..
Sugar, beet..................................	..	..	..	..	..	..	..	..	..	..	□○	..	..	..	..	..	△	..
Sugar, refining, cane.........................	..	..	..	..	..	..	..	..	..	..	○	..	..	..	..	..	..	..
Tanning materials, natural dyestuffs, mordants, and assistants and sizes.......................	..	..	..	..	○	..	..	..	..	..	..	..	..	..	..	..	..	..
Turpentine and rosin.........................	..	..	..	△	□	..	..	..	..	..	○	..	..	..	..	..	..	..
Wood distillation, not including turpentine and rosin....................................	..	..	..	..	..	..	..	..	..	..	..	△	..	..	..	..	..	..
Wool shoddy................................	..	..	..	..	..	○	..	..	..	..	..	..	..	..	..	..	..	..
Woolen and worsted..........................	..	..	..	..	..	..	..	..	..	..	△	..	..	..	..	..	..	..
Woolen goods...............................	..	..	..	○	..	..	..	..	..	..	..	..	..	..	..	..	..	..
Worsted goods..............................	..	..	..	○	..	..	..	..	..	..	..	..	..	..	..	..	..	..

* Declining by x per cent means that in the closing year of the subperiod, 1909, 1923, or 1929, the output of the industry was smaller by x per cent than in the first year of the subperiod, 1899, 1909, or 1923.

† Growing at a rate of x per cent of average means that from the first to the last year of the subperiod in question, the percentage rate of growth of the output of the industry, as computed from Professor Mills' data, corresponded to x per cent of the rate of growth of manufacturing output as computed from Professor Douglas' and Dr. Siegel's data (which in turn are based on the Day-Thomas index).

Some industries are marked only for one or for two of the three subperiods. This is because data are not available for all industries with respect to all three subperiods. The size of the sample is not the same for all subperiods.

△ = the subperiod, 1899–1909; □ = 1909–1923; ○ = 1923–1929.

APPENDIX III

Tables Underlying Figures 4-18, 23-25

TABLE 9

(For fig. 4)

CONSUMERS' OUTLAY AND NET PRIVATE CAPITAL FORMATION*

1919–1938, 1929 Prices

(in billions)

Year	Consumers' outlay	Net private capital formation
1919	48.9	6.5
1920	50.9	6.9
1921	53.6	1.7
1922	56.8	2.8
1923	62.5	7.2
1924	66.2	4.3
1925	65.1	7.4
1926	70.3	7.3
1927	71.6	6.3
1928	73.8	5.5
1929	77.0	8.2
1930	75.5	2.2
1931	69.1	−2.0
1932	61.1	−7.1
1933	61.6	−5.9
1934	65.7	−5.0
1935	65.2	−0.8
1936	69.5	3.2
1937	74.4	4.5
1938	75.8	0.6

* Data from Simon Kuznets, *National Income and its Composition, 1919–1938* (New York, National Bureau of Economic Research, 1941), Vol. I, pp. 147, 269, 272, and calculations therefrom.

TABLE 10 (For fig. 5)
CONSUMERS' OUTLAY AND NET PRIVATE CAPITAL FORMATION*
Quarterly, 1921–1938, Current Prices
(in millions)

Year	Quarter	Consumers' outlay	Net private capital formation
1921	I	14,381	2,063
	II	14,040	693
	III	13,886	509
	IV	13,583	−1,112
1922	I	13,655	1,120
	II	14,340	50
	III	14,487	295
	IV	15,474	1,061
1923	I	15,569	1,244
	II	16,133	1,930
	III	15,975	2,160
	IV	16,744	950
1924	I	17,046	1,243
	II	16,197	1,962
	III	16,464	863
	IV	17,076	536
1925	I	17,460	1,612
	II	17,439	1,121
	III	17,484	1,259
	IV	18,188	1,805
1926	I	18,142	2,227
	II	18,410	1,368
	III	18,623	1,071
	IV	18,402	1,817
1927	I	18,253	1,314
	II	18,417	1,219
	III	18,036	1,683
	IV	18,234	964
1928	I	18,966	1,625
	II	18,733	388
	III	19,014	1,153
	IV	19,183	2,013
1929	I	19,577	1,396
	II	19,463	1,356
	III	19,785	1,747
	IV	18,869	1,743
1930	I	18,361	1,672
	II	18,026	1,521
	III	17,083	1,267
	IV	16,232	−318

* Data from Harold Barger, *Outlay and Income in the United States, 1921–1938* (New York, National Bureau of Economic Research, 1942), pp. 114–119.

TABLE 10—*Continued*

Year	Quarter	Consumers' outlay	Net private capital formation
1931	I	15,906	−566
	II	15,230	−93
	III	14,524	−368
	IV	13,797	−1,054
1932	I	13,060	−1,229
	II	12,126	−1,040
	III	11,720	−2,199
	IV	11,139	−1,666
1933	I	10,772	−1,187
	II	11,831	−1,194
	III	12,589	− 876
	IV	11,753	−1,435
1934	I	12,659	− 768
	II	12,997	−387
	III	13,996	−1,043
	IV	13,664	−1,163
1935	I	13,667	−734
	II	13,831	−738
	III	14,008	−495
	IV	14,414	−132
1936	I	14,901	−183
	II	15,378	335
	III	15,834	463
	IV	16,430	1,094
1937	I	15,925	829
	II	16,124	1,617
	III	17,264	2,109
	IV	17,067	51
1938	I	14,998	−430
	II	14,749	−836
	III	15,517	−699
	IV	16,728	−300

TABLE 11

(For figs. 6 and 7)

CONSUMERS' OUTLAY AND CAPITAL FORMATION*

For Overlapping Decades, 1929 Prices

(in millions)

Decade	Consumers' outlay	Net capital formation	Gross capital formation
1879–1888............................	13,411	1,766	3,897
1884–1893............................	15,563	2,524	5,125
1889–1898............................	18,045	3,145	6,106
1894–1903............................	22,617	3,509	7,019
1899–1908............................	28,292	4,110	8,207
1904–1913............................	33,936	4,808	9,785
1909–1918............................	39,217	5,817	11,569
1914–1923............................	47,576	6,250	13,219
1919–1928............................	61,694	6,905	15,011
1924–1933............................	69,070	4,247	13,199
1929–1938............................	69,501	1,610	10,827

* Data from Simon Kuznets, *Uses of National Income in Peace and War*, Occasional Paper 6 (New York, National Bureau of Economic Research, March, 1942, pp. 30, 31, 35.

TABLE 12

(For fig. 8)

MARGINAL PROPENSITY TO CONSUME AND NET

CAPITAL FORMATION*

1929 Prices

Decade	Net capital formation (in millions)	$\Delta C/\Delta Y$
1884–1893.................	2,524	0.783
1889–1898.................	3,145	0.862
1894–1903.................	3,509	0.912
1899–1908.................	4,110	0.897
1904–1913.................	4,808	0.865
1909–1918.................	5,817	0.892
1914–1923.................	6,250	0.951

* Data from Kuznets, *Uses of National Income in Peace and War*, pp. 31, 35.

TABLE 13

(For fig. 9)

MARGINAL PROPENSITY TO CONSUME AND NATIONAL INCOME*

1929 Prices

Decade	National income (in millions)	ΔC/ΔY
1884–1893.................	18,087	0.783
1889–1898.................	21,189	0.862
1894–1903.................	26,126	0.912
1899–1908.................	32,402	0.897
1904–1913.................	38,744	0.865
1909–1918.................	45,034	0.892
1914–1923.................	53,826	0.951

* Data from Kuznets, *Uses of National Income in Peace and War*, pp. 31, 35.

TABLE 14

(For fig. 10)

CONSUMERS' OUTLAY AND NATIONAL INCOME*

1919–1938, 1929 Prices

(in billions)

Year	Consumers' outlay	National income
1919........................	48.9	57.0
1920........................	50.9	58.4
1921........................	53.6	56.5
1922........................	56.8	60.8
1923........................	62.5	70.7
1924........................	66.2	71.7
1925........................	65.1	73.9
1926........................	70.3	79.0
1927........................	71.6	79.6
1928........................	73.8	81.1
1929........................	77.0	87.1
1930........................	75.5	79.9
1931........................	69.1	69.3
1932........................	61.1	55.6
1933........................	61.6	56.7
1934........................	65.7	62.1
1935........................	65.2	65.6
1936........................	69.5	75.0
1937........................	74.4	80.8
1938........................	75.8	79.0

* Data from Kuznets, *National Income and its Composition, 1919–1938*, I, 147.

TABLE 15

(For fig. 11)

MARGINAL PROPENSITY TO CONSUME AND CONSUMERS' OUTLAY
AND NATIONAL INCOME*

1929 Prices

Decade	Consumers' outlay (in millions)	National income (in millions)	$\Delta C/\Delta Y$
1879–1888.........................	13,411	15,175	.....
1884–1893.........................	15,563	18,087	0.759
1889–1898.........................	18,045	21,189	0.806
1894–1903.........................	22,617	26,126	0.918
1899–1908.........................	28,292	32,402	0.905
1904–1913.........................	33,936	38,744	0.889
1909–1918.........................	39,217	45,034	0.841
1914–1923.........................	47,576	53,826	0.943
1919–1928.........................	61,694	68,598	0.959
1924–1933.........................	69,070	73,316	1.574
1929–1938.........................	69,501	71,110	−0.182

* Data from Kuznets, *Uses of National Income in Peace and War*, pp. 31, 35.

TABLE 16

CONSUMERS' OUTLAY AND INCOME PER CONSUMING UNIT AND
MARGINAL PROPENSITY TO CONSUME*

1929 Prices

Decade	Consumers' outlay per consuming unit	Income per consuming unit	$\Delta C/\Delta Y$
1879–1888.........................	358	406	.....
1884–1893.........................	368	429	0.435
1889–1898.........................	383	450	0.714
1894–1903.........................	434	501	1.000
1899–1908.........................	491	563	0.919
1904–1913.........................	534	609	0.935
1909–1918.........................	568	651	0.810
1914–1923.........................	639	722	1.000
1919–1928.........................	765	851	0.977
1924–1933.........................	796	844	−4.429
1929–1938.........................	757	775	0.565

* Data from Kuznets, *Uses of National Income in Peace and War*, pp. 31, 39, for data on consumers' outlay per consuming unit, consuming units, and national income. Income per consuming unit found by dividing national income by the number of consuming units.

TABLE 17

(For fig. 13)

CONSUMERS' OUTLAY AND AGGREGATE INCOME PAYMENTS,
INCLUDING ENTREPRENEURIAL SAVINGS, 1919–1938*

Current Prices (in billions)

Year	Consumers' outlay	Aggregate income payments
1919................	53.9	64.5
1920................	62.9	70.1
1921................	56.1	57.7
1922................	56.2	59.6
1923................	63.0	69.0
1924................	66.2	70.0
1925................	66.8	73.6
1926................	72.3	77.1
1927................	71.9	77.2
1928................	74.3	78.9
1929................	77.2	83.5
1930................	73.1	75.9
1931................	60.2	63.0
1932................	47.1	48.6
1933................	45.8	46.3
1934................	52.1	53.4
1935................	53.7	58.2
1936................	57.5	65.8
1937................	64.1	71.4
1938................	62.6	66.3

* Data from Kuznets, *National Income and its Composition, 1919–1938*, I, 137.

TABLE 18

(For fig. 14)

CONSUMERS' OUTLAY AND NATIONAL INCOME IN GREAT BRITAIN
FOR SELECTED YEARS*

Current Prices (in millions of pounds)

Period or year	Consumers' outlay	National income
1860–1869............	749	899
1907................	1692	1940
1924................	3708	4035
1929................	4070	4384
1930................	4139	4318
1931................	3855	3889
1932................	3815	3844
1933................	3901	3962
1934................	4014	4238
1935................	4205	4530
1937................	4986	5340

* Data from Colin Clark, *National Income and Outlay* (London, Macmillan, 1937) pp. 88, 185, and *idem, The Conditions of Economic Progress* (London, Macmillan, 1940), p. 397.

TABLE 19

(For fig. 15)

PERCENTAGE POPULATION GROWTH IN CONSUMING UNITS
AND NET CAPITAL FORMATION*

1929 Prices

Decade	Percentage population growth (averaged)	Net capital formation (in millions)
1884–1893.............	12.18	2,524
1889–1898.............	11.03	3,145
1894–1903.............	10.64	3,509
1899–1908.............	10.48	4,110
1904–1913.............	9.49	4,808
1909–1918.............	8.27	5,817
1914–1923.............	8.04	6,250
1919–1928.............	7.93	6,905
1924–1933.............	6.71	4,247

* Data from Kuznets, *Uses of National Income in Peace and War*, pp. 31, 39, and calculations therefrom.

TABLE 20

(For fig. 16)

ABSOLUTE POPULATION GROWTH IN CONSUMING UNITS
AND NET CAPITAL FORMATION*

1929 Prices

Decade	Absolute population growth (in thousands)	Net capital formation (in millions)
1884–1893..............	4835	2,524
1889–1898..............	4915	3,145
1894–1903..............	5275	3,509
1899–1908..............	5741	4,110
1904–1913..............	5726	4,808
1909–1918..............	5474	5,817
1914–1923..............	5773	6,250
1919–1928..............	6141	6,905
1924–1933..............	5585	4,247

* Data from Kuznets, *Uses of National Income in Peace and War*, pp. 31, 39, and calculations therefrom.

TABLE 21

(For fig. 17)

NATIONAL INCOME OR OUTPUT FOR OVERLAPPING DECADES*

1929 Prices (in millions)

Decade	National income
1879–1888............................	15,175
1884–1893............................	18,087
1889–1898............................	21,189
1894–1903............................	26,126
1899–1908............................	32,402
1904–1913............................	38,744
1909–1918............................	45,034
1914–1923............................	53,826
1919–1928............................	68,598
1924–1933............................	73,316
1929–1938............................	71,110

* Data from Kuznets, *Uses of National Income in Peace and War*, p. 31.

TABLE 22 (For fig. 18)
INDEXES OF MANUFACTURING OUTPUT AND UNIT LABOR COSTS
1899–1939* —(1899 = 100)

Year	Manufacturing output	Unit labor cost
1899.................	100.0	100.0
1900.................	100.2	106.4
1901.................	111.5	100.4
1902.................	121.2	106.2
1903.................	123.2	110.2
1904.................	123.4	104.8
1905.................	142.3	102.1
1906.................	150.8	108.2
1907.................	149.5	116.3
1908.................	133.2	115.6
1909.................	160.3	111.1
1910.................	157.2	117.4
1911.................	155.5	120.4
1912.................	174.5	117.6
1913.................	180.1	123.5
1914.................	170.6	123.2
1915.................	186.8	112.4
1916.................	217.6	119.4
1917.................	218.5	141.5
1918.................	237.3	160.4
1919.................	209.7	219.9
1920.................	223.6	246.0
1921.................	180.6	222.7
1922.................	229.2	188.1
1923.................	260.3	197.8
1924.................	247.1	197.2
1925.................	274.2	185.7
1926.................	284.9	184.6
1927.................	275.5	188.2
1928.................	291.2	181.0
1929.................	313.1	179.2
1930.................	250.5	182.8
1931.................	206.6	166.7
1932.................	165.9	143.4
1933.................	194.1	130.8
1934.................	206.6	159.5
1935.................	234.8	161.3
1936.................	281.8	154.1
1937.................	303.7	170.3
1938.................	234.8	168.5
1939.................	294.3	155.9

* Data from Paul H. Douglas, *The Theory of Wages* (New York, Macmillan, 1934), Tables I, V, and VII in the appendix for indexes of manufacturing output, employment, and money wages, respectively, for the period 1899–1926; Irving H. Siegel, "Hourly Earnings and Unit Labor Costs in Manufacturing, "*Journal of the American Statistical Association*, XXXV (September, 1940), 458 for index of manufacturing output and unit labor cost for the period 1927–1939. See above, note to figure 18 for the method employed in deriving continuous indexes for the entire period 1899–1939.

Appendix III

TABLE 23

(For fig. 23)

RESERVE RATIO OF MEMBER BANKS AND TREASURY BOND YIELDS
1933–1939*

Year	Quarter	Reserve ratio	Treasury bond yields
1933	II....................	12.6	3.21
1933	IV....................	14.4	3.53
1934	II....................	17.2	2.98
1934	IV....................	17.6	3.01
1935	II....................	19.5	2.72
1935	IV....................	21.0	2.83
1936	II....................	19.9	2.66
1936	IV....................	21.9	2.51
1937	I....................	22.3	2.60
1937	II....................	22.7	2.76
1937	IV....................	23.4	2.67
1938	II....................	26.6	2.52
1938	III....................	26.7	2.58
1938	IV....................	27.4	2.49
1939	I....................	28.6	2.34
1939	II....................	30.0	2.13
1939	III....................	33.2	2.65
1939	IV....................	32.7	2.35

* Data from *Twenty-Fourth Annual Report of the Board of Governors of the Federal Reserve System*, pp. 112–114, and *Federal Reserve Bulletins* for reserves and deposits; *Federal Reserve Bulletin* (December, 1938), 1045 and issues following for Treasury bond yields. Reserves include vault cash and reserves with Federal Reserve banks at call dates; deposits include demand deposits adjusted, United States government deposits, and time deposits at call dates.

TABLE 24

(For fig. 24)

INCOME VELOCITY OF MONEY AND TREASURY BOND YIELDS
1919–1929*

Year	Income velocity	Treasury bond yields
1919	3.05	4.73
1920	3.10	5.32
1921	2.79	5.09
1922	2.96	4.30
1923	3.21	4.36
1924	3.16	4.06
1925	3.07	3.86
1926	3.19	3.68
1927	2.89	3.34
1928	2.91	3.33
1929	3.04	3.60

* Data from James W. Angell, *Investment and Business Cycles* (New York and London, McGraw-Hill, 1941), pp. 337, 338 for income velocity; *Federal Reserve Bulletin* (December, 1938), 1045 and issues following for Treasury bond yields.

TABLE 25

(For fig. 25)

INCOME VELOCITY OF MONEY AND TREASURY BOND YIELDS
1933–1939*

Year	Income velocity	Treasury bond yields
1933	2.28	3.31
1934	2.29	3.12
1935	2.19	2.79
1936	2.18	2.65
1937	2.26	2.68
1938	2.10	2.56
1939	2.00	2.36

* Data from Angell, *Investment and Business Cycles*, p. 338 for income velocity; *Federal Reserve Bulletin* (December, 1938), 1045 and issues following for Treasury bond yields.

INDEX

Index

Hayek, F. A. von, relative price changes, 45
Hicks, J. R., quoted on underemployment equilibrium, 21, 74 n. 24
Higgins, Benjamin, 104 n. 1
Hoarding: liquidity requirement, 144; idle balances, 146–150 *passim;* speculative *vs.*
contingency, 146–151; interest elasticity of, 148, 168–173, 175–176, 191; increased contingency, with downward shift of profit expectations, 156, 164, 201; partly responsible for failure of investment and output, 171–172; overcome effects of, by changing money supply, 172; expansionary monetary policies and elasticity of, 174–180
Humphrey, Don D., concentration ratios, 91–92

Income: aggregate money, 8, 9, 10; expected, 8, 12, 27 and fig. 3; earned, defined, 9–10 and fig. 1; aggregate, rises with consumer demand, 24; consumption relationship, 55, 63, 65, 66; reaction to increase in, 61–62; velocity, 201–204 and figs. 24, 25; distribution bears on output and employment, 210–211, 212
Income: national for overlapping decades, App. III, 252; velocity of money and Treasury bond yields, App. III, 255
Industry: Federal Reserve Board chart of industrial production, 16 fig. 2, 17; output of, 85; Chamberlinian group, 85; relative significance of single firms within, 86; colluding by firms in, 86, 93; concentration ratios for, 86; concentration of production, 93–94; new production functions in, 115; probable outcome, 160–162
Inflation: policies to counteract, 183 ff.; possible to counteract by methods of credit policy, 183, 185; effect of raising interest rates, 184; threat of, with dishoarding of idle deposits, 227; and public investment projects, 228, 229; consumer subsidies a threat, 229; anticyclical spending policy might counteract, 229
Innovations: and the consumption function, 61; output and employment rise or decline with, 73–74; deepening or widening character of, 74–76, 216; per unit of output effects, 75–76; stimulate economic activity, 76–77; cost-saving effect of, 76; in monopolies, 88; result in new production functions, 115–116; theories, 115–118 *passim. See also* Shifts in composition
Institutional changes: for full employment, xii; not required to prevent recessions, xii; through mass unemployment or inflationary spiral of economic guarantee, xiii–xiv; result from government-made full employment, 227–228
Interest rates: lowering of, and business activity, xi; rigidity, 137 ff., 171–173; lowering of, may produce new investment, 138; failure to adjust downward during underutilization, 140, 167; rise in demand for liquidity and, 141; loanable funds theory in, 141, 142; Keynesian theory, 141–144 and fig. 20; elasticity and hoarding, 146, 148–151, 167, 175; zero rate discussed, 166, 169, 172, 232; long-run changes in, 167; determination of, 170 fig. 22; decline in, insufficient to maintain output, 171; and private investment, 172–176, 207; undesirable to interfere with upward rigidity, 173; sale of government securities to public raises, 174–175; decline in, through open-market purchases, 177, 181, 208; elasticity of private investment, 177, 178, 189; lower, and employment, 189; and business cycle, 189 ff.; leads and lags before Second World War, 189–191; elasticity of liquidity provisions, 200 ff.; liquidity ratios discussed, 204, 206–208; income velocity and, 204; gold influx and decline in, 206
Inventories, accumulation of unplanned: planned investment to avoid, 25, 26, 29; results in monetary and real contraction, 28
Investment for consumption: shift toward products stimulates, x; justified by consumer demand, 22, 23, 24, 29; contracting economy if only, 31–32; no relationship between time rate of change in consumption and, 35, 36, 42; corresponds to reduced output in low activity, 36; marginal propensity to consume does not govern, 42; psychologically determined, 43; effect of population growth on, 70; per unit of consumption varies inversely with money wage rates, 98. *See also* Capital Formation; Inventories